Désirée Kleiner-Liebau

Migration and the Construction
of National Identity in Spain

Ediciones de Iberoamericana

Serie A: Historia y crítica de la literatura
Serie B: Lingü.stica
Serie C: Historia y Sociedad
Serie D: Bibliografías

Editado por
Mechthild Albert, Walther L. Bernecker,
Enrique García Santo-Tomás, Frauke Gewecke,
Aníbal González, Jürgen M. Meisel,
Klaus Meyer-Minnemann, Katharina Niemeyer

C: Historia y Sociedad, 15

Désirée KLEINER-LIEBAU

Migration and the Construction of National Identity in Spain

IBEROAMERICANA – VERVUERT – 2009

© Iberoamericana, 2009
   Amor de Dios, 1 – E-28014 Madrid
   Tel. +34 91 429 35 22
   Fax +34 91 429 53 97
   info@iberoamericanalibros.com
   www.ibero-americana.net

© Vervuert Verlag, 2009
   Elisabethenstr. 3-9 – D-60594 Frankfurt am Main
   Tel. +49 69 597 46 17
   Fax +49 69 597 87 43
   info@iberoamericanalibros.com
   www.ibero-americana.net

ISBN (Iberoamericana) 978-84-8489-476-6
ISBN (Vervuert) 978-3-86527-503-5

Depósito legal: S. 1.116-2009

Diseño de la cubierta: Michael Ackermann
Imagen de la cubierta: Désirée Kleiner-Liebau

The paper on which this book printed meets the requirements of ISO 9706

Printed in Spain

Table of contents

To my parents

Acknowledgements

This book could not have been completed without the help of many people. First of all I want to thank Prof. Dr. Jürgen Rüland for accepting me as a doctoral student, for his support and guidance throughout the whole process of research and writing. Furthermore I thank Prof. Dr. Dieter Oberndörfer who inspired this work, for his helpful advice and constant encouragement. I am deeply indebted to all my friends and colleagues in Spain who always welcomed me with exceptional kindness. Lorenzo Cachón who opened many doors for me, introduced me to the right people and showed me the best coffeehouses in Madrid deserves particular mention. I thank all the interviewees, and all the persons and institutions in Madrid and Barcelona that provided assistance and advice. At home the Studienstiftung des deutschen Volkes gave me not only the opportunity to study and do research without having to worry about my livelihood, but also provided a forum for interchange of ideas across the disciplinary boundaries. In the past few years the Arnold-Bergstraesser-Institute in Freiburg has been like a second home to me. I enjoyed the pleasant and stimulating working atmosphere there and thank all my dear colleagues for their friendship and boosting my morale when necessary. I very much appreciate the many hours Anke Liebau, Jan Völkel, Ingrid Wehr, Eike Kleiner, and Margret Rae spent reading, correcting and doing the layout. I thank my family, my parents, my brothers, my in-laws, for believing in me and giving me their unconditional support. Finally I thank my husband for his love and patience, and for accompanying me through all the ups and downs of life.

Freiburg, 1.12.2008

List of abbreviations

AP	Alianza Popular
C.o.O.	Country(ies) of Origin
CAT	Catalonia
CCAA	Comunidad(es) Autónoma(s)
CDA	Critical Discourse Analysis
CDC	Convergència Democràtica de Catalunya
CIS	Centro de Investigaciones Sociológicas
CiU	Convergència i Unió
E	Central State
EC	European Communities
ERC	Esquerra Republicana de Catalunya
ETA	Euskadi Ta Askatasuna
EU	European Union
Gov	Government / governing party
GRECO	Programa Global de Regulación y Coordinación de la Extranjería y la Inmigración
HB	Herri Batasuna
IC	Iniciativa per Catalunya
IC-V	Iniciativa per Catalunya-Verds
INE	Institution Nacional de Estadística
IU	Izquierda Unida
L.O.	Ley Orgánica
LOAPA	Ley Orgánica para la Armonización del Proceso Autonómico
MIR	Ministerio del Interior
MTAS	Ministerio de Trabajo y Asuntos Sociales
NGO	Non-Governmental Organisation
Opp	Opposition

PCE	Partido Comunista de España
PNV	Partido Nacionalista Vasco
PP	Partido Popular
PPC	Partit Popular de Catalunya
PSC	Partit dels Socialistes de Catalunya
PSOE	Partido Socialista Obrero Español
PSUC	Partit Socialista Unificat de Catalunya
SIVE	Sistema Integral de Vigilancia Exterior
UCD	Unión de Centro Democrático
UD	Unió Democràtica
UGT	Unión General de Trabajadores
UK	United Kingdom
USA	United States of America

List of tables

List of figures

I.
Introduction

Almost thirty years after the transition to democracy, Spain is still struggling to find common ground in the conception of the Spanish State and its political system. Many of the disputes and controversies between the conservative party, Partido Popular (PP) and the socialist Partido Socialista Obrero Español (PSOE) can be attributed to the fundamental differences in their underlying assumptions about Spain's national identity. In particular the idea that there are various nations within the Spanish State, as defended by peripheral nationalist movements and supported by the PSOE, is highly controversial. The reasons for the still unsettled conflicts lie in Spain's past.

The country, until the beginning of the 20th century a weakly centralized monarchy with strong peripheral and regional movements, for the first time in the 1920s experienced a strong official version of Spanish nationalism under the authoritarian regime of Primo de Rivera. After a very short republican period and the destructive years of Civil War Franco took over, suppressed the peripheral nationalist movements in Catalonia, the Basque Country and Galicia and introduced strictly centralized governmental and administrational structures. He furthermore established a nationalist ideology which was based on conservative Catholic values and identified Spain with the Castilian heartland, its language, heroes and symbols. The peripheral nationalist movements, however, survived and became a synonym for the opposition and resistance to the regime. The "State of Autonomies" established after the transition to democracy with the Constitution of 1978 reflects the struggle for compromise between both, the idea of a unified Spanish nation and the existence of strong peripheral national identities. The recent debate about the reform of several statutes of autonomy, especially the Catalan, has shown once more that these internal controversies about the different constructions of national identity are still a prevailing topic in Spanish politics.

In addition, in the past fifteen years Spain has developed from a country of emigration to a country of immigration registering a fast increase in the numbers of immigrants from non-EU countries. Immigration is thus to be seen as another factor influencing the debate about national identity in Spain. In the political debate about immigration control or questions of immigrant integration politicians explicitly or implicitly define national identity and ascribe certain elements to it –either talking about the "Other" or about the own collective identity.

This book aims at analysing how national identity is constructed in the political discourse about immigration and immigrant integration in Spain. It examines therefore how much and by which means non-EU immigration influences the discursive construction of national identity in political discourse at both the central state level and the level of the Autonomous Community of Catalonia.

The extensive academic literature on nation-building, national identity, nationalism has studied in detail the relation between nationalism and categories such as demos, ethnos or ethnicity, and religion.[1] However, it has until now widely disregarded the field of migration research.[2] Thus "although the existence of the Other as part and parcel of the definition of the Nation has been widely accepted in scholarship, the relationship between the Other and the nation has not been investigated in depth".[3]

Vice versa, in migration research only a few studies have analysed the link between immigration, the delimitation against the "Other" and the construction processes of collective or rather national identities in a European context. Schnapper for instance, analysed the relationship between national identity and the treatment of immigrants comparing Germany, France and Great Britain.[4] Aiming at answering a similar question but using a different approach, Behr studied the migration policies of the United States, Germany and France.[5] Däu-

---

[1]   See for instance Hutchinson and Smith (1994): *Nationalism*, Oxford/New York: Oxford University Press; Smith (1991): *National Identity*, London: Penguin Books; Bendix (1996): Strukturgeschichtliche Voraussetzungen der nationalen und kulturellen Identität in der Neuzeit, in Giesen *Nationale und kulturelle Identität. Studien zur Entwicklung des kollektiven Bewußtseins in der Neuzeit*, Frankfurt a. M.: Suhrkamp; Smith (1971): *Theories of Nationalism*, London: Duckworth; Alter (1985): *Nationalismus*, Frankfurt a. M.: Suhrkamp; Hastings (1997): *The Construction of Nationhood. Ethnicity, Religion and Nationalism*, Cambridge: Cambridge University Press.

[2]   See Behr (1998): *Zuwanderung im Nationalstaat. Formen der Eigen- und Fremdbestimmung in den USA, der Bundesrepublik, Deutschland und Frankreich*, Opladen: Leske + Budrich, p. 18.

[3]   Triandafyllidou (2001): *Immigrants and National Identity in Europe*, London/New York: Routledge, p. 3.

[4]   See Schnapper (1994): The debate on immigration and the crisis of national identity, in Baldwin-Edwards and Schain *The Politics of Immigration in Western Europe*, Essex: Frank Cass.

[5]   See Behr (1998): *Zuwanderung im Nationalstaat*.

ble, moreover, interviewed teenagers stemming from migrant families to learn more about the sense of community of the Germans.[6] Against the background of critical theory Räthzel analyses which images of the "Other" go along with and determine the construction of the German nation.[7] Of particular interest are furthermore the works of Oberndörfer which point out the close relation between national identity and migration policy in Germany.[8]

Apart from these rare approaches in sociology, political science or pedagogy, a couple of critical linguists have addressed the discourse about immigration. In the tradition of critical discourse analysis the researchers around Ruth Wodak in Vienna studied the discursive construction of national identity in migration discourse in Austria.[9] In Germany, Jäger and others analysed the political and media discourse about immigration and asylum seekers aiming at revealing underlying racist and xenophobic tendencies in the different ways language is used.[10] Also the Dutch scholar van Dijk uses a critical approach of discourse

[6] See Däuble (2000): *Auf dem Weg zum Bundesrepublikaner. Einwanderung - kollektive Identität - politische Bildung*, Schwalbach/Ts.: Wochenschau Verlag.

[7] See Räthzel (1997): *Gegenbilder. Nationale Identität durch Konstruktion des Anderen*, Opladen: Leske + Budrich.

[8] See for instance Oberndörfer (2006): Nation, Multikulturalismus und Migration-auf dem Weg in die postnationale Republik? in *IMIS-Beiträge* 30; Oberndörfer (1993): *Der Wahn des Nationalen. Die Alternative der offenen Republik*, Freiburg/Basel/Wien: Herder; Oberndörfer (1996): Assimilation, Multikulturalismus oder kultureller Pluralismus-zum Gegensatz zwischen kollektiver Nationalkultur und kultureller Freiheit der Republik, in Bade *Migration-Ethnizität-Konflikt. Systemfragen und Fallstudien*, Osnabrück: Universitätsverlag Rasch; Oberndörfer (2003): Zuwanderung und nationale Identität, in Bundesamt für Anerkennung ausländischer Flüchtlinge *50 Jahre. Behörde im Wandel*, Nürnberg: Selbstverlag.

[9] See Wodak *et al.* (1998): *Zur diskursiven Konstruktion nationaler Identität*, Frankfurt a. M.: Suhrkamp; Matouschek, Wodak and Januschek (1995): *Notwendige Maßnahmen gegen Fremde? Genese und Formen von rassistischen Diskursen der Differenz*, Wien: Passagen-Verlag; Matouschek (1997): Soziodiskursive Analyse öffentlicher Migrationsdebatten in Österreich. Zu Theorie, Methodik und Ergebnissen einer diskurstheoretischen Untersuchung, in Jung, Wengeler and Böke *Die Sprache des Migrationsdiskurses. Das Reden über "Ausländer" in Medien, Politik und Alltag*. Opladen: Westdeutscher Verlag.

[10] See Jäger (2003): Die Kritik am Patriarchat im Einwanderungsdiskurs. Analyse einer Diskursverschränkung, in Keller, Hirseland, Schneider and Viehöver *Handbuch Sozialwissenschaftliche Diskursanalyse. Band II: Forschungspraxis*, Opladen: Leske + Budrich; Jäger (1993): *Brandsätze. Rassismus im Alltag*, Duisburg: Diss; Jäger and Link (1993): Die vierte Gewalt. Rassismus und die Medien. Einleitung, in Jäger and Link *Die vierte Gewalt und die Medien. Rassismus und die Medien*, Duisburg: Diss; Hell (2005): *Einwanderungsland Deutschland? Die Zuwanderungsdiskussion 1998-2002*, Wiesbaden: VS Verlag für Sozialwissenschaften; Carius (2004): Im "berechtigten Eigeninteresse". Die Konstruktion nationaler Identität, in Jäger and Januschek *Gefühlte Geschichte und Kämpfe um Identität*, Münster: Unrast-Verlag; Jung, Wengeler and Böke (1997):

analysis to uncover the discursive, often implicit construction of ethnic or racist categories.[11]

As to the research on nationalism in the Spanish context in general, Nuñez Seixas highlights that "the ideological, political and social presence of Spanish nationalism" "is one of the least researched areas".[12] Besides his own historio-graphical research, the studies of Fusi, Fox and Beramendi provide interesting insights into the historical development of national identity in Spain.[13] Further-more, Dolores Franco's anthology about the image of Spain in literature and philosophy[14] or Boyd's analysis of the transmission of collective representations of national history and identity in education are to be mentioned here. After the transition to democracy, the academic interest in national identity and na-tionalism focused rather on the analysis of the peripheral national identities in Catalonia, the Basque Country and Galicia.[15] Consequently, academic litera-ture concentrating on the history, development and current debate of national-ist movements in the Spanish peripheries is abundant.[16]

Die Sprache des Migrationsdiskurses. Das Reden über "Ausländer" in Medien, Politik und Alltag, Opladen: Westdeutscher Verlag.

[11] See van Dijk, Ting-Toomey, Smitherman and Troutman (1997): Discourse, Ethnicity, Culture and Racism, in van Dijk *Discourse as Social Interaction. Discourse Studies: A Multidisciplinary In-troduction. Volume II*, London/Thousand Oaks/New Delhi: Sage Publications; van Dijk (1984): *Prejudice in Discourse. An Analysis of Ethnic Prejudice in Cognition and Conversation*, Amsterdam/Philadelphia: John Benjamins Publishing Company.

[12] Nuñez Seixas (2001): What is Spanish nationalism today? From legitimacy crisis to unfulfilled renovation (1975-2000), in *Ethnic and Racial Studies*, 42: 5, p. 719.

[13] See Nuñez Seixas (1993): *Historiographical Approaches to Nationalism in Spain*, Saarbrücken: Verlag breitenbach Publishers; Nuñez Seixas (2001): *What is Spanish nationalism today?*; Fusi Aizpúrua (2000): *España. La evolución de la identidad nacional*, Madrid: Ediciones Temas de Hoy; Bera-mendi (2000): Identity, Ethnicity, and the State in Spain: 19th and 20th Centuries, in Safran and Máiz *Identity and Territorial Autonomy in Plural Societies*, London/Portland, OR.: Frank Cass; Fox (1997): *La invención de España. Nacionalismo liberal e identidad nacional*, Madrid: Ediciones Cátedra.

[14] See Franco (1980): *España como Preocupación. Antología*, Barcelona: Editorial Argos Vergara.

[15] See Flynn (2001): Constructed identities and Iberia, in *Ethnic and Racial Studies*, 24: 5, p. 744.

[16] In general see Keating (1993): Spain. Peripheral nationalism and state response, in McGarty and O´Leary *The Politics of Ethnic Conflict Regulation. Case Studies of Protracted Ethnic Conflicts*, Lon-don/New York: Routledge; Valandro (2002): *A Nation of Nations. Nationalities' Policies in Spain*, Frankfurt a. M.: Peter Lang; Guibernau (2006): National identity, devolution and secession in Canada, Britain and Spain, in *Nations and Nationalism*, 12; Guibernau (2007): *The Identity of Nations*, Cambridge: Polity Press; For details on Galicia see Losada (2000): National Identity and Self-government: The Galician Case, in Safran and Máiz *Identity and Territorial Autonomy in Plural Societies*, London/Portland, OR.: Frank Cass. For more information on the Basque

Also studies about immigration have proliferated in the last decade as Spain transformed into an immigration country receiving considerable numbers of non-EU immigrants. Nevertheless, only a few academic references can be found proximate to the analysis of the relationship between immigration and the construction of Spanish national identity.[17] There are, though, a couple of works studying, for instance, attitudes towards the immigrants or the implication of different integration policy concepts.[18] In Catalonia, however, the question of how internal Castilian-speaking migrants influence Catalan national identity has already in the 1960s led to a controversial debate among intellectuals and politicians. Explicit considerations about the relation between immigration and nation-building are hence still part of the current political debate at the Catalan level. Consequently, the question of how immigrants are integrated into societies under the influence of strong minority nationalisms, especially in the Basque Country and Catalonia has also aroused interest among Spanish

---

nationalist movement see Douglass *et al.* (1999): *Basque Politics and Nationalism on the Eve of the Millenium*, Reno: University of Nevada. A comparison between the Basque and Catalan nationalism is provided by Medrano (1995): *Divided Nations. Class, Politics, and Nationalism in the Basque Country and Catalonia*, Ithaca/London: Cornell University Press. Sources on Catalan national identity and nationalism are: McRoberts (2001): *Catalonia. Nation Building without a State*, Oxford: Oxford University Press; Keating (1996): *Nations against the State. The New Politics of Nationalism in Quebec, Catalonia and Scotland*, London: MacMillan Press; Estruch (1991): Die Soziale Konstruktion von nationalen Identitäten. Das Beispiel von Katalonien als Nation im spanischen Staat, in Fröschl, Mesner and Ra´anan *Staat und Nation in multi-ethnischen Gesellschaften*, Wien: Passagen Verlag; Llobera (1996): *The Role of Historical Memory in (Ethno)Nation-Building*, London: University of London; Balcells (1996): *Catalan Nationalism. Past and Present*, Houndmills, Basingstoke, Hampshire: MacMillan Press; Guibernau (1997): Nations without states: Catalonia, a case study, in Guibernau and Rex *The Ethnicity Reader. Nationalism, Multiculturalism and Migration*, Oxford: Blackwell Publishers.

[17] There is for instance Triandafyllidou's analysis discussed later on and various studies examining the historical and recent relation between national identity and Muslim immigration - often using the catchword "maurophobia". See for instance: Zapata-Barrero (2006b): The Muslim community and Spanish tradition. Maurophobia as a fact, and impartiality as a desideratum, in Modood, Triandafyllidou and Zapata-Barrero *Multiculturalism, Muslims and Citizenship. A European Approach*, London: Routledge.

[18] See Birsl *et al.* (2003): *Migration und Interkulturalität in Großbritannien, Deutschland und Spanien. Fallstudien aus der Arbeitswelt*, Opladen: Leske + Budrich; Agrela (2002): La política de inmigración en España: reflexiones sobre la emergencia del discurso de la diferencia cultural, in *Migraciones Internacionales*, 1:2; Zapata-Barrero (2008): Policies and public opinion towards immigrants: the Spanish case, in *Ethnic and Racial Studies*, URL: http://dx.doi.org/10.1080/01419870802302280.

scholars.[19] Zapata-Barrero, for instance, has published various studies analysing the link between autonomous government and immigrant accommodation in Catalonia.[20]

Against the background of the current literature in social sciences the book at hand ranges between two major areas of research examining the link between nation-building and immigration. Although, as described above, there are some studies that deal with similar questions in countries such as Germany, France and the United States, for Spain there can be found hardly any academic reference regarding the construction of national identity in view of the immigration from non-EU-countries. However, Spain is, because of the ongoing inner-Spanish debate about national identity, a very interesting case to look at. The concurrence of a rather complex situation of different nation-building processes and the fast development of immigrant numbers in the last years is without comparison in the EU.

This was certainly also one of the reasons for Triandafyllidou to include Spain into her comparative analysis of the nation-building processes in the three "old" immigration countries (Germany, France and UK) and the three "new" immigration countries (Spain, Italy and France).[21] Her study aims at investigating the role that immigrants play in the definition or re-definition of national identity in each country. The here presented analysis is based on similar theoretical assumptions and draws thus on Triandafyllidou's hypotheses. Yet there are considerable differences in the selection of the empirical material and in the assumptions the methodological approach is derived from. The press articles and interviews examined by Triandafyllidou date back to the mid-1990s when immigration from non-EU countries to Spain was still not very strong. Moreover, it was prior to the decisive debate about the new Law on Aliens which was

---

[19] See Shafir (1995): *Immigrants and Nationalists. Ethnic Conflict and Accomodation in Catalonia, the Basque Country, Latvia, and Estonia*, Albany: State University of New York Press.

[20] See Zapata-Barrero (2002): *El turno de los inmigrantes. Esferas de Justicia y Políticas de Acomodación*, Madrid: Ministerio de Trabajo y Asuntos Sociales; Zapata-Barrero (2004a): *Inmigración, innovación política y cultura de acomodación en España*, Barcelona: Fundació CIDOB; Zapata-Barrero (2005a): Construyendo una filosofía pública de la inmigración en Catalunya: los términos del debate, in *Revista de derecho migratorio y extranjería*, 2005:10; Zapata-Barrero (2006a): *Immigració i Govern en Nacions Minoritàries: Flandes, el Quebec i Catalunya en perspectiva?*, Barcelon: Fundació Ramon Trias Fargas; Zapata-Barrero (2007): Immigration, Self-Government and Management of Identity. The Catalan Case, in Korinman and Laugland *The long March to the West*, Vallentine: Mitchell.

[21] See Triandafyllidou (2001): *Immigrants and National Identity in Europe*, p. 78.

passed in 2000 and which for the first time directed the attention of a broad public to immigration issues and marked the beginning of serious considerations regarding the integration of immigrants.

Although the author mentions the multinational identity and the inner-Spanish diversity as a variable to explain the results of her analysis, the comparative approach constrains her to studying the Spanish context as a whole and leaving aside the perspective of the peripheral national identities. It is, however, necessary to cover both minority and majority national identity discourse, given that they are interdependent. In this study Catalan political discourse was chosen, because the Autonomous Community of Catalonia has received considerable numbers of immigrants, compared to other Spanish regions with strong minority nationalisms such as the Basque Country. Furthermore, Triandafyllidou chose distinct criteria for selecting the empirical material. On the one hand she analysed press discourse[22] and on the other hand the political discourse at the central state level. The latter based on eight interviews of NGO representatives of trade unions and administration officials. Apart from the small number of interviews, the choice of interviewees reflects a very broad definition of "political discourse",[23] whereas in the here presented study, statements and interviews of politicians were incorporated into the actual analysis while the interviews with administration officials, trade unionists and representatives of migrant organizations were used only to backup the results. The selection of empirical material chosen here makes it possible to distinguish between the different political parties and ideologies.

As to the actual methodological approach of her study Triandafyllidou shortly refers to discourse analysis, describing it "as a general analytical approach whose precise implementation depends upon the particular theoretical issues at hand",[24] without going into further details. As a matter of fact, discourse analytical approaches are an excellent instrument to study the construction of na-

---

[22] She quantitatively analysed 43 press articles referring to immigration from Spanish mainstream weekly press (Cambio 16, Sunday edition of El País, and Tribuna de Actualidad), between 1990-1995 (3 months each year).

[23] Triandafyllidou explains her selection of interviewees with the fact that they offered "privileged testimony" of immigration issues.

[24] Triandafyllidou (2001): *Immigrants and National Identity in Europe*, p. 123.

tional identity[25] and have recently also found their way into political sciences.[26] Nevertheless, it is important to explicate the applied concept of discourse, as there are distinct approaches to discourse analysis based on different underlying theoretical assumptions regarding their object of research. It is hence crucial to explain how the actual methodological approach is embedded into these overall discourse theoretical considerations.

Comparing Triandafyllidou's results for the mid-1990s with the recent data presented here in the chapters VI and VII enables me to draw conclusions about the development of migration discourse in the last decade and the changes in the constructions of national identity, at least from a central state perspective.

In chapter II the underlying theoretical assumptions regarding the construction of national identity and discourse analysis are explicated. National identity has been one of the most influential concepts of collective identity. The terms nation, national identity, nationalism are here used to describe categories which are subject to human construction-processes and must therefore be assessed in their actual representation.[27] In view of the extensive literature on nation-building and nationalism only a couple of relevant works are cited to present recurring general patterns of national identity-building such as for instance the reference to a common past. Furthermore, the idealtypical distinction of a civic nation and a cultural or ethnic nation is introduced and ideas are presented about how collective identity is constructed against an "Other", in this case the immigrants. After thorough thought, discourse analysis has turned out to be the most adequate fundament for analysing how national identity is actually constructed at the Catalan and central state level in Spain. Chapter II.2 thus deals with the basic assumptions of discourse analysis, the conception of discourse

[25] See Sutherland (2005): Nation-building through discourse theory, in *Nations and Nationalism*, 11:2.
[26] "Frames", "belief systems" or "discourse" are also used increasingly in political sciences as analytical variables, particularly in the field of International Relations. For an overview over discourse analytical approaches in political sciences see Kerchner (2006): Diskursanalyse in der Politikwissenschaft. Ein Forschungsüberblick, in Kerchner and Schneider, *Foucault. Diskursanalyse der Politik. Eine Einführung*, Wiesbaden: VS Verlag für Sozialwissenschaften, and Nullmeier (2001): Politikwissenschaft auf dem Weg zur Diskursanalyse? in Keller *et al. Handbuch Sozialwissenschaftliche Diskursanalyse. Band I: Theorien und Methoden*, Opladen: Leske + Budrich.
[27] Conscious of the fact that the categories nation, nationalism, nationalistic and national identity are differently defined in the distinct cultural and linguistic contexts. Especially in countries such as Germany and Spain, nationalism is often, also as a descriptive category, connoted negatively, delegitimised by the Nazi and Francoist past of these countries.

and frame followed here, and the particular relation of discourse, knowledge, ideology and power.

To better understand the context of the analysis, the past and recent developments in the two fields linked in this the study are outlined in chapter III and IV: on the one hand the constructions of national identity in Spain and particularly in Catalonia and on the other hand the change from an emigration to an immigration country in the last one and a half decades.

However, as discourse analysis provides only the theoretical framework for analysis, the methodological approach of how the empirical material was actually selected and coded, is described in chapter V. Moreover intermediate data on how politicians refer to immigration and immigrant integration are presented to allow in a next step the isolation and reconstruction of the frames of national identity in Spanish central state and Catalan political discourse.

The *frames* found at each level of government are presented in separate chapters, the ones found in central state political discourse in chapter VI and the ones found in Catalan political discourse in chapter VII. The frames were subsumed in each case under different areas of interest. Some of the frames showed furthermore various dimensions or variations and were thus classified into subframes.

Finally, in the last chapter, these different elements of constructions of national identity in Spain are examined in relation to each other: beginning with the historical dimensions, then asking for the principal categories attributed in each case to national identity, thirdly pointing out the respective definitions of who belongs to the "in-group" and who to the "out-group" and finally drawing conclusions regarding the question of how to classify these constructions of national identity with respect to the differentiation between civic or ethnic nation. In addition, the comparison with Triandafyllidou's results gives hints how to answer the question, if discourse about immigration at the central state level has changed in the last decade.

Due to the rapid changes in migration patterns over the last years, a change in discourse about migration and national identity is to be expected. To conclude, the most recent developments of the political discourse about immigration and immigrant integration in Spain are described and an outlook is given on the challenges to come.

II.
Theoretical assumptions

1. THE CONSTRUCTION OF NATIONAL IDENTITY

Since the nineteenth century national identity has been the most influential concept regarding the self-definition of larger social groups.[1] It was the time when in Western Europe nationalist movements grew stronger and promoted the formation of nation state. Up to then historical research had primarily the function to provide a legitimation basis for these nation-building processes. This is what characterizes, according to Kunze's classification, the first phase of research about nationalism. The second phase commencing in 1882 with Renan's famous lecture "Qu'est-ce qu'une nation?" at the Sorbonne[2] is marked by the differentiation between two types of nations, the political and the cultural nation. In 1983 the publication of Benedict Anderson's book "Imagined Communities"[3] heralded the third phase of research about nationalism and national identity promoting a constructivist turn in its theoretical approaches.[4]

The here presented analysis is hence grounded on a social constructivist approach, presuming that reality is constructed through social practices. In contrast to radical constructivism, social constructivism does not negate the physical existence of things. It focuses rather on the production of meaning and thus on the shared knowledge about them.[5]

---

[1] See Däuble (2000): *Auf dem Weg zum Bundesrepublikaner*, p. 33.
[2] Renan (1996): Was ist eine Nation? Rede am 11. März 1882 an der Sorbonne, in Groenewold *Ernest Renan: Was ist eine Nation? Rede am 11. März 1882 an der Sorbonne. Mit einem Essay von Walter Euchner*, Hamburg: Europäische Verlagsgesellschaft.
[3] Anderson (1983): *Imagined Communities. Reflections on the Origin and Spread of Nationalism*, London/New York: Verso.
[4] See Kunze (2005): *Nation und Nationalismus*, Dortmund: Wissenschaftliche Buchgesellschaft, p. 17.
[5] For the difference between Social Constructivism and Radical Construtivism see Höhne (2001): "Alles konstruiert, oder was?" Über den Zusammenhang von Konstruktivismus und empirischer Forschung, in Angermüller, Bunzmann and Nonhoff *Diskursanalyse: Theorien, Methoden, Anwendungen*, Hamburg: Argument Verlag, p. 24.

The research on the nation, nationalism, nation-building, and finally the construction of national identity has resulted in a broad and diverse academic literature. It is therefore inevitable to limit the discussion to a couple of relevant definitions and remarks about those theoretical concepts the research question and the analysis is based upon.

1.1 Collective identities

While identity usually refers to individual persons, collective identity refers to social systems, to groups. It is "the individual's knowledge that he/she belongs to certain social groups together with some emotional and value significance to him/her of the group membership",[6] thus the self-conception of an individual person as a group member, as a member of a common "We" that forms collective identity.[7] The crucial element here is the belief in belonging together as a group due to certain common characteristics.[8] In contrast to essentialist approaches[9] which assume that collective and especially national identities are naturally given, constructivist approaches rather emphasize the dynamic and continuous construction of social reality by humans.[10] Collective identities are thus not based on fixed variables but are constantly redefined and open to change. Cohen puts it this way:

> "Community exists in the minds of its members, and should not be confused with geographic or socio-graphic assertions of 'fact'. By extension, the distinctiveness of communities and, thus the reality of their boundaries, similarly lies in the mid, in the meanings which people attach to them, not in their structural forms."[11]

---

[6] Abrams and Hogg (1990): An Introduction to the social identity approach, in Abrams and Hogg *Social Identity Theory. Constructive and Critical Advances*, New York/London: Harvester Wheatsheaf, p. 2.

[7] See Ibid., p. 2.

[8] See Weber (1922): *Wirtschaft und Gesellschaft*, Tübingen: Mohr.

[9] The notion of collective or national identity as a primordial phenomenon has been generally discarded by scholars. See Armstrong (1995): Towards a Theory of Nationalism: Consensus and Dissensus, in Periwal *Notions of Nationalism*, Budapest/London/New York: Central European University Press, p. 35.

[10] See Calhoun (1994): Social Theory and the Poltics of Identity, in Calhoun *Social Theory and the Politics of Identity*, Cambridge, M.A.: Blackwell Publishers, p. 13.

[11] Cohen (1985): *The Symbolic Construction of Community*, London/New York: Routledge, p. 98.

The individual ascribes itself to multiple collective identities and roles, such as familial, regional, national, cultural, religious, ethnic, and gender identities.[12] These different group memberships are not necessarily competitive, though it depends on context and situation which of the offered group identity variables are selected and combined for self-identification.[13]

Both individual and collective identity, are built upon the implicit or explicit contrast to other individuals or groups. Their characteristics and categories are defined by reference to a "significant Other".[14] The "self" and its ascribed characteristics make only sense because an "Other", a contrasting image exists.[15] This contrasting image must not necessarily be adversarial, but can also be amicable or indifferent.[16] Besides, there can be various "Others" to which an individual or a community relates. Or they can relate differently to the same "Other" depending on the occasion.[17] Frederik Barth in his study about ethnicity highlights the relevance of symbolic and imaginary "boundaries" which are drawn by self-identification to delimit the group.[18] This process of inclusion and exclusion tends to homogenise intra group characteristics and to highlight intergroup distinctions.[19] Barth's assumptions about ethnic groups can be applied in general to the construction of collective identities, thus also to the definition of national identity.[20]

1.2 Nation, Nationalism and National identity

The definition and use of the analytical categories employed in this study –nation, nationalism, nation-building and national identity– have greatly varied in research. Not only are there differences in the underlying theoretical assumptions, but also are in the connotation of the terms. In US research, for instance,

---

[12] See Smith (1991): *National Identity*, p. 4.
[13] See Wodak *et al.* (1998): *Zur diskursiven Konstruktion nationaler Identität*, p. 59.
[14] See Cohen (1985): *Symbolic Construction of Community*, p. 115.
[15] Räthzel uses here in German the term "Gegenbild", see Räthzel (1997): *Gegenbilder*.
[16] See Ibid., p. 16.
[17] See Cohen (1985): *Symbolic Construction of Community*, p. 116.
[18] See Barth (1969): Introduction, in Barth *Ethnic Groups and Boundaries. The Social Organization of Cultural Difference*, London: George Allen & Unwin.
[19] See Kowert (1998): Agent versus Structure in the Construction of National Identity, in Kubálková, Onuf and Kowert *International Relations in a Constructed World*, New York/London: M. E. Sharpe, p. 107.
[20] See Triandafyllidou (2001): *Immigrants and National Identity in Europe*, p. 27.

nationalism is applied predominantly in a neutral way, whereas in Germany and Spain the term is at least ambivalent if not connoted rather negatively.[21] All the more is it necessary to define those terms for analytical purposes.

In accordance with the above explained constructivist approach to collective identity, nation is defined as a system of common beliefs, an "imagined community". Von Hirschhausen and Leonhard define, moreover, national identity as

"the sum of collective conceptions and images shared by a nation [...], which is expressed in common cultural codes, value systems, beliefs and interests, stabilized and updated by institutions and symbols, and whereby nations identify themselves and legitimize their actions inwardly and outwardly."[22]

The ideological concepts aiming at the construction of a nation and national identity are generally referred to as nationalism or nationalist ideologies. Nationalism is furthermore understood to be the "preferential treatment of the political, social and cultural interpretive pattern nation" to other interpretive patterns of collective identity,[23] functioning thereby as an ideology of integration for a large social group.[24]

Although the "nation is a community which normally tends to produce a state of its own",[25] not all nationalist movements have in historical perspective led to the formation of a nation-state. There are also minority nationalisms competing with the dominant definitions of the nation. For instance in the UK the Scottish nationalist movement, in Canada, Quebec or in Spain the Basque, the Galician and the Catalan peripheral nationalisms.[26] Consequently nationalism is an overall concept that describes quite different phenomena of social reality.[27]

---

[21] See von Hirschhausen and Leonhard (2001): Europäische Nationalismen im West-Ost-Vergleich: von der Typologie zur Differenzbestimmung, in von Hirschhausen and Leonhard *Nationalismen in Europa. West- und Osteuropa im Vergleich*, Göttingen: Wallstein Verlag, p. 13.

[22] Ibid., p. 15, translated from German.

[23] Ibid., p. 14.

[24] See Lemberg (1964): *Nationalismus II. Soziologie und politische Pädagogik*, Reinbek: Rowohlt Taschenbuch Verlag, p. 52.

[25] Weber (1948): The Nation, in Gerth and Wright Mills *From Max Weber: Essays in Sociology*, London: Routledge & Kegan Paul, p. 176.

[26] See Keating (1996) *Nations against the State*, pp. 18-22; Breuilly (1994): *Nationalism and the State*, Chicago: The University of Chicago Press.

[27] See Alter (1985): *Nationalismus*, p. 11.

Although the precise definitions of what and who constitutes the nation differ a lot[28] there are some abstract elements, categories and distinctions which are salient in many definitions of national identity, such as a shared culture, history, traditions, symbols, kinship, language, religion, territory, founding moment and destiny.[29] Nevertheless, as Lemberg points out, as a large social group having one or more of these characteristics in common, such as speaking the same language or stemming from the same ethnic descent, does not automatically conceive itself as a nation, there must be an ideology, a belief-system that attributes a particular value to these characteristics and constructs the nation around those elements.[30]

Various scholars have established typologies of nations or nationalisms depending on which of the mentioned elements is emphasized most in the concrete construction of the nation and national identity. Although these typologies tend to focus only on one particular element whereas the constructions of national identity are far more complex and diverse in reality, they can be used as idealtypes to guide the analysis.[31]

Most studies regarding the nation, nationalism or national identity are based on the distinction between two ideal types of nation. On the one hand the nation is defined on the basis of ethnic and cultural elements (ethnic nation), on the other hand on the political will to form a community, common values and institutions (civic nation).

The concept of *Kulturnation* and *Staatsnation*, made known by Friedrich Meinecke reflects this dualistic categorization.[32] The civic or political conception of nation, the *Staatsnation*, is defined as a collective enterprise which is based on common values and institutions.[33] Renan in his famous lecture "Qu'est-ce qu'une nation" at the Sorbonne in 1882 highlighted the subjective momentum: "The existence of a nation is an everyday plebiscite; it is, like the very existence of the individual, a perpetual affirmation of life".[34] In contrast,

---

[28] For an overview see Hutchinson and Smith (1994): *Nationalism*.
[29] See Guibernau and Hutchinson (2004): History and National Destiny, in *Nations and Nationalism*, 10:1/2, p. 134.
[30] See Lemberg (1964) *Nationalismus II*, p. 52.
[31] See Kunze (2005): *Nation und Nationalismus*, p. 25.
[32] See Meinecke (1908): *Weltbürgertum und Nationalstaat. Studien zur Genesis des deutschen Nationalstaates*, München/Berlin: R. Oldenbourg.
[33] See Keating (1996): *Nations against the State*, p. 5.
[34] Renan (1996): *Was ist eine Nation?*, p. 35; for the English translation of the relevant section see Hutchinson and Smith (1994): *Nationalism*, p. 17.

the *Kulturnation* (cultural nation) is independent of the state and defines itself through supposedly objective cultural criteria, such as common ethnic origin, language, and religion. For cultural nationalists "the essence of a nation is its distinctive civilization, which is the product of its unique history, culture and geographical profile".[35] Cultural nationalism hearkens back to the European romanticist movement, most prominently to Johann Gottfried Herder.[36] The nation is hence not seen rationalistically as a political unit but as a living personality which must be cherished passionately by its members. As a living organic principle the idea of the nation changes and must be renovated and morally regenerated continuously.[37] According to these conceptions a political nation (*Staatsnation*) can comprise different cultural nations (*Kulturnationen*) or vice versa a cultural nation (*Kulturnation*) can be distributed across different political nations (*Staatsnationen*). Both concepts must be seen again as ideal types, but cannot be found in social reality as such.

What above is subsumed under ethnic nation or *Kulturnation*, Oberndörfer sub-classifies furthermore in *Sprachnation, Geschichtsnation, Religionsnation* and völkische Nation. He speaks of *Sprachnation*, as the nation defining itself by means of a common language, of the *Geschichtsnation*, as the nation based on a common past, *Religionsnation*, as a nation constructed around a common religion, and *völkische Nation* as understood to be built on common ethnic descent.

To simplify matters here onwards the term ethnic nation will be used for nations that define themselves predominantly along ethnic and cultural dimensions, all the same following Oberndörfer by explicating which of the elements –language, common past, religion, or ethnic descent– is salient, whereas civic nation will be used for those nations that define themselves predominantly along civic and political dimensions.

A general strategy or pattern to construct and communicate national identity highlighted in many studies on nationalism and nation-building is what Anderson called a "narrative" or "biography" of the nation,[38] that is to say the

---

[35] See Hutchinson (1987): *The Dynamics of Cultural Nationalism. The Gaelic Revival and the Creation of the Irish Nation State*, London: Allen & Unwin, p. 13.

[36] See Barnard (2003): *Herder on Nationality, Humanity, and History*, London/Ithaca: McGill-Queen's University Press/Montreal & Kingston; Barnard (1965): *Herder's Social and Political Thought. From Enlightment to Nationalism*, Oxford: Clarendon Press.

[37] See Hutchinson (1987): *Dynamics of Cultural Nationalism*, pp. 12-19, 30-36.

[38] See Kunze (2005): *Nation und Nationalismus*, p. 75.

construction of a common past.[39] Halbwachs conceptualized this as collective memory.[40] While, according to Nora, the historical memory (*histoire*) as a result of scholarly and scientific research aims at the analytical reconstruction of a historical development as precisely and objectively as possible, collective memory (*mémoire*) is selective and is constituted only by the past events that are chosen to be significant. Collective memory is thus based on the continuous symbolic reproduction of events often situated in the far past.[41] However, this reproduction is not limited to real historical events, it can also result in a redefinition of the past. To describe this "process of formalization and ritualization" Hobsbawm introduced the term "invented traditions".[42]

> "'Invented tradition' is taken to mean a set of practices, normally governed by overtly or tacitly accepted rules and of a ritual or symbolic nature, which seek to inculcate certain values and norms of behaviour by repetition, which automatically implies continuity with the past. In fact, where possible, they normally attempt to establish continuity with a suitable historic past."[43]

Political institutions and ideological movements, nationalist movements in particular have constructed or invented historical continuity using either semi-fiction or forgery. Thus nations and their particular national identity were "invented" by political élites in order to legitimize their power. An important role in the emergence of the Western European nations played symbols and devices like flags, national anthems or the personification of "the nation" in symbol or image, e.g., the French Marianne or the Germania.[44] Even nowadays nations are reproduced daily by symbolical means.[45] Mainly, all these symbols and ceremonies can be subsumed under Hobsbawm's category of "invented traditions" and are thus rooted in the past.

---

[39] See Kolakowski (1995): Über kollektive Identität, in Michalski *Identität im Wandel. Castelgandolfo-Gespräche 1995*, Stuttgart: Klett-Cotta, pp. 47-51.

[40] See Halbwachs (1992): *On Collective Memory*, Chicago/London: The University of Chicago Press.

[41] See Nora (1998): *Zwischen Geschichte und Gedächtnis*, Berlin: Wagenbach.

[42] For concept of invented traditions see Hobsbawm (1983): Introduction: Inventing Traditions, in Hobsbawn and Ranger *The Invention of Tradition*, Cambridge: Cambridge University Press.

[43] Ibid., p. 1.

[44] See Ibid., p. 7.

[45] See the concept of "Banal nationalism", Billig (1995): *Banal Nationalism*, London/New Delhi: Sage Publications.

1.3 National identity and immigration

As explained before collective or, as in this case, national identity is constructed defining itself explicitly or implicitly in contrast to an "Other". Triandafyllidou conceives national identity therefore as a "double-edged relationship". Apart from the inward looking belief of forming a nation and the definition of common features, national identity is constructed as an "in group", distinguishing itself from an "Other", an "outgroup".[46] In the case of nationalist movements this "Other" can be both, an internal "Other", such as competing national identities or minority nationalisms, or an external "Other", such as other nations or supranational institutions. A minority nation within a multinational state might be perceived by the dominant nation as an internal, threatening "Other" or the other way round, the small nation might perceive the dominant nation as a threatening "Other" from which to distinguish itself and seek political autonomy.[47]

In addition, many nation-states face the challenge of immigration. Immigrants are "Others" within the own national territory,[48] who trigger the explicit or implicit reproduction of categories and characteristics of national identity. The definition of these categories and characteristics of national identity implies on the one hand the definition of who is a member of the community and on the other hand who is not, who is a foreigner.[49] There is hence a crucial link between the concept of the own national identity and the treatment of immigration. Confronted with or challenged by immigration, nations tend to redefine or reinforce what they believe to be the basic characteristics binding together the members of their particular "in group". As explained above, there are nations that emphasize ethnic and cultural features, such as ethnic origin, religion, language and on the other hand there are nations that highlight the civic aspects of their commonality.[50] Although the law on nationality has been changed recently towards a more open version, Germany is still presented within Europe as the

---

[46] See Triandafyllidou (2001): *Immigrants and National Identity in Europe*, p. 26.
[47] For a detailled description of internal and external Significant Others see Ibid., p. 36.
[48] See Ibid., p. 4.
[49] See Ibid., p. 2.
[50] For details on the relationship between the definition of national identity and immigration policy see Oberndörfer (1996): *Assimilation, Multikulturalismus oder kultureller Pluralismus*; Oberndörfer (1993): *Der Wahn des Nationalen*; Oberndörfer (2003): *Zuwanderung und nationale Identität*; Oberndörfer (2006): *Nation, Multikulturalismus und Migration*; Schnapper (1994): *Debate on Immigration Crisis*.

prototype of a nation that focuses on ethnic origin as a prerequisite for membership to the nation.[51] It is often compared and contrasted with France that is seen to be closest to the ideal type of a nation that highlights the civic dimensions and the republican values of the political community.[52] Civic nations are generally seen to be more open towards immigration and ethno-cultural diversity than ethnic nations.[53] Immigrants usually bring along their own language, culture and even a different religion. In a civic nation ethnic, cultural, linguistic and religious diversity does not threaten *per se* the self-definition of the nation as long as immigrants respect and follow the basic political and legal norms of the host society. This idea reflects the notion of *Verfassungspatriotismus* (constitutional patriotism), as introduced by Sternberger and postulated by Habermas and others, highlighting the role of the constitution as the decisive frame of reference for the construction of German national identity.[54] In contrast, ethnic nations tend to require assimilation and thus to abandon the idea of collective identity of origin to accept immigrants as full members of the nation.

In many countries public debate about the integration of immigrants has led to a raised awareness or even to a reconsideration and redefinition of self-constructions and ascriptions of national identity. In Germany, for example, facing the lack of integration of many immigrants, often residing in the country already in second or third generation, politicians and intellectuals have discussed in recent years which features of the German culture should be presented as guidelines (*Leitkultur*) to the integration of immigrants. This implied a debate about what is believed to be German.[55]

It is hence possible to reconstruct the concepts and ascriptions of national identity analysing public and political debate about immigration and immi-

---

[51] See Heckmann (2003): From Ethnic Nation to Universalistic Immigrant Integration: Germany, in Heckmann and Schnapper *The Integration of Immigrants in European Societies. National Differences and Trends of Convergence*, Stuttgart: Lucius & Lucius.

[52] See Schnapper, Krief and Peignard (2003): *French Immigration and Integration Policy. A Complex Combination*.

[53] See Däuble (2000): *Auf dem Weg zum Bundesrepublikaner*, p. 64.

[54] See Sternberger (1990): *Verfassungspatriotismus*, Frankfurt a. M.: Insel Verlag; Habermas (1992): Anerkennungskämpfe im demokratischen Rechtsstaat, in Taylor *Multikulturalismus und die Politik der Anerkennung*, Frankfurt a. M.: Fischer Verlag.

[55] For instance the debate of the 1990s in Germany labelled "Leitkulturdebatte". For details see Oberndörfer (2001): Leitkultur und Berliner Republik. Die Hausordnung der multikulturellen Gesellschaft Deutschlands ist das Grundgesetz, *Aus Politik und Zeitgeschichte*, 2001:B 1-2; Tibi (2001): Leitkultur als Wertekonsens. Bilanz einer mißglückten deutschen Debatte, *Aus Politik und Zeitgeschichte*, 2001: B 1-2.

grants, because the public, politicians, intellectuals and the media tend to define national identity in reference to immigrants.

2. Discourse analysis

As explained, in detail in the subsequent chapter there are different nationalist movements in current Spain. Apart from a weak central state nationalism, peripheral nationalism in Catalonia, the Basque Country and Galicia have regained strength after the breakdown of the Francoist regime. The construction of national identity in Spain must therefore be seen within the context of different "Others". On the one hand minority nationalisms perceive central state nationalism as an "Other" that threatens their distinct national identity and on the other hand minority nationalism is seen by conservative circles as threatening the unity of the Spanish nation. The recent radical change from an emigration to an immigration country has added non-EU-immigrants as yet another group of "Others" to the described scenery of inner-Spanish identity quarrels.

The analysis of the political discourse on immigration and immigrant' integration on both, the central state and the Catalan level aims at finding out how national identity is constructed on the side of minority and majority nationalism in view of these "new Others", the immigrants. The concrete categories and features that are defined to form the Spanish or Catalan national identity shall be identified and explained. Furthermore it is shown how the self-conception of national identity differs on both levels reflecting inner-Spanish identity-building processes and what new aspects are added by the need to integrate the immigrants.

Following a constructivist approach I have defined above national identity as a type of collective identity which is constructed by the belief in belonging together as a group due to having in common certain characteristics or features, such as language, culture, ethnic origin, religion, common history or various civic elements. The ideological concepts, aiming at the construction of national identity are referred to as nationalisms or nationalist ideologies.

To reveal and reconstruct these different concepts of national identity constructed vis-à-vis the immigration processes a discourse analytical approach seems most adequate, because it is based on the above explained constructivist assumption that collective identity as a part of social reality is constructed through social practices.[56] Discourse is understood as such a social practice, "signifying the world, constituting and constructing the world in meaning".[57]

However, the term discourse *per se* is a "fuzzy"[58] notion and must be defined before going into the details of discourse analysis. The concept is used to label rather different things. On the one hand in every day language or common sense understanding the term discourse refers to a form of language use, to public speeches or more generally to spoken language or ways of speaking. On the other hand, for discourse analysts discourse is a form of language use combined with functional and interactional aspects.[59] Gee denotes the first as "discourse with a little d" and the second, as discourse with a "Big D".[60]

In this study the terms migration discourse, political discourse, media discourse or public discourse are used in the sense of discourse with a little "d", assigning language use (talk and text) to a specific institutional arena or policy field and facilitating thus the selection of the empirical material.[61] Nevertheless, the object of investigation is the discourse on national identity in Spain –in the sense of discourse with a capital "D".

2.1 Basic assumptions of discourse analysis

Since the 1960s discourse studies have emerged in several disciplines in the humanities and the social sciences, for instance in Ethnography, Sociolinguistics and Pragmatics, Cognitive Psychology, Social and Discursive Psychology, Communication Studies and Sociology.[62] The great variety of approaches and the differences in their basic assumptions regarding discourse makes it difficult to find some common features. However, all discourse analytical approaches focus on

---

[56] See Sutherland (2005): *Nation-building through discourse theory.*

[57] See Fairclough (1992): *Critical language awareness,* London: Longman, p. 64.

[58] See van Dijk (1997d): The Study of Discourse, in van Dijk *Discourse as Structure and Process. Discourse Studies: A Multidisciplinary Introduction. Volume I,* London/Thousand Oaks/New Delhi: SAGE Publications, p. 1.

[59] See Ibid., p. 2.

[60] See Gee (1999): *An Introduction to Discourse Analysis. Theory and Method,* London/New York: Routledge, p. 17.

[61] See Angermüller (2001): Einleitung: Diskursanalyse: Strömungen, Tendenzen, Perspektiven, in Angermüller, Bunzmann and Nonhoff *Diskursanalyse: Theorien, Methoden, Anwendungen,* Hamburg: Argument Verlag, p. 8.

[62] For details on the emergence of the different approaches of discourse analysis, see van Dijk (1997d): *The Study of Discourse;* Keller (2004): *Diskursforschung. Eine Einführung für SozialwissenschaftlerInnen,* Wiesbaden: VS Verlag für Sozialwissenschaften.

written or spoken language use and study it regarding its formal characteristics and structures and/or their content elements.[63]

In general discourse analysis can be defined according to Paltridge as focusing

> "on the knowledge about language beyond the word, clause, phrase and sentence that is needed for successful communications. It looks at patterns of language across texts and considers the relationship between language and the social and cultural contexts in which it is used. Discourse analysis also considers the ways that the use of language presents different views of the world and different understandings. It examines how the use of language is influenced by relationships between participants as well as the effects the use of language has upon social identities and relations. It also considers how views of the world, and identities, are constructed through the use of discourse. Discourse analysis examines both spoken and written texts."[64]

This book in particular is based mainly on the assumptions of an important and well known "school" of discourse analysis, the Critical Discourse Analysis (CDA),[65] complemented with Keller's recent approach of a discourse analysis rooted in the sociology of knowledge of Berger and Luckmann.

Both, as many other approaches of discourse analysis, draw theoretically on the work of the French poststructuralist Michel Foucault.[66] In his writings, such as "The Archaeology of Knowledge" (1972), "The Birth of the Clinic" (1973), "Discipline and Punish" (1977), "The History of Sexuality" (1978) he studied not language "but discourse as a system of representation".[67] He conceptualized discourse as "a group of statements which provide a language for talking about –a way of representing the knowledge about– a particular topic at a particular

---

[63] See Keller (1997): Diskursanalyse, in Hitzler and Honer *Sozialwissenschaftliche Hermeneutik*, Opladen: Leske + Budrich, p. 312.

[64] Paltridge (2006): *Discourse Analysis. An Introduction*, London/New York: Continuum, p. 2.

[65] Critical Discourse Analysis is better to be called a "school", because it comprises a whole bunch of different approaches, based on distinct theoretical assumptions and methodologies. However, what makes discourse analysts critical discourse analysts is that they study discourse with respect to the underlying power relations. Important approaches of Critical Discourse Analysis have emerged around Norman Fairclough, Ruth Wodak, Siegfried Jäger, Teun A. van Dijk and others.

[66] Critical discourse analysis considers also, apart from Foucault, Marxist theory, the theoretical considerations of Gramsci, Althusser, the Frankfurt School (including Habermas) and others.

[67] Hall (2001a): Foucault: Power, Knowledge and Discourse, in Wetherell, Taylor and Yates *Discourse Theory and Practice. A Reader*, London/Thousand Oaks/New Delhi: Sage Publications, p. 72.

historical moment".[68] Discourses hence produce knowledge through language. They create meaning, make already existing things meaningful. According to Foucault "nothing has any meaning outside of discourse".[69] Physical things and objects exist, but it is only within discourse that they become objects of knowledge. Foucault was interested in the rules and practices which regulated discourse and thus the production of knowledge and meaning in different historical periods. Discourse therefore is thought to appear across different texts, actions and sources and never consisting of only one statement. Besides, it is not only language but also includes other social practices. Foucault wanted to "overcome the traditional distinction between what one says (language) and what one does (practice)".[70] This means that all social practices construct meaning and knowledge about the social reality and therefore comprehend discursive aspects.

Approaches of Critical Discourse Analysis are based on Foucault's assumption, defining discourse as a social practice, "signifying the world, constituting and constructing the world in meaning".[71] Although these approaches differ broadly in theoretical background and methodology, their common aim is to study the use of discourse in relation to certain social and cultural issues, preferentially race, politics, gender and identity, and highlight their respective implications.[72] Critical discourse analysts show, moreover, a particular interest in the relationship between language and power.[73] According to them power relations are negotiated and performed through discourse, because discourse both reflects and reproduces such social relations.[74] A critical approach of discourse analysis thus aims at revealing underlying and often hidden relations of power, dominance and hegemony reflected and (re)produced in discourse.

Context is another variable that plays a fundamental role in the description and especially in the explanation of discourse. Van Dijk defines the object of

---

[68] Hall (1992): "The west and the rest", in Hall and Gieben, *Formations of modernity*, Cambridge, Polity Press/The Open University, p. 291.

[69] Michel Foucault (1972): *The Archaeology of Knowledge*, London: Tavistock.

[70] Hall (2001a): *Foucault: Power, Knowledge and Discourse*, p. 72.

[71] See Fairclough (1992): *Critical language awareness*, p. 64.

[72] See Paltridge (2006): *Discourse Analysis*, p. 178.

[73] See Weiss and Wodak (2003): Introduction: Theory, Interdisciplinarity and Critical Discourse Analysis, in Weiss and Wodak *Critical Discourse Analysis. Theory and Interdisciplinarity*, Houndsmills, Basingstoke: Palgrave Macmillan, p. 12.

[74] See Paltridge (2006): *Discourse Analysis*, p. 187.

discourse studies in consequence as "talk and text in context".[75] The context of discourse is "the structure of all properties of the social situation that are relevant for the production or the reception of discourse".[76] Therefore, discourse analysis must take into account the historical, social and institutional context:

> "Describing discourse as social practice implies a dialectical relationship between a particular discursive event and the situation(s), institution(s) and social structure(s) which frame it. A dialectical relationship is a two-way relationship: the discursive event is shaped by situations, institutions and social structures, but it also shapes them."[77]

Furthermore, language users are members of different social categories and contexts or as explained above have different individual and collective identities. Such roles and identities are actively (re)constructed and displayed in discourse and must therefore be taken into account in the analysis.[78]

The approaches subsumed to Critical Discourse Analysis have developed basically in linguistic disciplines such as classical Rhetoric, Textlinguistics, Sociolinguistics, Applied Linguistics, and Pragmatics. However, representatives of CDA recognize that the relation between discourse and society can only be analysed adequately when linguistic and sociological approaches are combined.[79] Van Dijk stresses "that integral discourse analysis is necessarily an interdisciplinary task".[80]

Apart from that, he especially focuses on its cognitive processes and memory representations and argues that:

> "in order to relate discourse and society, and hence discourse and the reproduction of dominance and inequality, we need to examine in detail the role of social representations in the minds of social actors. More specifically, we hope to show

---

[75] See van Dijk (1997d): *The Study of Discourse*, p. 3.
[76] Ibid., p. 19.
[77] Fairclough and Wodak (1997): Critical Discourse Analysis, in van Dijk *Discourse as Social Interaction. Discourse Studies: A Multidisciplinary Introduction. Volume II*, London/Thousand Oaks/New Delhi: Sage Publications, p. 258.
[78] See van Dijk (1997a): *Discourse as Interaction in Society*, p. 3.
[79] See Weiss and Wodak (2003): *Introduction*, p. 7.
[80] van Dijk (1985): Introduction: Levels and Dimensions of Discourse Analysis, in van Dijk *Handbook of Discourse Analysis. Vol. 2: Dimensions of Discourse*, London: Academic Press, p. 11.

that social cognition is the necessary theoretical (and empirical) 'interface', if not the 'missing link', between discourse and dominance."[81]

Keller and colleagues also highlight the importance of these cognitive dimensions. Like van Dijk they draw on the sociology of knowledge of Berger and Luckmann. Discourse analysis is seen as an instrument to reconstruct, socially constructed and shared knowledge.[82] However, in contrast to Critical Discourse Analysis, the approach of a social discourse analysis of Keller ("Wissenssoziologische Diskursanalyse") concentrates rather on the content of discourse, the constructed knowledge as such (What?) than on the structures and rules of its formation (How?).[83] Social discourse analysis thus explores the processes of constructing, objectifying and legitimizing structures of meaning and symbolic systems, and asks for their social implications.[84]

2.2 Discourse, knowledge and ideology

As argued above, group identities, in this case national identity, are socially constructed. According to Berger and Luckmann's sociology of knowledge they are socially constructed knowledge on which our perceptions of the reality are based.[85] Van Dijk differentiates furthermore between knowledge and ideology, defining the latter more generally as the "underlying principles of social cognition". Accordingly, ideologies are a more general type of socially constructed knowledge, serving as the basis for the construction of more specific group-knowledge, beliefs and attitudes.[86] "Ideologies are group-specific 'grammars' of

---

[81] van Dijk (2001): Principles of Critical Discourse Analysis, in Wetherell, Taylor and Yates *Discourse Theory and Practice. A Reader*, London/Thousand Oaks/New Delhi: Sage Publications, p. 301.

[82] See Angermüller (2005): Sozialwissenschaftliche Diskursanalyse als interpretative Analytik, in Keller *et al. Die diskursive Konstruktion von Wirklichkeit. Zum Verhältnis von Wissenssoziologie und Diskursforschung*, Konstanz: UVK Verlagsgesellschaft, p. 29.

[83] See Ibid., p. 30.

[84] See Keller (1997): *Diskursanalyse*, p. 319; Keller (2005a): Wissenssoziologische Diskursanalyse als interpretative Analytik, in Keller *et al. Die diskursive Konstruktion von Wirklichkeit. Zum Verhältnis von Wissenssoziologie und Diskursforschung*, Konstanz: UVK Verlagsgesellschaft, p. 49.

[85] See Berger and Luckmann (2001): *Die gesellschaftliche Konstruktion der Wirklichkeit. Eine Theorie der Wissenssoziologie?* Frankfurt a. M.: Fischer Taschenbuch Verlag.

[86] See van Dijk (1997a): Discourse as Interaction in Society, in van Dijk *Discourse as Social Interaction. Discourse Studies: A Multidisciplinary Introduction. Volume II*, London/Thousand Oaks/New Delhi: Sage Publications, p. 28.

social practices"[87] which coordinate the acts or practices of the individual members of the group. They represent an overall self-definition of collective or social identity defining the shared characteristics of a social group, setting criteria of membership and group access, its norms and values, and its relative position to other groups in order to protect group interests.[88] These ideologically structured group schemata generally codify the specific identity of groups, such as, for instance national identity in relation to other groups, leaving specific tasks and domains to special mental representations. Variations and differences of opinion within the group depend on more specific beliefs and circumstances. Hence intra-group variation is tolerated as long as the basic ideological principles are shared.

What van Dijk describes as ideology or ideologically structured group schemata codifying collective identity, can also be conceived by the concept of frames.[89] According to Snow, Rochford, Worden and Benford a frame is defined as:

> "'schemata of interpretation' that enable individuals 'to locate, perceive, identify, and label' occurrences within their life space and the world at large. By rendering events or occurrences meaningful, frames function to organize experience and guide action, whether individual or collective."[90]

Frames are thus categories and schemata that are already present in the culture and the memories of social actors. Nevertheless, as frames are socially constructed knowledge they underlie the constant process of redefinition and reproduction through discourse. In discourse (media, public or political) social actors can use particular frames deliberately to define and construct social reality according to their interests.[91] This is what Entman denominated framing.[92]

---

[87] See Ibid., p. 28.
[88] See Ibid., p. 26.
[89] For the emergence and development of the concept in different disciplines see Dahinden (2006): *Framing. Eine integrative Theorie der Massenkommunikation*, Konstanz: UVK Verlagsgesellschaft.
[90] Snow *et al.* (1986): Frame Alignment Processes, Micromobilization, and Movement Participation, in *American Sociological Review*, 51:4, p. 464.
[91] See Donati (2001): Die Rahmenanalyse politischer Diskurse, in Keller *et al. Handbuch Sozialwissenschaftliche Diskursanalyse. Band 1: Theorien und Methoden*, Opladen: Leske + Budrich, pp. 151-152.
[92] Definition of framing: "To frame is to select some aspects of a perceived reality and make them more salient in a communicating text, in such a way as to promote a particular problem defi-

The here presented study aims at reconstructing the frames of national identity by analysing political discourse as a particular social practice.[93]

2.3 Discourse and power

To reconstruct the ideas and ideological beliefs of national identity in Spain, political discourse was selected for analysis, assuming that political actors and their discursive actions are crucial in giving rise to an ideological group, more or less coherent.[94] In historical perspective nationalist ideology aiming at the construction of national identity was promoted and shaped primarily by intellectuals and political entrepreneurs.[95] Political discourse alongside intellectual, academic and media discourse forms part of the public discourse. The different arenas of public discourse closely interact. For instance, the media cover political decisions, and political discourse or academia and intellectuals are discussing political and social issues in the media. Therefore, public discourse in general must be taken into account, along with the historical, institutional and social context when analysing political discourse.

An important factor which influences the construction of national identity in discourse and at the same time is influenced by it is the distribution and division of power between different social groups, institutions or political actors.[96] Stuart Hall stresses the following:

"Precisely because identities are constructed within, not outside, discourse, we need to understand them as produced in specific historical and institutional sites

---

nition, causal interpretation, moral evaluation and/or treatment recommendation." Entman (1993): Framing: Toward Clarification of a Fractured Paradigm, in *Journal of Communication*, 43:4, p. 52.

[93] The general and vague term *discourse* here not understood solely as language use, like in common-sense definitions but as embodying furthermore a cognitive dimension of communicating beliefs and a dimension of social interaction in speech or written texts.

[94] See Chilton and Schäffner (1997): Discourse and Politics, in van Dijk *Discourse as Social Interaction. Discourse Studies: A Multidisciplinary Introduction. Volume II*, London/Thousand Oaks/New Delhi: SAGE Publications, p. 214; Donati (2001): *Die Rahmenanalyse politischer Diskurse*, p. 147.

[95] See Eisenstadt (1996): Die Konstruktion nationaler Identitäten in vergleichender Perspektive, in Giesen *Nationale und kulturelle Identität. Studien zur Entwicklung des kollektiven Bewußtseins in der Neuzeit*, Frankfurt a. M.: Suhrkamp, p. 21.

[96] Political actors understood as political groups or as individuals acting as group members.

within specific discursive formations and practices, by specific denunciative strate-
gies. Moreover, they emerge within the play of specific modalities of power."[97]

Political actors, in particular political parties compete for political power.
They try to control and dominate political decisions by persuading the electorate to join their ideological beliefs and to support their objectives through discourse. As ideologies "monitor how language users engage in discourse as members of (dominant, or dominated, or competing) groups or organisations they
are also used to realize social interests and manage social conflict. At the same
time discourse is needed for the reproduction of the ideologies of a group".[98]

Power is here understood as the "power to mark, assign and classify", as the
power to "represent someone or something in a certain way" through repre-
sentational practices.[99] In this study the power to (re)construct and (re)define
frames of national identity in discourse is examined. Especially the question
of the competition between minority and majority nationalism for conceptual
hegemony will be of interest.[100]

The analysis of the frames of national identity discourse(s) in their historical,
social and institutional context also considers communicative power[101] and its
distribution between the different actors, including the access to the discourse
(re)constructing national identity. It must therefore be taken into account who
controls most economic, social, and symbolic resources and therefore has preferential access to public discourse, and who controls institutional discourse
structures.

Before getting into the empirical analysis by explaining the methodological
approach based on the theoretical assumptions above the context, such as the
Spanish historical development, the recent change from an immigration to an
emigration country, the development of Catalan nationalism, the interior migration and recent non-EU-immigration to Catalonia, migration and integration policy approaches, etc., will be described in the following.

---

[97] Hall (1996): Introduction: Who Needs "Identity"? in Hall and Du Gay *Questions of Cultural
Identity*, London: Sage Publications, p. 4.
[98] van Dijk (1997a): *Discourse as Interaction in Society*, p. 7.
[99] Hall (2001b): The Spectacle of the Other, in Wetherell and Taylor *Discourse Theory and Practice.
A Reader*, London/Thousand Oaks/New Delhi: Sage Publications, p. 338.
[100] See Sutherland (2005): *Nation-building through discourse theory*, p. 186.
[101] Ruoff (2007): *Foucault Lexikon*, Paderborn: Wilhelm Fink Verlag, p. 155.

III.
Constructions of national identity in Spain

In comparison to other European States nationalism had been quite weak in Spain prior to the Civil War (1936-1939). As the basic reasons, Payne identified that Spain had already been an independent empire since approximately the eleventh century, that it had not been confronted with a foreign threat since Napoleon and that the traditional Spanish monarchy had never managed to create fully centralized institutions.[1] Accordingly, until the late nineteenth century, Spain was held together only by a weak centralist administration and monarchy. There was no strong nationalist movement that could encourage social cohesion and a sense of national unity.[2]

Nevertheless, many politicians, intellectuals, and authors directed their attention to the question of Spain's collective identity, its past and future development. Until the late nineteenth century the preoccupation with the characteristics of Spanish collective identity, Spain's self-definition and its political, social and economic development was dominated by rather pessimistic views. In her anthology "España como preocupación" (Spain as a preoccupation) Dolores Franco has assembled literature of three centuries. The chapter headings such as "El Realismo: En busca del tiempo perdido" (Realism: In search for the time lost), "La Generación del 98: El dolorido sentir" (The Generation '98: The painful sensation) or "España como problema intelectual" (Spain as a intellectual problem) reflect the perception of Spanish identity as a problematic and complex issue.[3] The 20th century in contrast, generated the Francoist ideology constructing an idealized and homogenized image of Spain dominated by Catholic and Castilian values. Hence, constructions of national identity in Spain have varied and changed broadly over the last two centuries. However, this is not

---

[1] See Payne (1991): Nationalism, Regionalism and Micronationalism in Spain, in *Journal of Contemporary History*, 26:3/4, pp. 479-478.

[2] See Corkill (1996): Multiple National Identities, Immigration and Racism in Spain and Portugal, in Jenkins and Spyros *Nation & Identity in Contemporary Europe*, London: Routledge, p. 155.

[3] See Franco (1980): *España como Preocupación*.

to be seen as a mere succession of different ideas and ideologies about Spanish national identity; it is rather an accumulation of different elements of identity construction which appear and reappear in different periods, promoted by diverse political and social actors.[4] The present construction of collective identity in Spain can thus only be understood against the background of the preceding debates, and can only be explained appropriately having in mind the origin of recurrent national identity concepts. Therefore, beginning with the nineteenth century, a brief overview of the most important ideas and their historical and political context is given in the following with the emphasis on the post-authoritarian period (since 1975).

As to its identity construction processes the Spanish case is particularly interesting, because of its diversity and complexity.

> "Under the common banner of defending Spain as the sole sovereign entity enjoying collective political rights, very different political and social actors are to be found, as well as diverse worldviews and ideological programmes. There are Spanish ethno-nationalists, civic nationalists, cultural nationalists, etc., just as there are Catalan, Basque or Galician ethnic, civic and cultural nationalists, all of them in complex and intricate mixtures..."[5]

The constructions of Spanish national identity and the constructions of peripheral national identity in its different variations can not be treated as separate processes. They are interdependent and interacting interpretations of Spanish identity like two sides of a coin. Fradera describes the relation between both as a sole process of construction of national identity being interpreted in different ways:

> "I think it more reasonable to part from the idea that there was only one process of Spanish national construction which, however, was undertaken using very different interpretations of how and on what foundations it should be put in effect. These diverse interpretations were not exclusively or primarily the result of the opposition between a Spanish nationalism in construction —the normative— and the minor nationalisms of the irredentist peripheries —the exceptions, yet equally normative

---

[4]   See Nuñez Seixas (2001): *What is Spanish nationalism today ?*, p. 720.
[5]   Ibid., p. 725.

in their own way–, but the manifestation of very complex dynamics of interrelation, in which the local and the general dynamics were mutually dependent."[6]

Since it is not possible to include a detailed analysis of all peripheral nationalist ideas the analysis focuses here on the Catalan case. It is, however, not possible to exclude the Basque and Galician case entirely, because they, especially the separatist and violent tendencies of Basque nationalism, contributed crucially to the construction of certain views about Spanish national identity. References to these cases are made when necessary to explain corresponding reactions on the central state level.

1. Struggle for self-definition (19TH and beginning 20TH century)

Nationalism "as the enthusiastic exaltation of the unity of Spain, as an almost mystical faith in her destiny, as a glorification of her military and religious past"[7] only emerged in Spain in the twentieth century". This emergence of a broad common perception of a Spanish national identity was based on a long process of national assimilation in the nineteenth century which required the formation of a unified national market, and educational system, the expansion of mass communication and the construction of a narrow road and railway network.[8] Although, previous to that, the perception of a Spanish national identity was not broad-based, many Spanish authors and intellectuals, as well as foreigners, had focused on the interpretation of Spain's past, its future development and the definition of Spanish identity.

It was the loss of the last Spanish Colonies Cuba, Puerto Rico and the Philippines in 1898 that triggered of an intense analysis of Spanish national identity. The writings of the *Generation '98*, a group of Spanish intellectuals and authors,[9] and their direct intellectual pre- and successors reflect this deep crisis

---

[6] Fradera (2001): El proyecto español de los catalanes: tres momentos y un epílogo, in Morales Moya *Nacionalismos e imagen de España*, Madrid: Sociedad Estatal España Neuvo Milenio, p. 22.

[7] Fusi Aizpurúa (1990): Centre and Periphery 1900-1936: National Integration and Regional Nationalisms Reconsidered, in Lannon and Preston *Élites and Power in Twentieth-Century Spain*, Oxford: Clarendon Press, p. 43.

[8] See Ibid., p. 35.

[9] Important representatives of the *Generation '98* were Ángel Ganivet (1865-1898), Miguel de Unamuno (1864-1936), Antonio Azorín (1873-1967), Ramiro de Maeztu (1875-1936), Antonio Machado (1875-1939), Pío Baroja (1872-1957), Ramón Menéndez Pidal (1869-1968).

of national consciousness. These intellectuals thought of Spain primarily as a problem, a preoccupation and even a historical failure.[10] They called it a country which lacked any political will and moral, built upon a history of decadency and despotism. Spain, how they saw it, was a unique, marginalized and backward country at the periphery of a capitalist and industrialized Europe, the representation of abnormality.[11] They saw a need for the regeneration[12] of the Spanish national identity focusing largely on Castilian culture.[13] Thus, Castile emerged as the essence of Spanish national identity. In poetry, novels, paintings an idealized, mystic and bellicose image of Castile was constructed, a Castile represented by figures like the knights Don Quijote, and El Cid, a Castile of old towns and lonely roads, of vast desolate and inhospitable sceneries, priests and captains, a Castile as portrayed in the paintings of El Greco and Zuloaga.[14]

Apart from these Castilian-dominated images, the romanticist idea of an Andalusian Spain, constructed and distributed primarily by French and English travellers between 1830 and 1850, persisted.[15] They described Spain as a picturesque, exotic country, the country of gypsies and corridas (bullfights), the country of dramatic passion and religious pathos. As described in Mérimée's "Carmen" (1845),[16] in Washington Irving's "The Alhambra" (1833) or in Hemingway's novels "The Sun" (1926), and "Death in the Afternoon" (1932).[17]

The weak and inefficient Spanish central state of the nineteenth century inspired intellectuals not only to construct and reconstruct images of a unified Spanish national identity, but also promoted nationalist consciousness and sentiments in some of the more developed and culturally differentiated regions of the Spanish

---

[10] For more details and references see Varela (1999): *La Novela de España. Los Intelectuales y el Problema Español*, Madrid: Taurus, Chapter III: La Literature del Desastre o el Desastre de la Literatura, pp. 111-143.

[11] See Fusi Aizpúrua (2000): *España. La evolución de la identidad nacional*, pp. 24-26; Bernecker and Brinkmann (2004): Spaniens schwierige Identität. Geschichte und Politik zur Jahrtausendwende, in Bernecker and Dirscherl *Spanien heute. Politik -Wirtschaft- Kultur*, Frankfurt a. M.: Vervuert Verlag, pp. 123-125.

[12] Often referred to as *Regenerationism*.

[13] See Beramendi (2000): *Identity, Ethnicity and the State in Spain*, p. 92.

[14] See Fusi Aizpúrua (2000): *España. La evolución de la identidad nacional*, pp. 26-28; See Varela (1999): *La Novela de España*, Chapter IV: Castilla, Mística y Guerrera, pp. 145-176; See Fox (1997): *La invención de España*, pp. 202-204.

[15] See Varela (1999): *La Novela de España*, p. 177.

[16] The basis for the Libretto of Georges Bizet's widely known opera "Carmen".

[17] See Fusi Aizpúrua (2000): *España. La evolución de la identidad nacional*, p. 26.

periphery.[18] These regions claimed political reform of the central state authorities and more political and economic power. Nevertheless, the political implications of these peripheral nationalist movements were still quite weak in the nineteenth century, only growing stronger with the beginning of the twentieth century and parallel or rather in opposition to a Spanish "nationalization".[19] The development of the Catalan nationalism is elaborated in chapter III.6.

2. FRANCOISM (1939-1975)

During the first decades of the twentieth century and especially during the dictatorship of Primo de Rivera in the 1920s the ideological foundations for the fascist authoritarian rule of Franco were laid. However, as we have seen, some ideas and elements of the regime's centralized catholic nationalism derive from the nineteenth century debate about Spain's national identity. Through the Second Republic and up to the Civil War (1936-1939) Catholic intellectuals adopted the mission to fight the increasing secularization of the middle classes by enhancing the image of a traditionally catholic Spain which was threatened by laicist and Marxist ideas. They created the myth of Spain and Anti-Spain which served to explain the splitting up of the formerly complex and multiply fragmented Spanish society into two camps during the Civil War in the 1930s.[20] According to them it was a fight between "Spain" and "Anti-Spain", between religion and atheism, between Christian civilization and barbarianism. At the end, the "only true Spain" emerged victoriously, and a considerable part of the Spaniards, of Spanish history and intellectual life stayed behind, "brutally amputated" and oppressed until Franco's death in 1975.[21] The victorious fascist regime successfully constructed and distributed, via educational policy,[22] propaganda on certain symbols, and manipulation of mass-media, the "Catholic and traditionalist version of Spanish nationalism, which centered its nationalist dis-

---

[18] See Fusi Aizpurúa (1990): *Centre and Periphery 1900-1936*, p. 37.
[19] See Fusi Aizpúrua (2000): *España. La evolución de la identidad nacional*, pp. 234-236.
[20] See Juliá (1990): The Ideological Conversion of the Leaders of the PSOE, 1976-1979, in Lannon and Preston *Élites and Power in Twentieth-Century Spain*, Oxford: Clarendon Press, Chapter VII: Tarea del Intelectual Católico: Reconquistar para Cristo la Sociedad y el Estrado, pp. 275-315.
[21] Ibid., p. 288.
[22] A detailed description and analysis of educational policy and national identity is provided by Boyd (1997): *Historia Patria. Politics, History, and National Identity in Spain, 1875-1975*, Princeton, New Jersey: Princeton University Press.

course in the essentialist affirmation of a Catholic Spain basically identified with Castile".[23] The school book "España es así" (This is Spain) written by Augustín Serrano de Haro in 1946 provides a concrete example of Francoist discourse about the historical roots of Spanish Identity:

> "Spain had been Catholic since 589 and was eternally so despite the republican experience. The Arab conquest was possible only because the Moors were aided by Jews and traitors. The failure to expel the Arabs (for almost 800 years) was due to internal divisions. The moral is that all Spain's ills have stemmed from lack of unity. But for the zeal and patriotism of the Catholic Kings, Spain would never have emerged from the dark days of anarchy; order is solely possible under authoritarian rule...."[24]

As shown above, the construction of collective identity is not only based on the positive definition of its characteristics, it also needs to define negatively what it is not by contrasting it with an "Other" or "Others". In the case of the Francoist nationalist ideology, the external "Others" were the neighbouring Western European states and their political systems of multi-party, secular democracies. Since the End of World War II the Spanish authoritarian regime was an exception, an anomaly within Europe and became increasingly isolated.[25] Franco's strategy to face foreign pressure and critics was to emphasize Spanish uniqueness and its distinctive features and turn it into something positive. To promote tourism, a sector of growing importance since the 1960s, the Francoist regime propagated the slogan "España es diferente" ("Spain is different") highlighting the country's "ever shining" sun, its beautiful beaches, and the romanticist image of "Toros and Flamenco".[26]

Contrary to that, the opposition to the authoritarian regime in exile drew a dark and pessimistic picture of the conditions in Spain. They saw a miserable, underdeveloped, and left-behind society, a country which, isolated from other European countries, faced economic failure and which persisted in an anti-modern, narrow-minded ideological framework.[27]

Internally, all expressions of regional identity and peripheral nationalist movements questioning the idea of a unified national identity of Spain and the

---

[23] Nuñez Seixas (2001): *What is Spanish nationalism today?*, p. 720.
[24] Cited by Graham (1984): *Spain. Change of a Nation*, London: Michael Joseph, p. 39.
[25] See Fusi Aizpúrua (2000): *España. La evolución de la identidad nacional*, p. 29.
[26] Flynn (2001): *Constructed identities and Iberia*, p. 707.
[27] See Fusi Aizpúrua (2000): *España. La evolución de la identidad nacional*, p. 29.

features attributed to it were oppressed. This referred especially to the regions having already developed a strong peripheral national identity and autonomous institutions prior to the Civil War, the so-called "historical Nationalities" (the Basque Country, Catalonia and Galicia).[28] Not only was the whole administration settled and centralised again in Madrid, but it was also forbidden to use the regional languages, Euskadi, Gallego, and Catalá in public. It is therefore no surprise at all that opposition to the regime developed and grew strongest in these peripheral regions. The fight of peripheral nationalist movements against the Francoist domination and repression became a synonym for democratic opposition. That is why during the transition period, the aim of democratisation and the claim for recognition of regional autonomy were inseparably linked.[29]

3. THE FORMATION OF THE SPANISH "STATE OF AUTONOMIES"

The structure of Spain's current political system dates back to the transition period in the late 1970s and early 1980s. The democratisation process was based on a fragile "pact" between the "two Spains",[30] represented by the former Francoist elites on the one hand and the democratic opposition on the other hand. A peaceful transition was only possible, because a tacit agreement existed on leaving untouched issues concerning the cruelties and massacres committed during the Civil War and in its aftermath. Until recent years, there has not been a process of coming to terms with the past.[31] During transition the political actors concentrated on the future of the Spanish state.[32] They were able to negotiate a new constitution which reflected both, the idea of Spain as a single nation

---

[28] See Valandro (2002): *A Nation of Nations*, p. 14.

[29] See Sánchez Prieto (2001): Nación Española y Nacionalismos, in de Blas, Botti, Ezkerra and Pablo Fusi *La nación española: historia y presente*, Madrid: Fundación para el analisis y los estudios sociales, p. 156.

[30] The two Spains (Spanish: las dos Españas) is a phrase from an untitled short poem by Antonio Machado referring to the left-right political divisions in Spain. The idea of a divided Spain dates back at least to the nineteenth century. Santos Juliá, a Spanish historian, describes in detail the development of this idea in his book "Historias de las dos Españas". See Juliá (2004): *Historias de las dos Españas*, Madrid: Taurus.

[31] See Schlee (2008): *Die Macht der Vergangenheit. Demokratisierung und politischer Wandel in einer spanischen Kleinstadt*, Baden-Baden: Nomos-Verlag.

[32] See Nohlen and Hildenbrand (2005): *Spanien. Wirtschaft-Gesellschaft-Politik. Ein Studienbuch*, Wiesbaden: VS Verlag für Sozialwissenschaften, p. 255.

and the claim of peripheral nationalisms in the Basque Country, Catalonia and Galicia for regional autonomy.

After Franco's death in 1975 the newly enthroned King Juan Carlos set the course for a slow and cautious democratisation process.[33] So that in 1977, after 40 years of authoritarian regime, the first free elections could be held.[34] As the major political forces emerged the centrist UCD (Unión de Centro Democrático), led by Prime Minister Adolfo Suárez with 35 per cent and the PSOE (Partido Socialista Obrero Español) which gathered 29 per cent of the votes. Apart from these two formations, representing the democratic centre, two further political parties gained a remarkable number of votes: On the left-wing, the PCE (Partido Comunista de España), the communist party, with 9.2 per cent. On the right-wing, the Alianza Popular (AP), under the leadership of Manuel Fraga Iribarne, a former minister of Franco, obtained 8.3 per cent.[35]

The newly elected Spanish parliament initiated immediately the negotiation process and the drafting of a new constitution. The major political parties recognised the need to make concessions to Catalan and Basque nationalism, but wanted to limit autonomy to those regions and prevent a federalisation of the state.[36] The ambiguous and vague formulation of the second article of the Spanish Constitution reflects the obligation to reconcile the conservative idea of a centralist political system with the claim for a federal state structure, supported by the left-wing parties and the peripheral nationalist movements.[37]

---

[33] The Spanish transition process is often described in literature as the example of a so-called "transición pactada", a transition to democracy, negotiated between the elites of the authoritarian regime and the democratic opposition. See Merkel (1999): *Systemtransformation. Eine Einführung in die Theorie und Empirie der Transformationsforschung*, Opladen: Leske + Budrich, pp. 257-259.

[34] For more historical details see Schmidt (2005): *Kleine Geschichte Spaniens*, Bonn: Bundeszentrale für politische Bildung.

[35] See Ibid., pp. 484-485.

[36] See Keating (1993): *Spain. Peripheral nationalism*, p. 217.

[37] See Nuñez Seixas (2001): *What is Spanish nationalism today?*, p. 722.

Artículo 2[38]

La Constitución se fundamenta en la indisoluble unidad de la Nación española, patria común e indivisible de todos los españoles, y reconoce y garantiza el derecho a la autonomía de las nacionalidades y regiones que la integran y la solidaridad entre todas ellas.	The Constitution is based on the indissoluble unity of the Spanish Nation, the common and indivisible homeland of all Spaniards; it recognizes and guarantees the right to self-government of the nationalities and regions of which it is composed and the solidarity among them all.

On the one hand the constitutional text emphasizes the unity of the Spanish nation on the other hand it introduces the possibility of self-government for the so-called "historical nationalities", the Basque Country, Catalonia and Galicia, and the other regions. It does not provide however a clear definition of the terms nationality and nation, "though during the parliamentary debates the meaning of 'nationality' was reduced to that of a 'cultural and linguistic community', which was not a subject of sovereignty".[39] Until today, in every discussion about issues referring to the territorial organization of the state and the political system the same underlying concepts emerge. There are the conservatives still stressing the need to preserve the unity and uniqueness of the Spanish nation, and the left-wing parties defending the idea of Spain as a multinational state. The formula in between, seeing Spain as a "nation of nations",[40] is also heard frequently.

In spite of these fundamental ideological differences considering the national identity of Spain, and the disapproval of the AP and the Basque nationalists, the major political parties managed to adopt the new Spanish Constitution. It was afterwards, in December 1978, approved by referendum, with a clear majority of 87 per cent of the Spanish population. Herewith, the foundations of the post-authoritarian Spanish political system were laid.[41]

Spain is a parliamentary monarchy, limiting the king's role predominantly to representative tasks. The Spanish parliament (*Las Cortes*) consists of two cham-

---

[38] Congreso de los Diputados: *Constitución Española*, URL: http://www.congreso.es/funciones/constitucion/const_espa_texto.pdf, [19.02.2007].
[39] Nuñez Seixas (2001): *What is Spanish nationalism today?*, p. 723.
[40] A formula, popular also in social-sciences literature, e.g., see Valandro (2002): *A Nation of Nations*.
[41] For details about the Spanish political system see Nohlen and Hildenbrand (2005): *Spanien*.

bers, the Congress and the Senate. However, the latter is no typical territorial representation like the second chamber in Germany, the *Bundesrat*.[42] The
autonomous communities (*Comunidades Autónomas* = CCAA) appoint only
a small number of its members whereas the rest is elected directly along with
parliamentary elections.[43]

With respect to the territorial organization of the Spanish state the Constitution allows two different "types" of autonomous communities: The first is the
"usual" type, according to Article 143. It goes along with a low competence
level, but enables as well administrative as political decentralisation. The second
type, according to Article 151 of the Constitution, allows a higher competence
level, political autonomy, legislative competences. etc. At the beginning of the
process only the so-called "historical nationalities" were able to fulfil the demanding preconditions to follow the even more demanding path for autonomy.
They were granted a special status. However, the Constitution also includes the
opportunity for autonomous communities to follow the "slower" path in order
to reach the higher competence level.[44] As described below, for the Catalan case,
the negotiation process of the Statutes of Autonomy (Estatutos de Autonomía),
their adoption and the formation of an autonomous institutional structure took
a few years time. But since 1983 Spain has consisted of seventeen autonomous
communities, and the two North-African enclaves Ceuta und Melilla, which are
until present heavily disputed between Morocco and Spain.[45] The autonomous
communities, for their part, consist of provinces. Only ten of them contain various provinces, whereas the others are formed by a single province. Every autonomous community has its own government, headed by a president, its administrational body, and elects a unicameral parliament which functions in 4-year
parliamentary terms. The distribution of competences between the central state

---

[42] See Colomer (1998): The Spanish "State of Autonomies": Non-Institutional Federalism, in *West European Politics*, 21:4, pp. 49-51.
[43] For a detailed description of the Spanish Senate and its functions see Cordes und Kleiner-Liebau (forthcoming): Der spanische Senat-Wandel territorialer Repräsentation zwischen dezentralem Einheitsstaat und Föderalstaat, in Riescher, Ruß and Haas *Zweite Kammern*, München/Wien: R. Oldenbourg Verlag.
[44] See Article 148.2. See furthermore Hildenbrand (1993): Das Regionalismusproblem, in Bernecker and Collado Seidel *Spanien nach Franco. Der Übergang von der Diktatur zur Demokratie 1975-1982*, München: R.Oldenbourg Verlag, pp. 116-118.
[45] In theory, it would be possible for Ceuta and Melilla to become autonomous communities, according to Article 144 of the Spanish Constitution, but it is more likely that on the long run they will join the CCAA of Andalusia. See Congreso de los Diputados: *Constitución Española*, URL: http://www.congreso.es/funciones/constitucion/const_espa_texto.pdf, [19.02.2007].

and the autonomous communities results from four different elements: The regulations of the Constitution,[46] the respective Statute of Autonomy, special decrees (Reales Decretos de Traspaso) to transfer competences, and the decisions of the Constitutional Court with respect to competence conflicts.[47] Apart from the constitutional text all other elements are dynamic. The Statutes of Autonomy can be renegotiated with the central government. Thus in 2006 seven Statutes of Autonomy were in parliamentary process, and by 2008 six of them adopted: the Statutes of the autonomous communities of Catalonia, Valencia, the Balearic Islands, Castile-Leon, Aragon and Andalusia.[48]

In the years since transition, the transfer of competences has advanced remarkably. In 2002 only 5 per cent of the transferable competences remained with the central state. Nowadays, 45 per cent of state expenditures are assigned to the autonomous communities.[49] Nevertheless the distribution and transfer of financial resources constitute a permanent source of conflict between the autonomous communities and the central government and among the autonomous communities.

The asymmetries within the "State of Autonomies",[50] resulting from the varying historical and socio-economic background of each autonomous community, and the different legal status have led to a complex and inhomogeneous network of interests and potential conflicts within Spanish politics.

Catalonia, as one of the "historical nationalities" is a good example to better understand the development of the peripheral nationalisms and their influence in Spain.

---

[46] See in Article 148.1 and 149.1 the list of possible competences the autonomous communities are able to assume. For the "lower" competence level there are listed 22 materia in 148.1, for the "higher" competence level 32 could be transferred according to 149.1. See Congreso de los Diputados: *Constitución Española*, URL: http://www.congreso.es/funciones/constitucion/const_espa_texto.pdf, [19.02.2007].

[47] See Nohlen and Hildenbrand (2005): *Spanien*. For details on the distribution of competences between the Central state and the Autonomous Communities see Pérez Royo (1992): Die Verteilung der Kompetenzen zwischen Staat und Autonomen Gemeinschaften, in Nohlen and González Encinar *Der Staat der Autonomen Gemeinschaften in Spanien*, Opladen: Leske + Budrich.

[48] ELPAIS.com (2004): *Cuatro estatutos y 40 leyes*, 02.01.2007, URL: http://www.elpais.com, [04.01.2007].

[49] See Nohlen and Hildenbrand (2005): *Spanien*, p. 290.

[50] See González Encinar (1992): Ein assymetrischer Bundesstaat, in Nohlen and González Encinar *Der Staat der autonomen Gemeinschaften in Spanien*, Opladen: Leske + Budrich.

3.1 From "Spain versus Europe" to "Spain as a part of Europe"

It has always been an important part of the Spanish nation-building process and thus an element of national identity to define and position itself in reference to the other European states. Already in the nineteenth century, the Generation '98 observes, compared to other European countries, a Spanish backwardness in social, economic, and political developments. They oscillated between an "Europeanization" and a "Hispanization". The latter tended to adopt European influences not as such, but transform them into something genuinely Spanish. The first two decades of the twentieth century were determined by opening to influences from other European countries and liberal ideas. Many Spanish artists, intellectuals, and even politicians travelled, studied and worked abroad. But this was ended abruptly by the outbreak of the Civil War. As we have seen above, the Francoist regime again stipulated the divergence with respect to Europe.[51] While the regime propagated a defensive, self-sufficient anti-Europeanism in the 1950s, "this kind of discourse became more and more inappropriate in the 1960s due to the failure of autarkic economic policy and the need to open Spanish economy to European markets".[52] Yet the economic opening towards western European democratic systems in the latter half of Franco's authoritarian rule was not accompanied by a political opening.

Hence, during the transition to democracy the application for EC membership was derived from the strong will to become part of Europe again. On the one hand the inclusion into the Common Market was necessary in order to continue the path of economic modernization and growth on the other hand being a member of the EC would definitively end the political separation. Spain was to be no longer "different", but a "normal" European country.[53] It entered the European Communities in 1986.

4. THE POLITICAL DEVELOPMENT UNTIL TODAY

The UCD which dominated the transition period from 1976 until 1982 was an alliance of very heterogeneous interests. There were liberals and conservatives,

---

[51] See *Flynn (2001): Constructed identities and Iberia*, p. 707.
[52] Díez Medrano and Gutiérrez (2001): *Nested identities: national and European identity in Spain*, p. 762.
[53] See Bernecker and Brinkmann (2004): *Spaniens schwierige Identität*, pp. 127-129.

Christian and Social Democrats joined together by the consensus on democratisation. Soon these differences became more and more obvious and internal disputes divided the party. In 1981, Suárez resigned, among other things because of internal quarrels over the regionalization politics. This step accelerated the decline of the UCD which definitely disintegrated after the crushing defeat in the 1982 elections.[54]

The PSOE won the elections in 1982 with an absolute majority and stayed in power until 1996. Furthermore, it had transformed from a socialist party with a working class electorate to a social democratic party representing a broad political spectrum, including the bourgeois centre.[55] It even broke with the UGT (Unión General de Trabajadores), the socialist trade union which in 1988 even called for a general strike against the liberal economic policy of the PSOE government.[56] The PSOE government under Prime Minister Felipe González aimed at modernizing Spain. Although elements of social politics, like the improvement and reform of the social security and education system were important, it also reformed the military, the tax system and privatized state companies. The admission to the European Communities in 1986 contributed to an economic boom. Spain received considerable subsidies from Brussels and foreign investment increased. The biggest challenge for the PSOE government was to fight the ETA terror.[57] Although by cooperating with the French security forces it became easier to pursue the ETA activists who frequently have crossed the Spanish-French border, Spanish police and military were not really successful in this task. Over the fourteen years of socialist government 377 persons lost their lives in ETA attacks, most of them policemen and soldiers.[58]

The PSOE profited a lot from the fact that for many years there was no serious conservative opponent. The Alianza Popular under Fraga Iribarne was the only political party on the right that could have formed an opposition,

---

[54] See Baumer (2001): Jenseits der Pyrenäen: Parteiensysteme und gesellschaftliche Konflikte in Spanien und Portugal, in Eith and Mielke Gesellschaftliche Konflikte und Parteiensysteme, Opladen: Westdeutscher Verlag, pp. 147-148.

[55] See Gillespie (1989): The Spanish Socialist Party. A History of Factionalism, Oxford: Clarendon Press, pp. 299-367 and Müller (1994): Politische Parteien in Spanien (1977-1982). Interne Konflikte und Wahlverhalten, Saarbrücken: Verlag für Entwicklungspolitik Breitenbach, p. 42.

[56] See Baumer (2001): Jenseits der Pyrenäen, p. 148.

[57] ETA stands for Euskadi Ta Askatasuna (Basque Country and its Freedom). The terrorist organization was founded in 1959 to fight for Basque independence. For more details see Waldmann (1990): Militanter Nationalismus im Baskenland, Frankfurt a. M.: Vervuert Verlag.

[58] See Schmidt (2005): Kleine Geschichte Spaniens, p. 508.

but it never reached over 25-30 per cent of the votes. At the "Congreso de refundación" in 1989 the AP experienced a programmatic modernization and opened up to the political centre. It was renamed Partido Popular (PP).[59] Besides, a new generation of leaders emerged. In 1989 José María Aznar led the party into the general elections.

On the left wing the PCE had increasingly lost support. That is why in 1986 for the first time it presented itself in elections as part of a left-wing alliance, the Izquierda Unida (IU). The IU is a heterogeneous group representing communist, feminist, ecologist values.[60] Both, the Basque (PNV) and the Catalan nationalists (CiU) had influence on the central state level. They had various seats in the Spanish Congress and Senate. After the elections of 1993 the PSOE was only able to form a minority government and depended on the support of the CiU representatives in parliament.

Also the succeeding PP government under Prime Minister Aznar (1996-2000) had no absolute majority and was forced to sign a formal agreement with the Catalan nationalists.[61] Nevertheless, the Spanish conservatives continued their political discourse against the peripheral nationalisms, referring to the idea of a single Spanish nation and the threat peripheral nationalist movements posed to its unity. And the most obvious expression of this threat to the Spanish state was still the ETA. The ceasefire propagated in September 1998 was already broken by the ETA 15 months later, and the attacks and the bombing continued. In 2002 the PP government managed to forbid the political wing of the ETA, the party Herri Batasuna (HB). The PP won the elections in 2000 with an absolute majority and was thereafter able to govern without the support of the Catalan nationalists. With the help of the PP majority in the Spanish parliament, the government of Aznar could push through a number of important decisions, against the resistance of the other political parties and even against the Spanish public. Under the PP government the external relations of Spain were characterized by a growing self-confidence. Thus, the Spanish President aimed at playing a more important role in the EU. Along with Poland he voted against the draft of an EU constitution. It was not possible to find a compromise until the PSOE won the elections in 2004 and the EU Constitution

---

[59] See Jost (1994): *Die politische Mitte Spaniens. Von der Unión de Centro Democrático zum Partido Popular*, Frankfurt a. M.: Peter Lang, pp. 255-261.
[60] See *Baumer (2001): Jenseits der Pyrenäen*, p. 149.
[61] See McRoberts (2001): *Catalonia. Nation Building*, p. 76.

was adopted by referendum of the Spanish people.[62] The transatlantic relations changed under Aznar's leadership as well. He sought a close cooperation with the Bush Administration and supported its politics towards the Middle East. Although the majority of the Spaniards were against the Iraq war, Aznar sent Spanish troops. This decision caused large public protests and mass demonstrations. As to its southern neighbour Morocco, the Spanish government sharply defended its territorial claims. In 2002, a few Moroccan soldiers occupied the Isla Perejil, a very small uninhabited rocky island. Spain sent one of its warships and reconquered the island. Shortly before the next general elections, on March 11, 2004 a terrorist attack on Madrid's suburban trains afflicted Spain. Almost 200 people died and approximately 1,500 were injured in these attacks. At an early stage proves appeared that pointed to an Islamist background of the attacks, but the PP government omitted this information and solely blamed the ETA. Nevertheless, the information on a possible involvement of Islamist terrorists was made public and caused immediate protests and demonstrations against the government's restrained information policy. The general indignation was expressed by vote on the March 14 elections. Against all previous polls and surveys the PSOE won the election.[63] The PSOE government under President José Luis Rodríguez Zapatero immediately ordered the retreat of the Spanish troops from Iraq. It also offered the autonomous communities to renegotiate their Statutes of Autonomy.[64]

By that time, the Socialists had come to power in Catalonia. After 23 years of CiU government under Pujol, the PSC won the elections in 2003. As it could not reach an absolute majority it formed a coalition with the ERC and the IC-V (Iniciativa per Catalunya-Verds), the so-called *Tripartit*. The new Statute of Autonomy was drafted and negotiated with the central government.[65] The main conflicting issues were financial autonomy, the status of Catalan versus Castilian and the definition of Catalonia as a nation in the preamble of the Stat-

---

[62] See analysis Maihold and Maurer (2005): Neue Impulse aus Europas Süden. Spanien und Portugal stärken ihre Initiative im europäischen Einigungsprozess, in *SWP-Aktuell*, 2005:13.

[63] Süddeutsche Zeitung (2004): *Das Ende der Arroganz*, 16.03.2004, p. 3.

[64] See El País (2004a): *Las Reformas estatuarias que proyecto cada autonomía*, 24.05.2004.

[65] For a detailed description of the argumentative and legislative process of the new Catalan Statute of Autonomy see Nagel (2007): El debate sobre la relación entre centro y Autonomías en España, in Bernecker and Maihold *España: del consenso a la polarización. Cambios en la democracia española*, Madrid/Frankfurt a. M.: Iberoamericana/Vervuert, pp. 281-288.

ute.[66] Finally, in March 2006 the Statute was passed by the Spanish Congress and on June 18, 2006 the Catalans adopted it by referendum, 74 per cent voted "yes", approximately 21 per cent no.[67] Because of the change of their Statute of Autonomy, the Catalans called for premature elections which took place on November 16, 2006. Although the CiU could regain votes and the PSC lost, the latter was able to renew the coalition with the ERC and the IC-V, led by the new President José Montilla.[68] He is the first president of the *Generalitat* stemming from the Castilian immigration of the 1960s.[69]

5. RIGHT-WING AND LEFT-WING CONSTRUCTIONS OF NATIONAL IDENTITY

More than 30 years after Franco's death and the end of his authoritarian regime the debate about Spanish national identity and Spanish nationalism is still under way and probably more controversial than ever. Until the mid-1990s academic research emphasized the study of the peripheral national identity and nationalisms.[70] This reflects the way of dealing with it in the political arena where "any explicit affirmation of Spanish nationalism was automatically delegitimised and identified with the defence of the old tenets advocated by Francoism".[71] Until today, a widespread denial of the existence of a Spanish nationalism can be observed.

> "The purported non-existence of Spanish nationalism also constitutes a common belief which is currently reproduced by prominent intellectuals, politicians and the mass-media. Even for most Spanish opinion-makers, as well as for a large part of the Spanish academic community, Spanish nationalism is virtually a non-existent phenomenon, dissolved at the end of Francoism and the birth of the democratic Monarchy established by the 1978 Constitution."[72]

---

[66] NZZ (2005): *Tauziehen um die Autonomie in Katalonien*, 05.08.2005; El País (2005): *La Reforma del Estatuto Catalán. Comparación del Texto vigente y del proyecto*, 14.10.2005.

[67] Elmundo.es (2006): *Resultados Referendum Estatuto Catalán 18 Junio 2006*, URL: http://www.elmundo.es/especiales/2006/06/estatuto-catalan/resultados/globales/09/, [20.02.2007]. Parlament de Catalunya: *Organic Law 6/2006 of the 19th July, on the Reform of the Statute of Autonomy of Catalonia*, URL: http://www.parlament-cat.net/porteso/estatut/estatut_angles_100506.pdf, [19.02.2007].

[68] See TAZ (2006): *Wahlschlappe für Sozialisten in Katalonien*, 03.11.2006, 10.

[69] See Bernecker, Esser and Kraus (2007): *Eine kleine Geschichte Kataloniens*, Frankfurt a. M.: Suhrkamp, pp. 205-206.

[70] See Flynn (2001): *Constructed identities and Iberia*, p. 707.

[71] Nuñez Seixas (2001): *What is Spanish nationalism today?*, p. 721.

[72] Ibid., pp. 719-720.

Although, in reference to Spain, the terms nationalism, nationalist and national identity had almost disappeared from political and public discourse there was a need to redefine the characteristic of the newly democratic Spanish state during the transition period.[73] This happened over all implicitly by avoiding the controversial terms, using others instead, such as "patriotism" or "loyalty to the Constitution". Apart from the constitutional text itself which establishes "the indissoluble unity of the Spanish nation",[74] explicit self-reference as nationalist or nationalism is limited predominantly to the peripheral nationalist claims.[75] Nuñez Seixas names three reasons for the "invisibility", not "inexistence", of Spanish nationalism since 1975.[76] Apart from the already explained delegitimisation of expressions of Spanish national identity due to the propaganda use of the Francoist regime he mentions the merging of the ideas of the anti-Francoist left with the claims of the peripheral national movements and thus their alienation from an overarching Spanish national identity. But most important he refers to the controversial and fragmented conceptions of Spain's recent history, namely the Civil War and the succeeding authoritarian rule. As the transition did not imply a break with the former elites there was no explicit anti-fascist consensus like in Germany after 1945 which could have served as the foundation for the newly established democracy. Consequently, the interpretations of past events and the deduced implications for today's characteristics and elements of a Spanish national identity vary broadly among political actors. Nonetheless, the "two main tendencies of Spanish nationalism since 1975 correspond to the democratic right and the left. And within each of them, it is also possible to differentiate further currents of thought".[77] As it is not possible to cover all the multiple facets of Spanish identity construction, differing even on the individual level, the following categorization must be understood as a simplified idealtypical description of its main elements as described in academic literature.

---

[73] See Fusi Aizpúrua (2000): *España. La evolución de la identidad nacional,* p. 31.

[74] Congreso de los Diputados: *Constitución Española,* URL: http://www.congreso.es/funciones / constitucion/const_espa_texto. pdf, [19.02.2007], Art. 2.

[75] See Nuñez Seixas (2004): Gibt es einen spanischen Nationalismus nach 1975? Zur Rolle des historischen Gedächtnisses im spanischen "patriotischen" Diskurs, in Ruchniewicz and Troebst *Diktaturbewältigung und nationale Selbstvergewisserung. Geschichtskulturen in Polen und Spanien im Vergleich,* Wroclaw: Wydawnictwo Uniwersytetu Wroclawskiego, p. 229.

[76] See Ibid., pp. 230-231.

[77] Nuñez Seixas (2001): *What is Spanish nationalism today?,* p. 727.

5.1 The Spanish right

At the right-wing political spectrum different constructions and elements of national identity coexist.[78] There still can be found an almost nostalgic memory of the national Catholicism propagated by the Francoist regime. Although as an ideology it persists only within the far-right political parties and organizations some elements seem to have survived in the discourse of the conservative PP. For instance the importance which is given to the Catholic faith or the historic events it defines as constituting, such as the "Reconquista" or the conquest of Latin America.[79]

> "Intellectuals close to the Popular Party (Partido Popular, PP) still insist on the historical foundation of Spain as the outcome of the Christian kingdoms' fight against the Muslims during the Middle Ages, while also emphasizing the role played by the so-called Catholic Kings at the end of the fifteenth century, the unifying agency of the Spanish monarchy –which is supposed to be an essence of the Nation– and the intrinsically Catholic nature of the Spanish nation, whose moment of glory was the discovery and conquest of America."[80]

These concepts of Spain's historical and religious foundations are rarely openly displayed, but implicitly do still guide part of the political discourse and attitudes of politicians, as we will see below.

Nuñez Seixas differentiates between four main facets of what he calls "right-wing neo-nationalism": 1) "neo-nationalism" constructed as a continuous reaction against peripheral nationalisms, 2) the search for a regeneration of the historical foundations of Spanish national identity, 3) the inclusion of a regionalist variant of Spanish nationalism, and 4) the existence of a small variant, barely relevant which acknowledges the multinational character of Spain.[81]

The first facet listed by Nuñez Seixas shows that it is not only the peripheral nationalisms which are constructed in reaction to Spanish national identity, but also vice versa. According to that conservative politicians frequently refer to the discriminatory cultural and linguistic policies of Catalonia and the Basque country and advocate the defence of the individual right to use Castilian standing over the collective right of the Catalans and Basques to deliver their own

---

[78] For a detailed description see Ibid.
[79] See Nuñez Seixas (2004): *Gibt es spanischen Nationalismus nach 1975?*, p. 235.
[80] Nuñez Seixas (2001): *What is Spanish nationalism today?*, p. 729.
[81] See Ibid., pp. 729-731.

language and cultural identity. Peripheral nationalism is actually sometimes presented as tending toward totalitarianism imposing a monolithic culture. However, the outstanding element legitimizing the proliferation of Spanish unity and a strong Spanish national identity has been the persistence of the ETA terrorism and Basque separatist tendencies.

In view of the increasing support for the peripheral nationalisms and its questioning the national identity of Spain, academics and intellectuals, apparently supported by the governing PP, attempted to explain and justify the existence of a unified Spanish nation.[82] In search of the historical foundation and legitimacy of Spain as a plural, diverse but unified nation the conservatives try to ignore as far as possible the recent Spanish history of Francoism and the Civil War. This part of the Spanish history is seen as "abnormal" and must be overcome and forgotten. Although, since the 1990s and even more intensely since 2000, an increasing interest in a historical investigation of these periods, both in academia and the public, has set in, the official discourse of the Spanish conservatives emphasizes that Francoism lies in the past and should be treated as such. The efforts of restoring the memory of the victims cause, according to them, the persisting political cleavage in the present Spanish society.[83] It was not until the year 2000 that for the first time the Spanish government condemned the Franco dictatorship with unanimity of all political parties.[84] And there is still a strong resistance within the Spanish right against the implementation of the recent Spanish Law of Historical Memory (Ley de Memoria Histórica) which promotes a policy of finally coming to terms with the country's militant and dictatorial past.

For the historical foundations of today's Spanish national identity conservatives rather go further back in time. They refer to the generation '98 and their notion of "unity in diversity" which now has been realized in the present State of Autonomous Communities. Moreover, Spain is seen as the

"true outcome of historical experience, and its objective 'body' has adopted different forms over time. In contrast, the stateless nationalisms are accused of being based upon

---

[82] See Bernecker and Brinkmann (2004): *Spaniens schwierige Identität*, p. 132.
[83] See Nuñez Seixas (2004): *Gibt es spanischen Nationalismus nach 1975?*, pp. 236-237.
[84] See Silva Barrera (2004): *The Importance of Remembrance in the Transition to Democracy in Spain*, p. 71.

historical fantasy and non-scientific literary imagination, due to the inventions of second-rank intellectuals."[85]

According to that, the Spanish nation has existed prior to the 1978 constitution and can be traced back till the Reconquista in the late fifteenth century.

"According to Aznar, Spain is a historical reality forged in the fifteenth century and unified by the agency of the Monarchy and the existence of a common project, whose best expression would be the benign and generous Spanish conquest of America."[86]

Supported by conservative circles, a generation of revisionist historians, both professional and non-professional, recently have contributed to a shifting in the historical self-conception of the Spanish public. Emphasising the glorious Siglo de Oro (Golden Age), they neglect the more recent history.[87]

Even though the official discourse of the Spanish right constructs national identity in reaction to the nationalisms in the peripheral regions, as explained above, there also exists, however, a "regionalist variant" of Spanish nationalism within the PP.[88] In Galicia and the Balearic Islands the PP governments have implemented moderate policy of defence of the peripheral languages and cultural and promoted a regional cultural identity.

"This 'self-identification' includes the conscious pride of being Galician and loving the dignified language and traditions of the region, combined with the promotion of folklore, popular culture and the 'recognition of own personality', from which a right to 'a real self-government and administration' emerges."[89]

While the promotion and maintenance of a regional cultural heritage within a unified Spanish nation is welcomed, self-determination and separatist tendencies are fiercely rejected. This variant of Spanish nationalism thus refers to

[85] Nuñez Seixas (2001): *What is Spanish nationalism today?*, p. 731.
[86] Ibid., p. 731.
[87] See Sáez Arance (2004): Auf der Suche nach einem neuen "demokratischen Zentralismus"? Nationalkonservativer Geschichtsrevisionismus im Spanien der Jahrtausendwende, in Ruchniewicz and Troebst *Diktaturbewältigung und nationale Selbstvergewisserung. Geschichtskulturen in Polen und Spanien im Vergleich*, Wroclaw: Wydawnictwo Uniwersytetu Wroclawskiego, p. 268.
[88] See *Nuñez Seixas (2004): Gibt es einen spanischen Nationalismus nach 1975?*, p. 235.
[89] Nuñez Seixas (2001) *What is Spanish nationalism today?*, p. 733.

pre-Civil War regionalist intellectuals and politicians which stand for moderate positions.[90]

5.2 The Spanish left

Nuñez Seixas detects constructions of national identity using the label "patriotism" also in the Spanish left, particularly within the PSOE.[91] Characteristic for the left-wing discourse about Spain's national identity starting with the mid-1980s is the emphasis of Spain as a political nation embracing diverse cultural nations.[92]

> "According to this definition, the multiple character of Spanish identities and the combination of cultural nations in a single political nation represented by the 1978 Constitution allows some intellectuals, politicians and opinion-makers to refer to Spain as a 'nation of nations', whose existence is legitimized in History."[93]

This concept legitimizes a Spanish national identity and at the same time permits to accommodate the claims of peripheral nationalists for more political autonomy.

As to the basis of this political national identity the Socialists have adopted the concept of *Verfassungspatriotismus* (constitutional patriotism).[94] This means, as explained above, that the political community is based upon universalistic principles which were laid down in a constitution. Hence, the democratic legitimization of Spain as a nation is attributed to the Constitution of 1978.

The concept of "constitutional patriotism" has been used in the past at some occasions also by PP politicians. However, the underlying strategy and interest in referring to this concept and to the constitution has been quite different. The conservatives, for instance, deduced the inflexibility regarding the Status Quo of the "State of Autonomies".[95]

---

[90] See Nuñez Seixas (2004): *Gibt es spanischen Nationalismus nach 1975?*, p. 235.

[91] See Nuñez Seixas (2001): What is Spanish nationalism today?, p. 735.

[92] Following the concept of Friedrich Meinecke explained in chapter II.2.

[93] Nuñez Seixas (2001): *What is Spanish nationalism today?*, p. 736.

[94] See for the use of the term "constitutional patriotism" in Spanish discourse: Velasco (2002): Patriotismo Constitucional y Republicanismo, in *Claves de la Razón Práctica*, 125.

[95] See Bernecker and Brinkmann (2004): *Spaniens schwierige Identität*, p. 139.

In spite of the reference to "constitutional patriotism", the Spanish left, like the Spanish right fall back on a certain historical determinism, searching for an inherited historicist legacy of the Spanish nation. Nuñez Seixas states that

> "instead of building on the consent of the governed, Spain is conceived as an old nation constructed upon the existence of a common culture and history dating back to the early Renaissance. [...] In other words, the Spanish left still fears that the constitutional State will be unable to survive if deprived of its 'emotional', cultural or historical appeals to a common citizen identity, and based solely on the citizens' will. Hence, a form of Spanish 'patriotism' –which avoids the label 'nationalism'– is considered to be a necessary element to maintain the social cohesion Spain as a political community."[96]

Essentialist attitudes which believe that Spain is an "objective reality created by previous generations of Spaniards, whose national spirit was already expressed in positive terms (discovery of America in 1492) and in negative terms (expulsion of the Jews by the end of the fifteenth century)"[97] represent a minority position within the Spanish left-wing.

But also in Socialist discourse an increasing importance has been given to the construction of a collective memory. During the government of Felipe González the Socialist party renounced to cultivate the memory of the victims of Civil War and Francoist dictatorship, because they did not want to risk the tacit agreement not to touch the recent past. Instead, they focused on the future, on the modernization, and the Europeanization of Spain. On official occasions representatives of the left-wing political parties tended to search for historical roots prior to the Civil War. This changed in the 1990s in response to the growing attempts of the Spanish right to give Spanish national identity a historical foundation. The left-wing political parties began to demand an official condemnation of the cruelties and massacres committed during Civil War and the authoritarian regime.[98] They supported initiatives which tried to reconstruct the happenings, they claimed to finally demolish Francoist monuments, to change Francoist street names, and to open up burial pits and recover the bodies of executed opposition members.[99] This has helped to slowly recover the memory

---

[96] See Nuñez Seixas (2001): *What is Spanish nationalism today?*, pp. 737-738.
[97] Ibid., p. 739.
[98] See Nuñez Seixas (2004): *Gibt es spanischen Nationalismus nach 1975?*, pp. 234-236.
[99] For more information see *Silva Barrera (2004): The Importance of Remembrance in the Transition to Democracy in Spain.*

of the Civil War and the period of authoritarian rule for a broad public, even though this process is still in its early stages. In 2007 the adoption of the Ley de Memoria Histórica (Law of Historical Memory) was an important step en route to recovering and dealing with the crimes and massacres of the Civil War and Francoism. For instance it sets aside all verdicts due to political and ideological reasons pronounced by Francoist courts, it increases the compensations for victims and their families, it promotes the finding and opening of mass burial pits, and it provides that all symbols linked to the Francoist past shall be removed from the public sphere. The current PSOE-government has made quite clear that it is determined to push the implementation of the new law's provisions albeit the strong opposition of the PP.

Recapitulating the previous pages, it can be stated that both on the left and right of the political spectrum "Spanish nationalist discourse exists today as a multifaceted and plural set of ideas".[100] Those diverse constructions of Spanish national identity are constructed explicitly or implicitly in reference to the stateless nationalisms of the peripheral regions. In the following "the other side of the coin", the construction of Catalan identity, its historical development and its diverse elements are presented.

6. CATALONIA "FER PAÍS"[101]

As shown above, nation-building processes often imply the attempt to construct collective memory.[102] Likewise, Catalan nationalists make frequent use of historical events to emphasize the long tradition of a distinctive national identity in Catalonia.

---

[100] Nuñez Seixas (2001): *What is Spanish nationalism today?*, p. 743.

[101] "Fer país" (Building a country) is the term Jordi Pujol introduced to describe the Catalan nation-building process, restoring Catalan culture and language, and Catalonia's historical memory. See Centre d'Estudis Jordi Pujol: Activist, in: URL: http://www.jordipujol.cat/en/jp/activista [23.01.2007].

[102] See concept of Halbwachs, explained in chapter II.2.

6.1 Historical roots[103]

In the fifteenth century Catalonia formed part of the Kingdom of Aragón-Catalonia. By then, it included the territories of Sardinia, Sicily, and southern Italy and had become one of the most important mercantile powers in the Mediterranean area.[104] Catalonia experienced an economic and cultural boom. Besides, in earlier centuries it had developed a powerful political and administrative structure. King Ferdinand I not only accepted the *Usatges* (a kind of a Catalan constitution established in 1150), but approved of the existence of the *Corts Reials Catalanes* (Royal Catalan Corts). This parliamentary institution already dated back till the early thirteenth century and had an advisory and legislative function. He also laid down the definitive legal form of an executive government body, the *Generalitat*. Both are seen as predecessors in the long republican tradition of Catalan self-government.[105] With the marriage of Isabella of Castile and Ferdinand II of Aragón, the so-called "Catholic Kings" in 1469 a process of centralization set in during which Catalonia lost its political, economic and cultural influence. Between 1640 and 1651 the Catalan rebellion against the Bourbon contender to the Spanish throne, Philip V marked an important date in the history of Catalonia. The so-called *Guerra dels Segadors* (War of the Mowers) ended with the Catalan capitulation. However, this rebellion against the centralist monarchical system is remembered by a popular song, *El Cant dels Segadors* which is today the official Catalan national anthem. The wars for hegemony in Europe continued and Catalonia was the plaything of the major European powers. In 1714 Barcelona fell to Philip V, king of Spain. He abolished the Catalan institutions, centralized administration, and substituted Catalan by Castilian as official language. The date, September 11, 1714, is remembered as a symbol for the Catalan will to survive as a people and as a nation. It was made Catalonia's National Day (*La Diada*).[106]

Although Catalonia had existed as a distinctive entity already for centuries, the ideology of Catalan nationalism did not develop until the nineteenth cen-

---

[103] For detailed information on the history of Catalonia see Valandro (2002): *A Nation of Nations,* Chapter 4.2; Balcells (2004): *Breve historia del nacionalismo catalán,* Madrid: Alianza Editorial; Ferreres i Calvo and Llorens i Villa (1992): *Història de Catalunya,* Barcelona: Grup Promotor.
[104] See Keating (1996): *Nations against the State,* p. 115.
[105] For more details of this early Catalan institutions see McRoberts (2001): *Catalonia. Nation Building,* p. 10.
[106] See Llobera (1996): *The Role of Historical Memory,* pp. 9-10.

tury when modernisation and industrialisation transformed the Catalan society.[107] Influenced by the "Romantik" (e.g. Herder)[108] and the nationalist movements in other European countries, the new Catalan bourgeoisie promoted a revival of Catalan language and literature, the *Renaixença*.[109] Along with a new sense of pride in Catalonia and its historical achievements, claims for political self-government grew louder. In 1892 the first draft statute for a Catalan self-government, the *Bases de Manresa*, was released. It outlined a Catalan government with substantial powers.

But it was not until 1914 that the four Catalan provinces were granted self-government. The *Mancomunitat* was established as a union of the four Provincial Councils (Barcelona, Girona, Lleida and Tarragona) under the overall control of Enric Prat de la Riba. It had more symbolic than real political power,[110] and was abolished in 1925 under the dictatorship of Primo de Rivera (1923-1931). The Second Republic offered a new chance for establishing Catalan autonomy. On the April 14, 1931 the leader of the left-wing nationalist party ERC (Esquerra Republicana), Lluís Companys[111] proclaimed the Catalan Republic. But it was not until 1932 that the first Catalan Statute of Autonomy was adopted. The newly created *Generalitat* was only given administrative responsibilities and no legislative power. Since its origins, Catalan nationalism "had undergone a remarkable transformation, and a new version, rooted in republican and leftist forces, had become dominant".[112] The bourgeois-led movement had committed the error of supporting the regime of Primo de Rivera. Therefore, after it was overthrown, leftist groups rooted in the lower middle classes took over the Catalan movement and formed the ERC. In 1934, Lluís Companys went as far as to proclaim an independent Catalan Republic. As a result, the Spanish government suspended the Statute of Autonomy and Catalan institutions until 1936 when a new left-wing government re-established them.[113] During the Civil War,

---

[107] See McRoberts (2001): *Catalonia. Nation Building*, p. 2.
[108] For instance the Catalan thinker Francesc Xavier Llorens i Barba drew upon Herder's notion of a *Volksgeist*. See Fèlix Villagras i Hernàndez (2006): *Frances Xavier Llorens i Barba: cultura i política a la Catalunya del segle XIX*, PHD thesis presented to the Universitat de Barcelona, Facultat de Geografia i Història, Departament d'Història Contemporània the April 28, 2006, URL: http://www.tesisenxarxa.net/TDX-0615106-114946/#documents, [07.02.2008]
[109] See Payne (1991): *Nationalism, Regionalism, Micronationalism in Spain*, p. 482.
[110] Valandro (2002): *A Nation of Nations*, p. 60.
[111] From 1933 until the end of the Second Republic, President of the Generalitat.
[112] McRoberts (2001): *Catalonia. Nation Building*, p. 35.
[113] See Valandro (2002): *A Nation of Nations*, p. 61.

Catalonia fought on the republican side. In defence of the Republic, anarchists and Marxist forces, rooted in the Catalan working-class, won more and more power. Although the ERC was the leading force in the *Generalitat* until the end of the Second Republic, the political power of the left-radical forces grew steadily. The final defeat by Franco's troops in February 1939 ended the first period of Catalan self-government.

6.2 Catalan nationalism under Franco

The former leaders and supporters of Catalan nationalism were either executed, imprisoned or went into exile. Franco suspended all Catalan institutions and made Castilian the sole official language. The use of Catalan was forbidden in public, and children were taught solely in Castilian. McRoberts describes in detail to what extent all expressions of Catalan identity were suppressed:

> "The Catalan flag and anthem were outlawed, and patriotic monuments were destroyed. The public use of Catalan was banned, and Catalan-language signs and notices were removed. Public employees were forbidden to use Catalan either in public buildings or outside. Catalan culture was banned as a subject at the University of Barcelona, and cultural institutions such as the Institut d'Estudis Catalans were closed. Teachers suspected of Catalanist sympathies were transferred elsewhere and were replaced by teachers from other regions of Spain, who, having no knowledge of Catalan language and culture, could be counted upon to advance the cause of assimilation. Signs were erected on trains and in other public places inciting people to 'Speak Spanish! Speak the Language of the Empire!' Mail was censored, and correspondence in Catalan was destroyed. Catalan could not be used in the civil register; Catalan first names were banned and Catalan family names were transcribed in Castilian."[114]

In spite of the strong repression, different forms of passive resistance emerged. In private circles and organisations the Catalan cultural heritage was preserved and cultivated. The Abbey of Montserrat became a symbol of a conservative, catholic Catalan nationalism. The hymn of the football club F.C. Barcelona substituted the prohibited Catalan national anthem *Els Segadors*.[115] The musical

---

[114] McRoberts (2001): *Catalonia. Nation Building*, p. 41.
[115] For the importance of the C.F. Barcelona for Catalan identity-building see Bernecker, Esser and Kraus (2007): *Kleine Geschichte Kataloniens*, pp. 202-203.

movement, *Nova Cançó* managed to transport political demands for free expression of Catalan culture and identity via their songs.[116]

In the 1960s the Francoist regime opened up to an economic liberalisation and modernisation process. Thus Catalonia entered a process of rapid industrial expansion and Franco reduced his economic and political pressure. As a result a cultural revival set in. Under the auspices of the Catholic Church, especially at the Abbey of Montserrat, a new, distinct Catholic version of Catalan nationalism emerged. Jordi Pujol, son of an upper-class Barcelona family, became the leader of this new generation of Catalanists. He wanted to create a modern Catalonia. In order to provide the foundations for political action, he intended to build a strong Catalan identity based on cultural and economic process. He called this Catalan nation-building process "fer país" (build a country).[117]

At the political left, Catalan nationalism was treated ambiguously. The ERC had disappeared under Franco, and the PSUC (Partit Socialista Unificat de Catalunya), following the example of the Spanish Communist Party (PCE), rather highlighted issues concerning class-conflict and did not officially support Catalan autonomy until 1965. The PSOE, having a strong electorate of non-Catalan immigrant workers, was cautious about assuming Catalanist claims.[118] Nevertheless, by the late 1960s a strong demand for democracy and autonomy existed, which was institutionalised in 1971 by forming the *Assemblea de Catalunya* (Catalan Assembly). Likewise in 1971, the ERC was reorganised and the formation of other Catalan political parties was to follow.

6.3 Formation of the Autonomous Community of Catalonia

As already shown above, the Catalan claim for autonomy was linked inseparably to the pressure for democratisation. In the first democratic elections after Franco's death, in 1977 the Catalans demonstrated their support for democratic transition and Catalan autonomy voting for the socialist and communist parties. The governing party of Prime Minister Suarez won in all Spain except in the Catalan provinces.[119] Pujol's electoral coalition Pacte Democrátic per Catalunya

---

[116] Its leading figures were Lluís Llach , Joan Manuel Serrat, and Raimon. See Esser (2007): Diguem yes! Vom Protestlied zum Mestizo-Sound. Musik in Katalonien, in Esser and Stegmann *Kataloniens Rückkehr nach Europa 1976-2006*, Berlin: Lit Verlag, pp. 186-189.
[117] See Keating (1996): *Nations against the State*, p. 121.
[118] See Keating (1993): *Spain. Peripheral nationalism*, pp. 215-217.
[119] Balcells (2004): *Breve historia del nacionalismo catalán*, pp. 234-235.

(Democratic Pact for Catalonia), which most nationalist parties had joined, won 16.8 per cent of the vote in Catalonia and filled eleven seats in the Spanish Parliament (*Las Cortes*).[120] This led to a strengthening of the Catalan cause. In October 1977 the *Generalitat* was restored provisionally. Josep Tarradellas (ERC), formerly president of the Catalan government in exile, was appointed transitional president.[121] After the adoption of the new Spanish Constitution a commission of the *Asamblea de Parlamentarios de Cataluña* elaborated a Statute of Autonomy which was adopted by referendum in 1979.[122] The Spanish Constitution and the Statute establish the following institutions of self-government for the Autonomous Community of Catalonia (*Comunitat Autónoma de Catalunya*): The *Generalitat*, consisting of a unicameral parliament (*Parlament de Catalunya*) with 135 members, elected every four years, its President (*President*) and an Executive Council or regional government (*Govern*).[123] Due to its special status as a "historical nationality" Catalonia was also granted a high court of justice (*Tribunal Superior de Justicia de Catalunya*) to guarantee limited judicial autonomy. Furthermore, the Catalan Statute of Autonomy of 1979 laid down the competences exclusively limited to the Catalan self-government. The most important areas besides the organisation of its political institutions are: education and research, language policies, cultural affairs, archives, museums and libraries, tourism and leisure, social welfare, health and hygiene, public works, infrastructure and transport, and finally various competences in regional economy matters.[124]

The first elections were held in Catalonia on the March 20, 1980. Under the leadership of Jordi Pujol's CiU (Convergència I Unió), a moderate nationalist Christian Democrat formation uniting the CDC (Convèrgencia Democràtica de Catalunya) and the UD (Unió Democràtica) won the elections with 27.7 per cent, followed by the Catalan Socialist party, the PSC-PSOE[125] (22.3 per

---

[120] See Valandro (2002): *A Nation of Nations*, p. 63.

[121] For more details on the pre-autonomous regime see Hildenbrand (1993):*Das Regionalismusproblem*.

[122] See Balcells (2004): *Breve historia del nacionalismo catalán*, p. 237.

[123] For details on the Catalan political system see Valandro (2002): *A Nation of Nations*, Chapter 4.5.

[124] Generalitat de Catalunya: *Estatut d'autonomia de 1979*, URL: http://www.gencat.cat/generalitat/cat/estatut1979/index.htm, Art. 9, [19.02.2007]

[125] In 1978, the Catalan Socialists (PSC, Partit Socialista de Catalunya) had affiliated to the Spanish socialist party, the PSOE.

cent), and the PSUC (18.7 per cent).[126] As the PSC rejected the offer to form part of a governing coalition, the CiU was forced to establish a minority government supported by the votes of the ERC and the UCD. Nevertheless the CiU was able to push through Catalan interests in exchange for their support of the UCD government in the Spanish parliament. However, this initial phase of the autonomy process, favourable for Catalan nationalism, was followed by a second phase of stagnation.[127] After the failed coup d'état, the Spanish government of the UCD wanted to cool down the process of autonomy and prevent a further weakening of the central state. It successfully negotiated with PSOE the *Ley Orgánica para la Armonización del Proceso Autonómico* (LOAPA, Organic Law for the Harmonization of the Autonomous process), a law to harmonise the various types of autonomy.[128] The Catalan and the Basque government challenged this law in the constitutional court. Several of its main provisions were disallowed.[129] With the 1984 elections an era of consolidation as to Catalan autonomy began. The CiU secured an absolute majority and managed to preserve it in the two succeeding elections.

6.4 Strengthening Catalonia's national identity

The system of political parties is rather complex in Catalonia, because it is not only determined by the axis "left-right", but also by the nationalist axis "Catalanismo-españolismo",[130] whereas Catalan nationalism, in its different variations, predominates.[131]

After the transition to democracy Catalan nationalism emerged in various forms. The most important ones are: First of all, a moderate, conservative nationalism embodied by the CiU, secondly, a radical, left-leaning Catalan nationalism aiming at Catalonia's independence within a European framework, represented by the ERC, and finally, a radical, separatist form of Catalan nationalism. The latter lacked support in the Catalan society and had hardly any po-

---

[126] For electoral results 1980 see Balcells (2004): *Breve historia del nacionalismo catalán*, p. 243.

[127] See Valandro (2002): *A Nation of Nations*, p. 20.

[128] See Keating (1993): *Spain. Peripheral nationalism*, pp. 219-220.

[129] See Keating (1996): *Nations against the State*, p. 123.

[130] See Kraus (1996): *Nationalismus und Demokratie. Politik im spanischen Staat der Autonomen Gemeinschaften*, Wiesbaden: Deutscher Universitäts Verlag, p. 224.

[131] Shafir speaks in the Catalan case of a "nationalist hegemony". See Shafir (1995): *Immigrants and Nationalists*, pp. 61-63.

litical influence in Catalonia.[132] The extremist group *Terra Lliure*, for example, which tried to imitate the Basque organisation ETA, was forced to give up their armed struggle for independence.[133]

Of all political parties in Catalonia,[134] the CiU has been playing the most important role in reconstructing an autonomous Catalonia within the Spanish state. The long-standing president of the Generalitat, Jordi Pujol shaped its ideas about the collective identity of the Catalans as no one else did.[135] That's why CiU's national ideology is often termed as "Pujolisme".[136] McRoberts describes the outstanding position of Pujol as follows:

> "…who, through both a charismatic political style and his lenght of time in office, has come to personify Catalonia not only to Catalans but to most Spaniards as well. His political world view, which has profoundly shaped Catalonia's existence as an autonomous community, has made the 'national' question a continuing issue in Catalan politics and has positioned the CiU in a way that so far has put its competitors at a distinct disadvantage."[137]

Pujol's nationalist discourse intends to carefully balance different positions. It is therefore described in academic literature as an ideological syncretism, as nationalism without attributes standing for political pragmatism.[138] Thus, on the one hand it tries to prevent being accused of separatism and on the other hand it defines Catalonia as a nation with its own language and culture.[139] Catalonia is seen as one of various nations forming a plurinational Spanish state. Referring to the autonomy level reached, the moderate nationalists believe, that there is still a lot to be done. However, they reject a further generalization of the autonomy processes for all autonomous communities. According to them, the

---

[132] See Valandro (2002): *A Nation of Nations*, p. 77.
[133] See Keating (1993): *Spain. Peripheral nationalism*, p. 221.
[134] For tables on the objectives of the Catalan political parties see Brinck (1995): *Regionalistische Bewegungen zwischen internationaler Integration und regionaler Eigenständigkeit: Baskenland und Katalonien*, Hamburg: LIT-Verlag, pp. 92-101.
[135] For a detailed description of Pujol's ideology see Guibernau (2002): *El nacionalisme català. Franquisme, trancisió i democràcia*, Barcelona: Pòrtic, pp. 228-244 and the overview of Pujol's writings Pujol and Pi (1996): *Jordi Pujol. Cataluña-España*, Madrid: Espasa Calpe.
[136] At its homepage the *Centre d'Estudis Jordi Pujol* presents, under the motto "Thoughts into facts", life, writings, and ideology of Jordi Pujol. See Centre d'Éstudis Jordi Pujol, URL: http://www.jordipujol.cat.
[137] McRoberts (2001): *Catalonia. Nation Building*, p. 66.
[138] See Bernecker, Esser and Kraus (2007): *Kleine Geschichte Kataloniens*, p. 178.
[139] See Guibernau (1997): *Nations without States*, p. 151.

newly created autonomous communities should not be treated equally to the so-called "historical nationalities" which are rooted in the past and have their own languages, cultures, and a strong sense of identity.[140] Pujol's definition of national identity is not based on ethnic and racial factors, but on language, culture, social cohesion, collective consciousness, common projects and country pride, and an opposition against absorption and homogenizing policies. He links identity, progress, and economic success and emphasizes the positive attitude of Catalans towards hard work, innovation, and modernization. Catalonia should aim at being one of Europe's most dynamic economic regions.[141] As to the European Union, Pujol defends the idea of a Europe of the Regions, because it allows "nations without states",[142] like Catalonia to play a key part in European decision processes. Consequently, the CiU government always tried to maintain, independently of the central government, direct relationship with the European Institutions and member states.

The major opponent of the CiU is the PSC-PSOE. This has been confirmed by the results of general and communal elections. It has so far had the largest popular vote in Catalonia and consequently the largest number of Catalan seats in the Spanish Parliament. Barcelona as well has been governed by the PSC since the democratic transition.[143] With the PSOE governing on the central state level (between 1982-1996) the Catalan Socialists had to deal with the dilemma of representing the Catalan interests on the one hand and complying with the general guidelines of the PSOE leadership on the other hand. Thus they were permanently torn between central and peripheral interests and therefore ambivalent in the questions concerning autonomy and the national identity of Catalonia.[144]

Among the Catalan political parties the ERC represents the most radical form of Catalan nationalism. In 1989 the party committed itself formally to promote the independence of Catalonia through a step-by-step expansion of autonomy within Spain. Besides the ERC, there is on the left wing another smaller party, the Initiative for Catalonia or in Catalan, Iniciativa per Catalunya (IC). It was formed in 1987 to replace the PSUC thus following the example of

---

[140] See Ibid., p. 148.

[141] See Ibid., pp. 144-146.

[142] See title of the Article of Montserrat Guibernau Ibid.

[143] Pasqual Maragall, President of the Generalitat 2003-2006, was formerly mayor of Barcelona between 1982 and 1997. See McRoberts (2001): *Catalonia. Nation Building*, p. 62

[144] See Kraus (1996): *Nationalismus und Demokratie*, pp. 221-222.

the IU (Izquierda Unida) at the central state level and is allied with Els Verds, the green party, forming hence the Iniciativa per Catalunya Verds (ICV).

The opposite pole to the ERC on the "Catalanism-españolismo" axis is represented by the Partido Popular (PP). As explained above it explicitly rejects Catalan nationalism and a multinational Spain and emphasizes, like on central state level, the importance of preserving Spain's unity.

From the first Catalan elections until their defeat in the 2003 elections, Catalonia was dominated by the moderate nationalist party, CiU and its president Jordi Pujol. Due to the fact that for the Catalan nationalists language had always been the most important characteristic of national identity, their major political project was the linguistic "normalization" (normalització lingüística), meaning the return of the Catalan language to normal usage in all spheres.[145] But they had to deal with the problem that "the linguistic entity does not correspond with the political borders" of the Autonomous Community Catalonia.[146] Also in Valencia and at the Balearic Islands a variant of Catalan is spoken, but there, in the course of time, they have developed their own regional identity and are ruled by their own autonomous government.[147] The promotion of the use of Catalan by the *Generalitat* only went for parts of the Catalan speaking persons in Spain, namely in the territory of the Autonomous Community of Catalonia. There, the Statute of Autonomy (1979) established Catalan, along with Castilian, as official language of Catalonia.[148] The *Generalitat* launched campaigns to introduce Catalan in education, public administration, media, and cultural life.[149] In 1980 it created a directorate for language policy in its department of culture (*Direcció General de Política Lingüística*). The Law for Linguistic Normalization (*Llei de Normalització Lingüística a Catalunya*), passed in 1983 with the consent of all political groups in Catalonia, aimed at encouraging

---

[145] See Balcells (1996): *Catalan Nationalism*, p. 188.

[146] Valandro (2002): *A Nation of Nations*, p. 53.

[147] All Catalan speaking Spanish regions together are referred to as *Països Catalans* (Catalan countries).

[148] Generalitat de Catalunya: *Estatut d'autonomia de 1979*, URL: http://www.gencat.cat/generalitat/cat/estatut1979/index.htm, Art. 3, [19.02.2007].

[149] The Catalan government created its own television and radio stations, e.g., TV3, Canal 33, Catalunya Radio. It promoted the publication of newspapers and literature in Catalan, and 'typical' Catalan activities like the folk dance *Sardana*, and the human tower-building, *Castellers*. For details on the development of communication media see Keating (1996): *Nations against the State*, pp. 136-137.

and supporting an official bilingualism,[150] thus normalizing the use of Catalan in all areas of social communication. The subsequent law, the Law of Linguistic Politics (*Llei de Política Lingüística*), finally approved in 1998 was preceded by a fierce debate. The *Generalitat* was accused of monopolizing the use of Catalan in education and the public sphere.[151] Indeed there is a "contradiction between the formal equality of Catalan and Castilian as official languages, and the promotion of one of them, Catalan, as Catalonia's 'proper' language".[152] However, the language policy of the Catalan government has had the effect that the percentage of people living in Catalonia understanding and writing Catalan, has risen remarkably.[153] The official use of Catalan has spread, although in the world of business and professions Castilian and English are still preferred.

Apart from its efforts in the area of linguistic "normalization", the *Generalitat* under the CiU attempted to engage in low-level international activities and to position itself as an independent actor within the European Union. It aimed at positioning Catalan representatives in the major European cities and at the EU institutions.[154] Furthermore, Catalonia has its own program for development aid and a large number of joint programs with other regions and states, such as the "Four Motors of Europe" it forms along with Baden-Württemberg, Rhône-Alps, and Lombardy.[155] The Olympic Games in 1992 in Barcelona were an excellent opportunity for Catalonia to present itself to the world as a culturally distinct part of Spain, open and tolerant.

The nationalist identity politics of the CiU government was largely sucessful. Today, a wide spread identification with a distinctive Catalan identity can be found there.

"Catalonia has retained a marked sense of national identity, which has grown stronger over the last twenty years. It is, by and large, not an exclusive but a dual

---

[150] See Ibid., p. 136.
[151] For a detailed description of the legislation process of the Llei de Política Lingüística see Gergen (2000): *Sprachengesetzgebung in Katalonien. Die Debatte um die "Llei de Política Lingüística" vom 7. Januar 1998*, Tübingen: Max Niemeyer Verlag.
[152] McRoberts (2001): *Catalonia. Nation Building*, p. 158.
[153] See table 17.5 Balcells (1996): *Catalan Nationalism*, p. 189.
[154] See Bernecker, Esser and Kraus (2007): *Kleine Geschichte Kataloniens*, p. 188.
[155] See homepage: Four Motors for Europe, URL: http://62.101.84.82/4motori.nsf/framesweb/index, [19.02.2007].

identity, as a distinct nation within Spain with, at the elite level, a strong commit-ment to Europe."[156]

Regularly conducted surveys have shown that the percentage of Catalans with a dual identity, that means who identify with both Catalonia and Spain, has not changed much over the last two decades. From the approximately 70 per cent of Catalans expressing dual identification, in the year 2003 only 40 per cent identified equally strong with Catalan and Spanish identity, whereas 24 per cent felt more Catalan than Spanish and 8 per cent more Spanish than Catalan. Of all Catalans 16 per cent perceive themselves exclusively as Catalans and 12 per cent exclusively as Spaniards.[157]

---

[156] Keating (1996): *Nations against the State*, p. 160.
[157] See Bernecker, Esser and Kraus (2007): *Kleine Geschichte Kataloniens*, p. 204.

IV.
Migration to Spain

In the last chapter different and varying constructions of national identity and their development have been outlined. They are aiming at a definition of Spanish national identity in reference to the peripheral national identities or at a definition of Catalan national identity in reference to Spanish national identity. However, they also do refer to external "Others". Not only the neighbouring states, or the EU can represent this "Other", as explained above in chapter II in detail, also immigration can provoke explicit or implicit reproduction of categories and characteristics of national identity. Since the mid-1990s Spain faces an increasing number of immigrants from non-EU countries. Traditionally an emigration country, within a few years Spain has developed into an immigration country, with figures comparable to other European countries. The following chapter exemplifies this development on the basis of statistical data and examines the political response to the new "phenomenon".

1. SPAIN, FROM EMIGRATION TO IMMIGRATION

Until the mid-1970s Spain was a typical country of emigration. Since colonial times, the main destinations for Spanish emigrants were the Latin American countries. This changed after the World War II. Due to the economic boom, western European countries like France, Germany or Switzerland started to recruit foreign workers to prevent labour shortages. In the 1960s and early 1970s, over two million Spaniards moved to other European countries as so-called "guestworkers". This migration flow ended abruptly when the oil crisis in 1973 and the resulting economic recession forced the corresponding governments to stop recruitment of foreign workers and even to introduce incentives for them to return to Spain. Many of them actually did return. That is why in 1975 the emigration rate fell dramatically and stabilized between 15,000 and 20,000 emigrants per year.[1] In the last decade, emigration has decreased to a symbolic level and concentrated on temporary[2] migration.[3] At the same time immigration has increased.

The early immigrants to Spain were North or Western Europeans who came for tourism or settled there after retirement. In the mid-1980s non-European immigration from Latin America and North-Africa set in. After the fall of the Iron Curtain immigrants from Eastern European countries, especially from Romania joined them. By then Spain had become an attractive destination for immigrants. The country's continued economic growth and the raised standard of living created a need for foreign labour. Foreign workers were especially needed for the jobs that are usually described as "3-D-Jobs" (dirty, dangerous, demeaning), e.g., picking fruit and vegetable, because the locals were no longer willing to do them. Because of Spain's interest to attract tourists and of its historical ties to the Latin American countries, the country still had a very liberal immigration policy when other European countries or the United States already restricted accession. Another important factor why Spain like Italy became an attractive destination for migrants is its geographical situation at the outer border of the European Union,[4] a border which separates two regions with enormous differences in demographic and economic development. All this led to a shift of migration movements to Spain. Within a short period of time the Southern European country reached the highest yearly immigration rate within the EU. Figure 1 shows how rapidly the net migration to Spain grew in the last decade compared to all the EU-15 countries together.[5] Although Spain in absolute numbers has not yet reached the level of foreign residents in the "older" European immigration countries it has experienced a remarkable growth.

---

[1] See Blanco Fernández de Valderrama (1993): The New Hosts: The Case of Spain, in *International Migration Review*, 27:1, p. 169.
[2] Between 3 months and one year.
[3] See Puyol (2001): La Inmigración en España ¿Un problema o una necesidad?, p. 12.
[4] See Blanco Fernández de Valderrama (1993): *The New Hosts*, p. 171.
[5] EU-15 members: Germany, Italy, Spain, Portugal, Greece, Belgium, Netherlands, United Kingdom, France, Denmark, Sweden, Finland, Luxembourg, Republic of Ireland, and Austria.

FIGURE I. Net Migration in EU-15 and Spain
(difference between emigrants and immigrants per 1,000 inhabitants)

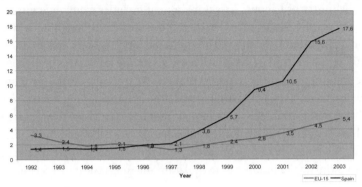

Source: Eurostat

Table 1 shows the absolute numbers of working and residency permits issued by the Ministry of Labour, corresponding to the number of foreign residents in legal situation. The percentage of foreign residents ascended within a few years from 1.8 per cent of the total population in 1998 to 8.6 per cent in 2007.

TABLE I. Foreign Residents in Legal Situation (1998-2007)

Year	Total population	Foreign residents	% of total population
1998	40,202,160	719,647	1.8
1999	40,499,791	801,329	2.0
2000	41,116,842	895,720	2.2
2001	41,837,894	1,109,060	2.7
2002	42,717,064	1,324,001	3.1
2003	43,197,684	1,647,011	3.8
2004	44,108,530	1,977,291	4.5
2005	44,708,964	2,738,932	6.1
2006	45,200,737	3,021,808	6.7
2007	46,063,511	3,979,014	8.6

Source: MTAS and INE

Yet in Spain another government body, the National Institute of Statistics (INE) also gathers information about foreign residents on the basis of the local registers (*Padrón Municipal*). As Figure 2 shows, the absolute number of foreign residents registered at the local level is much higher than the number published by the Ministry of Labour. That is, because it includes many migrants without residency permit, but registered in their municipality. Although since 2000, the national police has been allowed access to the local registers, many municipalities still refuse to hand in the information about the legal status of their citizens, as the amount of financial resources they receive from the central government is based on the number of people registered. The irregular immigrants on the other hand also profit from registering in their municipality. Once they are registered they have certain rights e.g. for free basic health care or to send their children to school. Therefore the discrepancies between the two kinds of official data can be used to estimate the number of irregular immigrants residing in Spain.

FIGURE 2. Foreign Residents in Spain (1998-2007)

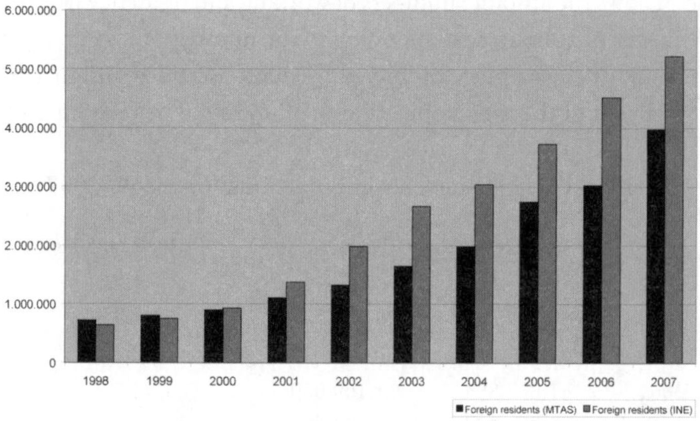

Source: MTAS and INE

Regarding the countries of origin there was a clear shift from European immigration to non-EU immigration. In 1996 the proportion of EU citizens was still 46 per cent of all foreign residents living in Spain. In 2006 only 21.9 per cent of the legal foreign residents came from other EU member states.[6] Due to the enlargement of the EU in 2007 and the associated inclusion of two important immigrant sending countries, Romania and Bulgaria, EU citizens today

---

[6] Even though the EU has enlarged during this period from 15 to 25 member states.

again constitute the major immigrant group in Spain (see Figure 3). The main continents of origin, apart from the EU, continue to be Latin America and Africa.

FIGURE 3. Foreign Residents per Continent (31.12.2007)

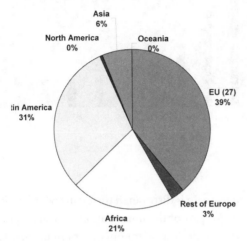

Source: MTAS

As to the main countries of origin the data show that, comparing the absolute numbers of immigrants (legal status) according to their country of origin in 2000 and in 2007 the composition of immigration to Spain has changed remarkably within only a few years. Nowadays, the Moroccans represent the biggest immigrant group, followed by the Ecuadorians, Colombians and Romanians. Figure 4 shows that there has been a clear growth in the number of the latter. Even though in absolute numbers they are still not very important, the numbers of immigrants coming from Bulgaria and Ukraine have lately grown quite rapidly. Also the African immigration has changed in recent years. The number of people coming from Sub-Saharan countries is increasing steadily. As to the Asians living in Spain, almost half of them are of Chinese origin.

FIGURE 4. Main Countries of Origin (31.12.2000/31.12.2007)

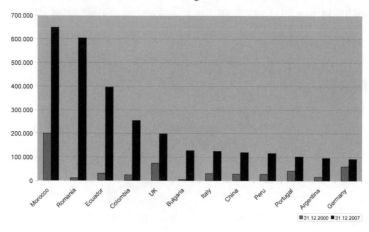

Source: MTAS

The immigration to Spain is distributed unequally between the autonomous communities. The major part of the immigration to Spain, approximately two thirds (see Figure 5) settle in four autonomous communities, Catalonia, Madrid, Valencia and Andalusia. For Catalonia, detailed information will be given in IV.3. While the EU immigrants looking for warmth and sun concentrate at the Mediterranean Coasts and the Canary Islands, non-EU-immigrants like Latin Americans, North Africans and Eastern Europeans tend to settle where their work force is needed, in the conurbations of Madrid and Barcelona, and in agricultural zones.

The composition according to sex is more or less balanced with 54.4 per cent men and 45.6 per cent women. However, among the immigrants coming from Latin America female, and among the North-Africans male immigrants predominate. Usually the immigrants are younger than the average of the Spanish population. For 2007 the average age of legal immigrants was 33.2 years.[7]

---

[7] Source: Ministry of Labour, URL: http://www.mtas.es, 31.12.2007.

FIGURE 5. Foreign Residents by Autonomous Communities (31.12.2007)

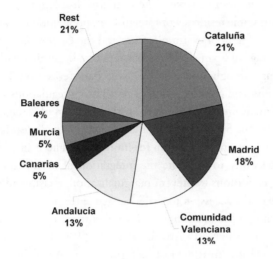

Source: MTAS

The level of education among immigrants is quite similar to the one of the Spanish Population, when compared to Spaniards of the same age, with one major exception: the African and Asian immigrants show an inferior level of education.[8] Irrespective of their level of education, most immigrants work in unqualified jobs in construction, agriculture, domestic service, and gastronomy or hotels.[9]

2. SPANISH IMMIGRATION POLICY

Most authors distinguish three stages of Spanish immigration policy.[10] During the first stage, until 1985, Spain still had very little immigration. Therefore, migration issues were no priority for the political agenda. Nevertheless, the accession to the EU forced Spain to regulate the immigration of non-EU citizens. In 1985, the first Law on the Rights and Freedoms of Foreigners in Spain (*Ley*

---

[8] See tables Cachón Rodríguez (2003): La Inmigración en España: Los desafíos de la construcción de una nueva sociedad, in *Migraciones*, 2003:14, pp. 243/245.
[9] See Consejo Económico y Social (2004): *La inmigración y el mercado de trabajo en España*, pp. 50ff.
[10] See Cachón Rodríguez (2003): *La Inmigración en España*, p. 221.

de Extranjería)[11] was adopted, wherein the focus lay on the regulation of immigrants' access to the labour market. The restrictive legislation regarding family reunification and stable residency of foreign-born population reveals the underlying conception of temporary immigration and the *Gastarbeiter* principle.[12]

The second stage of Spanish immigration policy, beginning with the Law of 1985 and lasting throughout the 1990s, was characterized by the differentiation, consolidation and concretization of the existing regulations. In 1990, the Spanish government presented a report on the situation of foreigners in Spain and guidelines for the Spanish immigration policy. It concludes that Spain will be in future an important destination for immigrants, and it introduces for the first time the necessity to promote the integration of immigrants and assure dignified living conditions to prevent marginalization, racism and xenophobia. In consequence of the accession to the Schengen agreement in 1991 Spain was forced to tighten up its regulations on Visa and entry to its territory, e.g., it had to introduce visa for the North African states in 1991. However, it was able to maintain the privileged treatment of its former Latin American colonies for a few years more. Besides, the socialist government enacted a whole lot of regulations concerning migration issues. For instance, it introduced the first quota for labour immigrants in 1993. In 1996, an amendment to the 1985 law for the first time recognized immigration as a structural phenomenon and acknowledged certain immigrants' rights, such as the access to education, the right for legal council and an interpreter. It also established the possibility of permanent residency and formally included family reunification.[13]

A milestone in Spanish migration policy, the Law on Rights and Freedoms of Foreigners in Spain and their Integration (*Ley Orgánica 4/2000*)[14] which took the place of the 1985 law, marked the beginning of the third stage of Spanish immigration policy. The negotiations of this law for the first time led to a broad public debate and awareness of migration issues. According to Huntoon's four

---

[11] *Ley Orgánica 7/1985, de 1 de Julio, sobre derechos y libertades de los extranjeros en España*, URL: http://extranjeros.mtas.es/es/normativa_jurisprudencia/nacional/ley7_1985.pdf, [19.02.2007].

[12] See Ortega Pérez (2003): *Spain: Forging an Immigration Policy*, Migration information Source, URL: http://www.migrationinformation.org , [10.09.2004], p. 3; For details on the Ley de Extranjería, 1985 see Corredera García (1994): La política de "extranjería" en España, in Contreras *Los retos de la Inmigración. Racismo y pluriculturalidad*, Madrid: Talasa.

[13] See Ortega Pérez (2003): *Spain: Forging an Immigration Policy*, p. 3.

[14] *Ley Orgánica 4/2000, de 11 de enero, sobre derechos y libertades de los extranjeros en España y su integración social*, Boletín Oficial de Estado Nr. 10, 12.03.2000, URL: http://extranjeros.mtas. es/es/normativa_jurisprudencia/nacional/leyorganica_dchos_libertades.pdf, [19.02.2007].

stage model of policy responses in new countries of immigration this marks the step towards the fourth stage, the implementation of a control regime as immigrant populations begin settlement.[15]

Starting with the new millennium immigration is finally acknowledged as a social fact and institutionalized through legislative regulations.[16] The legislation process to the Law 4/2000 which was initiated in January 1998, although criticised by the ruling PP government, was supported by a broad political consensus in the Spanish Parliament. It no longer focuses solely on controlling immigration flows but highlighted the integration of immigrants. It extended the political and social rights to non-EU foreigners.[17] In the 2000 election migration was used for the first time as a controversial topic for the campaign. The PP heavily criticised the new Law which in its opinion was too permissive and against the restrictive standards set by the European Union. After winning an absolute majority, the new PP government passed the Law 8/2000[18] as an amendment of the Law 4/2000. This new law restricted certain rights (e.g., to health care, to education for their children, to apply for scholarships) which were conceded previously to all foreigners on Spanish territory to immigrants with a legal status. Besides, it focused on the control and prevention of irregular immigration. It was followed by further restrictive regulations regarding repatriation, internment, family reunification, etc.

Although the change of government in 2004 did not lead to a further reform of the Law 8/2000 the PSOE government liberalized some of its regulations through the Royal Decree of December 2004.[19] This marks the beginning

---

[15] The four stages according to Huntoon are: 1) low levels of entry matched by tolerance, 2) growth of immigration met by no official response, 3) acceleration of immigration met by public awareness and design of controls, 4) implementation of a control regime as immigrant populations begin settlements. See Huntoon (1998): Immigration to Spain: Implications for a Unified European Union Immigration Policy, in *International Migration Review*, 32:2, p. 427.

[16] See Cachón Rodríguez (2003): *La Inmigración en España*, p. 226.

[17] For a detailed description of the legislation process and the content of the Law see Charro Baena and Ruiz de Huidobro de Carlos (2000): La Ley Orgánica 4/2000: Análisis técnico-jurídico de sus principales novedades, in *Migraciones*, 2000:7; Ruiz de Huidobro (2000): La Ley Orgánica 4/2000, in *Migraciones*, 2000:7.

[18] *Ley Orgánica 8/2000, de 22 de diciembre, de reforma de la Ley Orgánica 4/2000, de 11 de enero, sobre derechos y libertades de los extranjeros en España y su integración social*, Boletín Oficial de Estado Nr. 307, 23.12.2000, URL: http://extranjeros.mtas.es/es/normativa_jurisprudencia/nacional/ley_organica_8-2000.pdf, [19.02.2007].

[19] *Real Decreto 2393/2004, de 30 de diciembre, por el que se aprueba el Reglamento a la Ley Orgánica 4/2000, de 11 de enero, sobre derechos y libertades de los extranjeros en España y su integración social*,

of a fourth stage of Spanish immigration policy.[20] Based on this Royal Decree the new government also initiated a regularization campaign of irregular immigrants, the so-called "Normalización" (normalization). Between February and May 2005 employers were able to solicit residency permits for their employees. Regarding the social integration of immigrants the PSOE government for the first time allocated a well-remunerated fund (2005: 120 million €; 2006: 182 million €) to be distributed among the autonomous communities and municipalities.[21] In 2006 the integration fund was included in the new plan for integration policy measures, the "Plan Estratégico de Ciudadanía e Integración 2006-2009". This plan was equipped with approximately two billion Euros for its four-year time period.[22]

In the following, the four most important and distinctive issues of the Spanish immigration policy, irregular migration, asylum, migration and labour market, social integration and citizenship will be presented in detail. In analogy to other Southern European countries, particularly Italy, the challenges to immigration policy concerning these issues differ crucially from other Western European countries. Italy and Spain are both responsible of controlling EU-borders which are not only long but also particularly difficult to control because they are coastal borders. Both countries also show relatively high levels of economic informality and irregular migration.[23]

2.1 Irregular immigration

The high number of so-called "sin papeles"[24] –foreigners living in Spain without having a residency permit– has been one of the major problems Spanish migration policy had to face in the last two decades. On the occasion of the "normalization" process the government estimated the numbers of irregular immigrants

---

Boletín Oficial de Estado Nr. 6, 07.01.2005, URL: http://extranjeros.mtas.es/es/normativa_jurisprudencia/Nacional/RD2393-04.pdf, [19.02.2007].

[20] See Kreienbrink (2006): *Länderprofil Spanien*, pp. 3-5.

[21] ELPAIS.es (2005): *El Gobierno aprueba 120 millones para el fondo de ayuda para la integración de inmigrantes*, 20.05.2005, URL: http://www.elpais.es, [23.05.2005].

[22] Kreienbrink (2008): Länderprofil Spanien, in Focus Migration, Hamburgisches Weltwirtschafts-institut.

[23] See Geddes (2003): *The Politics of migration and immigration in Europe*, London/Thousand Oaks/New Delhi: Sage Publications, p. 150.

[24] In analogy to the French term "sans papiers".

in Spain between 800,000 and one million.[25] Thus it is not surprising that irregular immigration and its restriction has been one of the main issues in public and political debate. While the attempts of illegal border crossing are often emphasized, the major part of the irregular immigrants are so-called "overstayers", which means that they enter Spanish territory with a tourist visa, thus legally, but stay on in the country after it has expired. However, the media focus primarily on the irregular border-crossing of African boat migrants. The dramatic pictures of small fisher boats packed with immigrants landing at the Spanish coasts seem to have evoked fears of an African mass immigration to Europe. The Spanish government, pressed by other EU member states, reacted by enforcing the border controls. With EU funds a technologically highly advanced surveillance system for the Strait of Gibraltar, the SIVE (Sistema Integral de Vigilancia Exterior) was installed by the end of the 1990s.[26] Due to the intensified border controls on both sides of the Strait, the Spanish and the Moroccan side, migration flows shifted first to Ceuta and Melilla. The incidents in September/October 2005 when hundreds of sub-Saharan Africans managed to climb the fences of Ceuta and Melilla and a great number of them got hurt while doing so shocked the European public.[27] As a consequence the Spanish government heightened and strengthened the fences of Ceuta and Melilla. Table 2 shows how the attempts to enter Spanish territory illegally by boat have increased since 1999 and have shifted at the same time towards the Canary Islands. During the year 2006 31,787 boat migrants, mostly sub-Saharan immigrants arrived at the Canary Islands and only 7,456 at the coasts of the Spanish mainland or at Ceuta and Melilla.[28] After the intensification of the offshore controls also at the Canary Islands the number of irregular boat migrants has decreased 55 per cent in the first 7 months of 2007, compared to the first 7 months of the previous year.[29]

---

[25] El País (2004b): *Los inmigrantes con contrato podrán solicitar la regularización a partir del 31 de enero*, 14.12.2004, p. 32; El País (2005): *"Ésta es la última oportunidad para los empresarios que contratan a 'sin papeles'"*, Interview with Consuelo Rumí, 07.02.2005, p. 22.

[26] For more information on migration control at the Spanish-African Borders see Carling (2007b): Migration Control and Migrant Fatalities at the Spanish-African Borders, in *International Migration Review*, 41:2.

[27] El Periódico (2005): *La tanca de Melilla pateix el pitjor assalt de la història*, 28.09.2005, p. 34.

[28] See Córdoba (2006): *La ola de cayucos en el 2006 deja 800 cadáveres en el Atlántico*, 28.12.2006, www.diariocordoba.com. [26.11.2007].

[29] See El País (2007b): *La llegada de inmigrantes por mar cae und 55% tras el refuerzo de controles fronterizos*, 08.08.2007, p. 19.

TABLE 2. Irregular Boat Migrants (1999-2006)

Year	Total	Spanish Mainland (incl. Ceuta and Melilla)	Canary Islands
1999	3,569	2,694	875
2000	15,195	12,785	2,410
2001	18,517	14,405	4,112
2002	16,670	6,795	9,875
2003	19,176	9,788	9,388
2004	15,675	7,245	8,426
2005	11,781	7,066	4,715
2006	39,246	7,456	31,787

Source: MTAS, MIR[30]

In a relatively short period of time the migration routes adapted to the increased border controls. Agreements with Morocco and Mauritania established joint naval patrols. Also other EU member states started to support the Spanish security forces with boats, equipment and staff, coordinated by the new Agency for Border Control, Frontex.[31]

Apart from increased border-controls the Spanish government was forced to adapt its visa-policy to EU norms. Consequently Spain had to introduce visa also for countries it had special historical ties with, like the Latin American countries. It was torn between EU regulations and its national interest to maintain good relations with these countries and managed to delay the introduction of visa. For instance Ecuadorians were not asked any visa to enter Spain until 2003. For Bolivia only in 2007 visa were introduced.

To facilitate the repatriation of irregular immigrants Spain signed bilateral readmission agreements with various countries of origin, e.g. Morocco (1992), Bulgaria (1996), Romania (1996), Nigeria (2001), Algeria (2002), Mauritania (2003), Guinea Bisseau (2003). However, it was not able until now to negotiate such bilateral agreements with the Latin American countries from where the

[30] See Ministerio de Trabajo y Asuntos Sociales (2006): *Nota de Prensa*, URL: http://extranjeros. mtas.es/es/general/NOTA_BALANCE_PATERAS_20051.pdf, [13.02.2007]; Ibid. (2007a): *Nota de Prensa*, URL: http://www.mir.es/DGRIS/Notas_Prensa/Ministerio_Interior/2007/ np022103.html, [27.11.2007].
[31] For details on current border control projects see MTAS Dirección General Guardia Civíl, Oficina de Relaciones informativas y Sociales: Proyectos para el Control de la Immigración Irregular, URL: http://www.guardiacivil.org/prensa/actividades/mauritania/especial.pdf, [13.02.2007].

major part of irregular immigrants in Spain stems. In total between 2001 and 2004 approximately 330,000 immigrants, mostly nationals of Morocco and Bulgaria were repatriated.[32]

TABLE 3. Repatriations from Spain 2001-2006

Year	Total Repatriations
2001	45,544
2002	74,467
2003	92,951
2004	121,121
2005	92,638
2006	99,445

Source: Spanish Ministry of Home Affairs

Having a closer look at the numbers of expulsions the difference between expulsions ordered and expulsions carried out is striking. For instance in 2004, 73.7 per cent of the ordered expulsions were not carried out.[33] This shows how ineffective the measures are.

To reduce the numbers of foreigners in illegal status there is another practice which, apart from Spain at least five other European countries[34] have used as part of their immigration policy, regularization processes. Usually, the irregular immigrants fulfilling certain requirements were given the opportunity to solicit a residency and working permit. Thus Italy has regularized 20,000 foreigners in the past 20 years.[35] Spain has had in the last two decades six regularisation campaigns in 1985/86, 1991/92, 1996, 2000, 2001 and 2005. The latter was the largest regularization campaign ever in Europe with almost 700,000 appli-

---

[32] See Serra (2005): Spain, in Niessen, Schibel and Thompson *Current Immigration Debates in Europe: A Publication of the European Migration Dialogue*, Brüssel: Migration Policy Group, p. 10.

[33] In 2003, 53,778 expulsions were ordered and only 14,104 actually carried out.

[34] Belgium (2000), France (1981-1982/1997-1998), Greece (1997-1998/2001), Italy (1987-1988/1990/1996/1998/2002), Portugal (1992-1993/1996/2001), see Consejo Económico y Social (2004): *La inmigración y el mercado de trabajo en España*, pp. 77-79. For more information on regularization processes around the world see Sunderhaus (2007): Regularization programms for undocumented migrants, in *Migration Letters*, 4:1.

[35] See Pastore (2004): *To Regularize or Not to Regularize: Experiences and Views from Europe*, in Migration Information Source, URL: http://www.migrationinformation.org, [27.01.2004].

cations, 577,159 of them approved.[36] In contrast to the former regularisation processes this time not the immigrant him or herself but solely his or her employer could hand in an application. This shows that the focus of the campaign lay on economic and labour related issues.[37] The basic requirement for regularisation was to have a work contract with a further duration of at least 6 months. Also the immigrants had to prove that they were registered at the local register of their municipality before August 8, 2004 and had been living in Spain ever since. The Spanish government announced this regularisation to be the last and introduced severe sanctions for employers who kept on contracting irregular immigrants.[38]

2.2 Asylum

As mentioned above, most immigrants enter Spain with tourist visa and "stay over". Another regular way to enter, seeking asylum, has never been very important in Spain. Figure 6 shows that, although the number of asylum seekers in certain years reached remarkable levels, e.g. after the fall of the iron curtain in 1990, the rate of approved applications has been low.

---

[36] See Ministerio de Trabajo y Asuntos Sociales (2005): *Proceso de Normalización de Trabajadores Extranjeros*, 30.12.2005, URL: http://www.mtas.es/balance/Proceso_norm. pdf, [19.02.2007].

[37] See Serra (2005): *Spain*, p. 12.

[38] For details on the latest regularization process in Spain see Arango and Jachimowicz (2005): *Regularizing Immigrants in Spain: A New Approach*, in Migration Information Source, URL: http://www.migrationinformation.org, [26.05.2006].

FIGURE 6. Asylum in Spain (1984-2007)

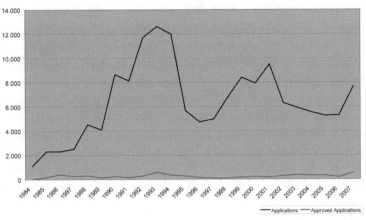

Source: Spanish Ministry of Home Affairs:
Anuario estadístico de extranjería 1993-2003, Ministry of Labour and Social Affairs:
Anuario estadístico de inmigración 2004-2005.

For instance, in 2007 of the 7,658 applications for asylum only 570, 7.4 per cent, were approved. In the 1990s, the biggest groups according to nationality of asylum seekers came from Eastern Europe and Latin America (Poland, Peru, Dominican Republic, Romania, etc.).[39] Recently an increasing number of asylum seekers originate from sub-Saharan States. For some years Nigerians even represented the biggest group and are currently only outnumbered by Iraqis and Colombians, the latter seeking new possibilities of entering Spain, given that a tourist visa is required since 2002.[40]

Nevertheless, since the numbers of accepted asylum seekers are so small, asylum is, compared to other countries of the EU of little relevance in Spanish immigration policy.

2.3 Immigration and labour market

The Spanish labour market is characterised by relatively high unemployment rates, particularly among women and young people, a high rate of temporary

---

[39] See table 19 in Kreienbrink (2004): *Einwanderungsland Spanien. Migrationspolitik zwischen Europäisierung und nationalen Interessen*, Frankfurt a. M./London: IKO-Verlag für Interkulturelle Kommunikation, p. 310.
[40] See Kreienbrink (2008): *Länderprofil Spanien*, 6.

jobs, a high level of informality and black economy, big regional differences, and low levels of mobility.[41] Apart from these characteristics there is a need for foreign work force, particularly for unqualified jobs in sectors like construction, industries, services, and agriculture. Therefore Spanish immigration policy not only focuses on the restriction of irregular migration, but also promotes a controlled regular immigration of foreign labour to cover jobs that can not be covered by nationals. In 1993, for the first time an annual quota to recruit foreign labour was established. Its number is determined by the administration taking into consideration the report on the nation's employment situation, issued by the National Employment Institute (Instituto Nacional de Empleo)[42] and the open job offers reported by the employers' organizations or employers themselves. Table 4 shows the quota for 2008 according to the sectors of the Spanish economy.

TABLE 4. Quota System 2008

Sector	Total
Construction	1,818
Hotels, hotel Service, etc.	4,267
Transport	818
Trade	2,570
Agriculture	659
Metal industry	2,445
Textil manufacturing	35
Wood industry	225
Food industry	305
Other industries	112
Fishing industry	200
Services	2,277
Total	15,731

Source: Boletín Oficial de Estado, Nr. 11, 12.01.2007

---

[41] See Consejo Económico y Social (2004): *La inmigración y el mercado de trabajo en España*, pp. 33f.

[42] The National Employment Institute issues annually the numbers of open job offers which can not be covered by unemployed Spanish workers. These open positions may be considered for the annual quota.

Until 2002 the annual quota system was de facto used as a possibility to regularize foreigners already living in Spain. But after that, this wasn't allowed any longer and the foreign workers had to be contracted in their countries of origin. The quota system has been criticised frequently for its inadequacy. In the last years there has been a large gap between supply and demand of foreign labour.[43] However, the quota system is not the only instrument to recruit foreign work force. It is also possible for employers to contract particular persons by themselves or make temporary or seasonal contracts. Adding the three instruments of recruiting foreign workers in their countries of origin, the government predicted 180,000 new working contracts for the year 2007.[44]

To facilitate the recruitment of workers in their countries of origin the Spanish government has signed agreements on the regulation of migratory flows with various countries of origin e.g. in 2001 with Morocco, Colombia, Ecuador, the Dominican Republic, in 2002 with Romania and Poland, in 2003 with Bulgaria. These agreements regulate migratory labour flows, especially of temporary and seasonal workers, establishing mechanisms for communicating job offers and guaranteeing social and labour rights for foreign workers in Spain. In view of the increasing numbers of Sub-Saharan immigrants, Spain has started negotiating agreements including the declaration of intent to cooperate in the field of legal migration, also with West-African countries, such as Senegal, Ghana, and Nigeria. It has already signed agreements with Gambia, Guinea-Conakry and Mali, Mauritania and Cape Verde.[45] These agreements form part of a new strategy presented in the so-called "Plan África" which links migration and development policy directed at the African countries of origin.[46]

---

[43] See Serra (2005): *Spain*, p. 10.

[44] See Ministerio de Trabajo y Asuntos Sociales (2007b): *Nota de Prensa: El Gobierno aprueba el Contingente de trabajadores extranjeros de régimen no comunitario en España para 2007*, URL: http://www.tt.mtas.es/periodico, [14.02.2007].

[45] El País (2007b): *Malí firma el martes un acuerdo con España que incluye repatriaciones*, 20.01.2007, URL: http://www.elpais.com, [26.01.2007]; ELPAIS.es (2006): *Moratinos dona 10 millones a Guinea-Conakry y Gambia a cambio de acuerdos de repatriación*, 10.10.2006, URL: http://www.elpais.es, [13.10.2006].

[46] Ministerio de Asuntos Exteriores y de Cooperación: *Plan África 2006-2008. Resumen Ejecutivo*, URL: http://www.mae.es/NR/rdonlyres/C4C81869-0E32-470D-8D5F-7A49AD84D5C0/0/planafrica.pdf, [14.02.2007].

2.4 Social integration and citizenship

As already mentioned above Spanish migration policy at the central state level has been secondary to the control of migration flows. Nevertheless, since the decisive year 2000 it has constantly been a subject of the public and political debate. The Programa GRECO (Global Programme to Regulate and Coordinate Foreign Residents' Affairs and Immigration),[47] a multi-year initiative that was adopted by the Spanish government in March 2001 mentions one of its four key areas the integration of foreign residents and their families as active contributors to the growth of Spain.[48] It acknowledges also the vital role of regional and local government with regard to the social integration of immigrants.[49] However, neither the financing of the proposed measures, nor the terms in which the objectives should be reached were specified. Monitoring and evaluation of its implementation was not incorporated in the Programa GRECO.[50]

The integration of immigrants was, in spite of these formal declarations, not made an important issue on the central state political agenda until the change of government in 2004. The PSOE government under Zapatero initiated a consultation process and elaborated in cooperation with the autonomous communities, municipalities, social agents, migrant associations and NGOs the Plan Estratégico de Ciudadanía e Integración 2007-2010 (Strategic Plan for Citizenship and Integration 2007-2010). The Plan, approved by the Ministerial Council in February 2007, addresses the whole Spanish society which includes both immigrants and autochthonous population. It aims at promoting social cohesion through public policies, in a close cooperation with the civil society and immigrants' organizations. Its twelve areas of action are 1) Reception, 2) Education, 3) Employment, 4) Housing, 5) Social Services, 6) Health, 7) Childhood and Youth, 8) Equal Treatment, 9) Women, 10) Participation, 11) Awareness Raising, 12) Co-development. Special importance is given to educa-

---

[47] Ministerio del Interior: *Programa Global de Regulación y Coordinación de Extranjería e Inmigración*, aprobado 30.03.2001, BOE núm. 101, 27.04.2001.
[48] The other three areas were: global planning and coordination of immigration as a desirable phenomenon for Spain, within the framework of the EU; regulation of migratory flows to guarantee the peaceful cohabitation in the Spanish society; maintenance of the protection system for refugees and displaced persons. See Ministerio del Interior: *Programa Global de Regulación y Coordinación de Extranjería e Inmigración*, aprobado 30.03.2001, BOE núm. 101, 27.04.2001, chapter III.
[49] See Ortega Pérez (2003): *Spain: Forging an Immigration Policy*, pp. 3-5.
[50] See Zapata-Barrero (2002): *Inmigración, innovación política en España*, p. 180.

tion (40 per cent), reception (20 per cent) and employment (11 per cent). The Plan provides also instruments for the monitoring and evaluation of its implementation. With the Strategic Plan for Citizenship and Integration for the first time a central state government provides integration policy measures with a considerable budget, over 2 billion euro for the 4-year period.[51] Providing the financial resources and the framework it furthermore delegates the actual execution of political measures to the regional and the local level.

Due to the Spanish peripheral nationalisms and their own languages and cultures, the regional and local approaches of integration policy have differed a lot. In IV.3 the Catalan immigration and integration policy, the respective programmes and plans will be presented briefly.

Another aspect closely linked to the social integration of immigrants, is the question of naturalization and its requirements.[52] Here the Spanish law differentiates according to the origin of the immigrant to be naturalized. Latin Americans can request the Spanish nationality after two years of legal residence in Spain, whereas the requirement for immigrants from other countries is ten years. It is therefore not surprising that more than half of the naturalization since 1975 correspond to immigrants originating from Latin America.[53]

Altogether, Spanish immigration policy has adapted in the last years to the restrictive standards set by the European Union. However, torn between EU and national interests, it oscillates between more liberal measures like the regularization campaigns and policies for the social integration of irregular immigrants and an increasingly restrictive immigration policy.[54]

3. IMMIGRATION TO CATALONIA

As above mentioned, the Autonomous Community of Catalonia presents today, along with Madrid, the highest proportion of non-EU immigrants within Spain. Immigration and the challenges it poses to Catalan national identy has been one of the priority issues of the *Generalitat* in recent years. However, to be able to

---

[51] See Ministerio de Trabajo y Asuntos Sociales (2007c): *Strategic Plan for Citizenship and Integration 2007-2010–Executive Summary*, Madrid: MTAS.

[52] For details on the nationality law see Pajares (2005): *La Integración Ciudadana. Una perspectiva para la inmigración*, Barcelona: Icaria Editorial, pp. 19-33; Zapata-Barrero (2004b): *Multiculturalidad e inmigración*, Madrid: Editorial Sintesis, pp. 52-62.

[53] See Kreienbrink (2006): *Länderprofil Spanien*, p. 6.

[54] See Baldwin-Edwards (2004): *The Changing Mosaic of Mediterranean Migrations*.

understand the current public and political migration discourse in Catalonia it is necessary to explain shortly its historical background.[55] Long before the immigration of non-EU foreigners to Spain began, Catalonia faced a remarkable influx of internal migrants from other econonomically less developed Spanish regions, mostly Andalusia, Castilla y León, Extremadura, Aragón, Galicia, Murcia, etc. Starting in the 1940s these internal migration flows increased steadily until they reached their highest numbers in the 1960s (700,000). Between 1941 and 1975 more than 1.3 million migrants settled in Catalonia (see Table 5).

TABLE 5. Migration to Catalonia (1941-1975)[56]

Year	Number of migrants
1941-45	160,874
1946-50	95,844
1951-55	199,877
1956-60	239,997
1961-65	354,162
1966-70	366,280
1971-75	231,831

By 1970, 37.7 per cent of the population resident in Catalonia was not born there, not counting their children, the so-called second generation. Due to the enormous population growth of 75 per cent between 1950 and 1975,[57] many ghettoes formed in the outskirts of the larger cities, particularly around Barcelona where the migrants lived under often precarious circumstances. It is not surprising at all that this enormous change in population composition created certain integration problems, espeficically because most of the new citizens were Castilian-speaking. A number of books were published adressing the implications of immigration for Catalonia and the effects it could have on Catalan identity.[58] These publications, for instance "Els Altres Catalans" by Francisco Candel published 1964 or "Els no Catalans I nosaltres" by Manuel Cruells,

[55] For a more detailed description see Zapata-Barrero (2007): *Immigration, Self-Government and Management of Identity. The Catalan Case*, pp. 181-185.
[56] See Ferreres i Calvo and Llorens i Villa (1992): *Història de Catalunya*, p. 364.
[57] See McRoberts (2001): *Catalonia. Nation Building*.
[58] See Ibid., p. 133.

published in 1965, initiated a public debate about how to handle Castilian-speaking immigration. Candel proposed an interbreeding of cultures and being himself the son of migrants, advocated respect for the immigrants' own values. He warned that the bad living conditions of the immigrants would hinder an identification with the Catalan society.[59] Manuel Cruells ("Els no Catalans I nosaltres", 1965) criticised Candel sharply. He accused him of underrating the importance of learning Catalan and questioned the ability of the immigrants to make new roots in Catalonia.[60] Jordi Pujol who also treated this issue in his writings praised Candel's book.[61] Yet he emphasized, according to the national-ist ideology he represented, the importance of linguistic incorporation:

> "Our central problem is immigration and, hence, integration. The basic objective is to build up a community valid for all Catalans. And I would add that by Catalan I mean everybody who lives and works in Catalonia, and who makes Catalonia his/her own home and country, with which he/she incorporates and identifies."[62]

These opinions show how controversial internal migration to Catalonia was perceived by then. However, the predominant reaction was inclusive, constitut-ing "a new form of Catalan nationalism that was based on the realistic assess-ment that, to be viable, any national project would have to win the suport of immingrants".[63]

Apart from the consequences of the past internal migration movements which are still felt and have to be dealt with, Catalonia faces currently, like other Spanish regions a significant influx of non-EU immigrants. Since 1998 the ab-solute number of regular immigrants in Catalonia has more than quadrupled (see Figure 7).

---

[59] See Candel (1965): *Els altres catalans*, Barcelona: edicions 62.
[60] See Balcells (1996): *Catalan Nationalism*, p. 153.
[61] About Pujols writings regarding internal immigration see Termes (1984): *La immigració a Cat-alunya i altres estudis d'història del nacionalisme català*, Barcelona: Editorial Empúries, pp. 154-156.
[62] Jordi Pujol (1966): *La immigració, problema i esperança*, Barcelona: Nova Terra cited by Conversi (1997): *The Basques, the Catalans and Spain*, London: Hurst & Company, p. 195.
[63] McRoberts (2001): *Catalonia. Nation Building*, p. 131.

FIGURE 7. Foreign Residents in Catalonia (1998-2007)

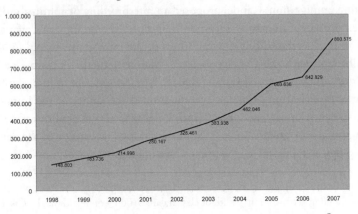

Source: MTAS

In the two autonomous communities with the greatest proportion of immigrants in Spain, Madrid and Catalonia the main groups of immigrants according to their country of origin differ largely. In Catalonia the North-Africans, specifically the Moroccans outweigh the Latin American immigrants, in Madrid it is vice versa. Another remarkable difference between the two autonomous communities according to the composition of their immigrant communities is that, except for a few individuals all Pakistanis and all Gambians registered in Spain live in Catalonia (see Figure 8).

FIGURE 8. Main Countries of Origin of Foreign Residents (non-EU) in Catalonia and Madrid (2007)

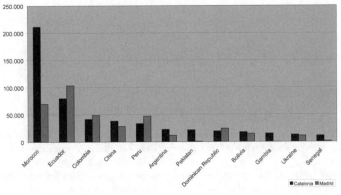

Source: MTAS

According to provinces, over two thirds of the regular immigrants in Catalonia live in Barcelona (province) and the other third in the three remaining Catalan provinces (see Figure 9).

FIGURE 9. Foreign Residents according to Province (Catalonia)

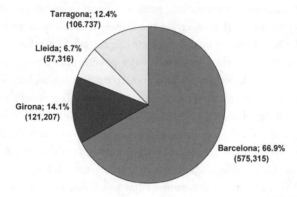

Tarragona; 12.4%
(106.737)

Lleida; 6.7%
(57,316)

Girona; 14.1%
(121,207)

Barcelona; 66.9%
(575,315)

Source: MTAS, 31.12.2007

Due to its limited authority in migration policy matters, the *Generalitat's* approach to immigration has concentrated on measures for the integration of the immigrants on the regional and local level, with special emphasis on the acquisition of the Catalan language. Integration policy is, moreover, not treated as a specific policy field but as an issue within the different areas of Catalan politics, such as health care, education, housing, etc. Hence there is no specific budget for immigration policy.[64] With the Pla Interdepartamental d'Immigració 1993-2000 (Interdepartmental Plan for Immigration 1993-2000)[65] a commission to coordinate the policy measures of the different departments of the *Generalitat* concerning the integration of immigrants (Comissió Interdepartamental d'Immigració) was created. The second plan, the Pla Interdepartamental d'Immigració 2001-2004 (Interdepartmental Plan for Immigration 2001-2004) addresses the same objectives as its precursor introducing yet further aspects. The general principals it establishes are thus a) balance between rights and obligations, b) normalization and universality of public services, c) collaboration

---

[64] See Rigau i Oliver (2003): La inmigración extranjera en Catalunya: presente y futuro, in Aubarell *Perspectivas de la Inmigración en España. Una Aproximación desde el Territorioa*, Barcelona: Icaria editorial, p. 20.
[65] The first plan of this kind in Catalonia.

and social participation, d) cooperation and coordination between the public authorities, and e) integration. Following these basic guidelines it more specifically aims at global politics of integration, at enhancing the participation of the immigrants in the Catalan society, at awareness-raising about the migration reality among the Catalans in general, at fighting against social, political and economical exclusion, at promoting equality of opportunities and it establishes various programmes and services for the immigrants' integration into Catalan society.[66] The *Secretaria per a la Immigració* (Secretary's Office for Immigration), by than allocated with the Presidency, since government change in 2003 part of the *Departament de Benestar i Família* (Department for Welfare and Family), was created to coordinate the policy measures concerning immigration matters of the different departments of the *Generalitat*.[67] In 2004 the PSC-led government elaborated a third plan, the Plan for Citizenship and Immigration (Pla de Ciutadania e Immigració 2005-2008) which centres on a new conception of a Catalan citizenship, independent of the Spanish nationality.[68] Since the elections in 2006 the Catalan government has promoted two important projects regarding its immigration policy. The first is to elaborate a National Pact on Immigration (Pacte Nacional per a la immigració) in a broad participatory process. This pact shall define the short, middle and long term general public policies and specific programmes and measures of all relevant actors. Moreover, it shall include a new Plan for Citizenship and Immigration for the years 2009-2012. The second objective is to pass a law on the reception and accommodation of immigrants (Llei d'Acollida).

The three Catalan plans for immigration and the recent initiatives for a National Pact on Immigration and a "Llei d'Acollida" show that, although the control of immigration and the related security issues still exclusively lie in the hands of central state authorities, the Catalan government has been able to promote a Catalan nationalist approach to integration policy rather independently.

---

[66] See Zapata-Barrero (2004): *Inmigración, innovación política en España*, pp. 182-183.
[67] For details on the policy action of the different departments concerning immigration issues see Aubarell, Aragall and Padilla (2003): *Gestionar la diversitat. Reflexions i experiències sobre les polítiques d'immigració a Catalunya*, Barcelona: Institut Europeu de la Mediterrània.
[68] For further explanation of the new concept of citizenship in Catalonia's official documents see Zapata-Barrero (2005): *Una filosofía pública de la Inmigración en Catalunya*, pp. 18-32.

V.
Methodological approach
& political discourse on migration

As the above described assumptions of discourse analysis are only a theoretical framework, a research programme which implicates as such no concrete method of data collection or data analysis, its methodological realisation must be chosen according to the actual research questions.[1] In the following the methodological approach to reconstruct the frames of national identity in Spanish and Catalan political discourse about migration is presented.

1. SELECTION OF THE EMPIRICAL MATERIAL

Political discourse is understood as the sum of public statements of politicians belonging either to the government and governing party (Gov) or to the opposition (Opp). The political discourse was analysed at the central state level (E) and at the level of the Autonomous Community of Catalonia (CAT). At the central state level only statements of politicians belonging to the two major political parties, PP (Partido Popular) and the PSOE (Partido Socialista Obrero Español) were included, because they have dominated Spanish politics ever since the transition to democracy. In Catalonia politics have been defined by five political parties, the CiU (Convergència y Unió), PSC (Partit dels Socialistes de Catalunya), ERC (Esquerra Republicana de Catalunya), IC-V (Iniciativa per Catalunya Verds), y (PPC (Partit Popular de Catalunya) (see III.1.6). Sources for the statements of politicians about immigration were parliamentary debates, public speeches and conferences, party platforms, interviews given to the media, newspaper articles written by politicians themselves, press conferences, government plans, and official declarations of political parties.[2]

---

[1] See Keller (2005b): *Wissenssoziologische Diskursanalyse. Grundlegung eines Forschungsprogramms*, Wiesbaden: VS Verlag für Sozialwissenschaften, p. 188.

[2] It should be kept in mind that the system of representative democracy implicates already a democratic selection process. Only the dominant political parties and politicians have access to these fora, e.g., parliament, where their opinion is heard. This discourse analysis can thus only

The year 2000 was chosen as starting point for analysis, because it was a decisive year for migration policy (see IV.1). As the empirical material for the chosen time-span between 2000 and 2005 was excessive in the case of the central state, it was necessary in a first step to pick out those time periods in which migration was an important political issue. A chronological list showed that one can distinguish two periods in 2000 and two periods in 2005.

Time period	Spain (E)
I.	Jan-March 2000 (Ley 4/2000, El Ejido, Elections)
II.	Nov/Dec 2000 (Ley 8/2000, End of regularization process)
III.	Jan-March 2005 (Regularization process)
IV.	Sept/October 2005 (Melilla/Ceuta)

This selection allows us to see if there has been a transformation in migration discourse over the five years and if the migration discourse transformed with the change of government in 2004. The analysis of four periods, furthermore, avoids that the results reflect only a single event.

For Catalonia the list of events related to migration issues showed that it was impossible to make out certain periods of time in which the subject migration was considerably more important than in others. Considering the fact that in Catalonia the gathered empirical material for the years 2000 until 2005 was less extensive than on the central state level it was possible to include all found documents.

Thus, for both central state and regional level the relevant interviews, press conferences, articles, speeches, conferences, official documents of the political parties within the above mentioned time periods were selected by searching the documents with the two syllables migra.[3] These syllables are both part of the Spanish words inmigrante, emigrante, migración, inmigración, emigración, migratorio, migratoria, inmigrado, inmigrada, migrar, inmigrar, emigrar + plu-

---

include statements that have already overcome the obstacles of representative democracy. See van Dijk (2001): *Principles of Critical Discourse Analysis*, p. 304.

[3] This is a kind of a simplified keyword list as suggested for instance by *Donati (2001): Die Rahmenanalyse politischer Diskurse*.

ral, as of the Catalan words concerning migration issues: immigrant, emigrant, migració, immigració, emigració, migratori, migratòria, immigrat, immigrada, migrar, immigrar, emigrar + plural.[4] Furthermore, the chapters of government plans/programmes and platforms which highlight migration issues and measures to deal with those were analysed for both government levels. With respect to the parliamentary debates, all parliamentary initiatives (in plenum and committee) dealing explicitly with immigration within the four selected time periods were included for the central state level whereas for Catalonia all sessions of the relevant parliamentary committees (Commissió d'Estudi sobre la Política d'Immigració a Catalunya/Commissió Permanent de Legislatura sobre Immigració) were included and all parliamentary initiatives dealing explicitly with immigration, too.

To back up the results of the analysis the author conducted eighteen interviews: twelve in Barcelona in 2005 and six in Madrid in 2007. In Catalonia, four members of the Catalan Parliament, two party representatives, two trade union representatives, three experts on migration and one representative of the Autonomous Administration, and in Madrid, three members of parliament, two representatives of immigrant associations and one representative of central state administration were interviewed. All interviews were given in Spanish, recorded and afterwards transcribed.

2. Coding in ATLAS.ti

The here presented interpretative-analytical compilation and reconstruction of frames of Spanish and Catalan national identity in the political discourse on migration draws on a multi-step approach suggested by Keller.[5] The first step consists in the description of the phenomenon or subject "migration" as it is presented in political discourse.

---

[4] Documents were not included when the syllable "migra" either formed part of the word "emigration" and the document contained only declarations about the Spanish emigration to other countries and does not mention immigration, or was found but the word which contained it was merely part of an enumeration of e.g. Political problems to deal with, global and national challenges, etc.

[5] See Keller (2004): *Diskursforschung*, pp. 93-114.

To facilitate the analysis, all selected documents, except the interviews, were coded with the software programme ATLAS.ti 5.0. The two government levels were each treated in separate files (in Atlas.ti: Hermeneutic Units).

Codes or categories were developed inductively of the material itself to make sure that all important dimensions were captured and no virtual categories constructed accidentally by the analyst.[6] Some smaller exceptions of the inductive approach were made: formal categories (four for the central state level and nine for the Catalan level) were introduced to mark of which political party the speaker is member and if this political party forms the government or the opposition at the time the statement was made ("Form Gov *Political Party*" or "Form Opposition *Political Party*"). These top-down categories make it possible to answer the following questions: Does the migration discourse of a political party changes over time? Does the migration discourse vary between different political parties? Does it make any difference if the political party is in government or in opposition?

The inductive coding took place in various steps going forth and back through the material. The names of the codes are in English or in Spanish/Catalan. In some cases it was necessary to stick to the Spanish or Catalan wording to avoid all kind of change in meaning at this stage (set off by quotation marks).

The categorization of the material at the central state level brought forth five overall categories. The first is, when politicians talk abstractly about migration, expressing what migration means to them (Migration is…). Talking about the human beings involved, the migrants, is the second overall category (Migrants are…). The Third is the explicit self-definition of the Spanish state and society (Spain is…). Migration policy in present and future is the fourth block (Migration policy is…) which is linked closely to the last summarizing category of the political parties talking about each other and about them handling migration issues (Political parties criticising each other…).

In addition to the already existing categories referring to the political parties and their responsibilities as part of the government or opposition, and a newly introduced category "Catalonia =", the five overall categories were used as top-down categories for the analysis of *discourse* at the regional level. The whole

---

[6] Following hence the methodology of open coding as suggested by "Grounded Theory". See Strauss and Corbin (1996): *Grounded Theory: Grundlagen Qualitativer Sozialforschung*, Weinheim: Beltz Psychologie Verlags Union.

material for Catalonia was first coded with these top-down categories and then in various following steps all other categories were evolved inductively.

The results of this coding process, the categories and dimensions of "migration" as a subject of the political discourse are presented briefly in the following.

3. THE POLITICAL DISCOURSE ON MIGRATION

Here a brief outline of the political discourse on migration and its different dimensions will be given as it is understood to be an important intermediate step towards the analysis of the constructions of national identity, presented in chapter VI and VII.

The discursive elements which appear when politicians talk about migration are all in some way linked to each other. That is why some dimensions appear in various varieties subsumed under different categories. Where further explanation is needed regarding the self-definition of collective identity it will be given in chapter VI and VII.

3.1 Central state level

Migration is...

All statements referring to migration, to the nature of migration, to what migration means for Spain, etc. were subsumed under the Category Migration =.

There are a series of words with which the speakers substitute the term migration ("migración" = migration/"inmigración" = immigration). When talking about migration in general the word fenómeno (= phenomenon) is used quite frequently. Other terms which I believe to have neither negative nor positive connotations are asunto (= subject), situación (= situation) and tema (= topic). The latter two were used only by the PSOE in its role as governing party. In contrast to these three terms the notion problema (= problem) used to describe migration is connoted more often negatively. Both political parties use it equally, whether or not in government or opposition.

Legal and illegal immigration are two different dimensions of migration which appear quite often in political discourse. For illegal migration the word ilegal (= illegal) is used as well as the term irregular (= irregular) which is generally thought to be a more neutral adjective. It seems though that there has been a change between the year 2000 in which migration is named "irregular" only by the opposition and the year 2005 when both, PP and PSOE, use it. Clandestina (= clandestine) is another adjective which means more or less the same. Illegal migration is said to exert a pressure (presión) on Spanish borders. Besides, the metaphors avalancha (=avalanche), flujos (= flows) and oleada (= wave) are used to describe the movements of migrants trying to cross the Spanish borders illegally.

The debate on migration prospects for the future depends widely on the discursive context. The PP government highlights the growing importance of migration to defend future political measures. Concerning the evaluation of the amount of migrants, politicians in governing positions tend to stress that the result of their migration policy is or will be less irregular migration. On the other hand the PP talks about a growing number of irregular immigrants as a result of the regularization process of the PSOE government in 2005. In the case of the massive border crossing in Ceuta and Melilla in 2005 the government emphasizes their circumstantial and short term character. The PSOE also mentions the change in migration patterns with the migrants originating to a growing extent from the sub-Saharan countries.

Migration is described often as a fenómeno reciente (= recent phenomenon) to which the Spanish society and politics must adjust. It is also mentioned as the signo más reconocible de nuestro tiempo (= the most obvious characteristic of our time), one of the big political issues of the 21st century, and as an effect of globalization. Referring to the political options to handle migration politicians find it to be a very complex field and difficult to manage. Illegal migration is even said to be imparable (= unstoppable). There is a broad consensus over political parties and over time that migration is a complex subject which needs complex answers and solutions. Migration is seen therefore as a big challenge (reto/desafío) for the present and future. And that is why PSOE, as well in opposition as in government, is postulating that in migration policy should be found a broad consensus between all political and social actors. It should be treated as what is called in Spanish cuestión de Estado (= state matter).

Migration is not only a security problem, but it has also other dimensions. With respect to the migrants coming by boat to the Canary Islands or the migrants trying to enter Ceuta and Melilla, migration is described in terms of a drama (drama) and human tragedy (tragedia humana).

The causes and motives for migration mentioned are various. As *pull factors* one can isolate the demand of the Spanish labour market for workforce and the regularization program of the PSOE government in 2005. The latter is stressed by the PP opposition which accuses the government of provoking the so-called efecto llamada (= attracting effect) by the legalization of illegal workers. The idea behind this slogan is that more illegal migrants are attracted because they see possibilities to get working and resident permissions in a future regularization process. But talking about causes and motives, what is highlighted most are the economical *push factors* which drive people to leave their home searching for a better life, e.g. demographic causes. People, over all young persons, migrate because they see no perspective in their home countries due to immense population growth and unemployment. The political reasons, such as persecution due to a different political opinion play only a minor role in political discourse.

There is seen also the positive contribution of migration to Spanish society and economy. Politicians of both political parties emphasize that economic growth in Spain needs migration. Another positive contribution considering the low birth rates in Spain are the children born from migrant parents. In addition members of the PSOE talk about the contribution to Spain's cultural richness.

Migrants are…

All statements concerning the immigrants' characteristics, role, status, etc., were coded with the category Migrant =.

The neutral and most frequently used term "inmigrante" (= immigrant) is substituted by different other words having various connotations. Both, PP and PSOE, tend to speak of migrants as seres humanos (= human beings) when talking about the victims of mafias which traffic migrants and exploit them or when highlighting the desperate economic situation the migrants are in or flee from. Another term used to emphasize migrants as human beings is persona (= person). When debating the integration of migrants they are defined as the new neighbours and new citizens (nuevos vecinos/nuevos ciudadanos). On the other hand in the context of the illegal border-crossings in Ceuta and Melilla the exceptional use of the word intruso (= intruder) can be found.

As already mentioned above one perspective to talk about migration is the economic contribution it renders. As a consequence, talking about immigrants in political discourse, means in the case of the analyzed documents often talking about them as foreign workforce (mano de obra). Having in mind the special context of Spanish labour market and its need for unqualified or low qualified workforce, in the debate about migrant workers they are implicitly not defined as highly-qualified professionals but as migrants working in a few sectors, e.g. the building, service, and domestic sector.

Explicitly or implicitly migrant workers are meant to be legal residents in Spain. This is made very clear in the debate about the 2005 regularization programme, when only irregular migrants already having a job were given the residency and working permit. The legal status of migrants is addressed usually when talking about migrants who enter illegally into Spanish territory or who are already residing and working in Spain without having the necessary documents. The words used are similar to those used when speaking of migration in general: ilegal (= illegal), irregular (= irregular), and indocumentado (= having no documents). There cannot be found any striking patterns about the use of either of these terms. Both are used in various contexts and by both political parties. The PSOE in their role as opposition and with respect to the irregular migrants claims that those should not be treated as criminals and they accuse the PP government of doing so.

Apart from defining migrants as workers, there are some other views outlined in political discourse. On the one hand they are seen as actors contributing to the development of their home countries (Migrant = actor of codesarrollo) and to the cultural diversity and richness of the host country. On the other hand, referring explicitly or implicitly to the irregular immigration from Africa trying to enter Spanish territory at the Canary Islands, the Strait of Gibraltar or the Spanish enclaves Ceuta und Melilla, they are refugees; refugees fleeing from the bad living conditions in their home countries, trying to survive, and searching for a better life in Europe (Migrant = victim-of conditions of life in C.o.O/searching for a better life). They are willing to make long and dangerous journeys (Migrant = victim-long/dangerous journey) and even risk their lives to reach it (Migrant = victim-risk and loose their lives). On their way they are victims of mafias and exploitation (Migrant = victim-of mafias/exploitation). This view highlights the humanitarian aspects and the vulnerability (Migrant = vulnerable/desprotegido) of the African immigrants.

Spain is...
Apart from talking about migration and the migrants the politicians also refer to their own country and society in a sort of self-reflection. These statements were subsumed under the category Spain =.

Spain is territorially defined in migration discourse to form part of the community of developed countries, of the so-called first world (Spain = developed country/part of first world). Besides, politicians emphasize the fact that Spain is a part of the European Union (Spain = EU-Part of EU) which is seen as a fortress of wellbeing and prosperity (Spain = EU-fortaleza de bienestar y de prosperidad) As such, all members of the European Union are likewise affected by migration (Spain = EU-all countries affected by migration) but it is highlighted that the patterns and dimensions of migration to Spain are unique (Spain = EU-patterns and dimensions of migration to Spain are unique in EU). This is due to the fact that Spanish borders are simultaneously the borders of the European Union to the south making Spain an access point for migration to the EU (Spain = EU-External borders of EU/Access point to EU). Those borders are borders separating the developed EU member states from developing countries in North Africa (Spain = border between rich and poor). Therefore the regions named as most affected by irregular migration from Africa are the Canary Islands and Ceuta/Melilla (Spain = most affected regions = Ceuta/Melilla; Spain = most affected regions = Las Canarias).

In addition to these characteristics linked to the Spanish territory there are some values and norms mentioned that are thought to be the foundations of the Spanish state and society. In migration discourse the democratic nature of the Spanish state (Spain = Values-Democracy) based on its constitution (Spain = Values-Constitution) and the rule of law (Spain = Values-Estado de derecho) is emphasized. At a certain point, when debating the massive border-crossings in Ceuta and Melilla in parliament, the PP brings up the question of the Spanish unity and sovereignty defending these two enclaves against Moroccan claims of territory (Spain = Values-Unity/Sovereignty).

With regard to Spain as an immigration country the quite common formula of Spain as a país/tierra de acogida (= country/land of welcome) can be found also in the political discourse about migration. Cultural diversity is believed to be something inherent throughout the history of the Iberian Peninsula (Spain = Values-cultural diversity based in history). Spanish society is therefore thought of as tolerant, open, plural, generous, advanced in adapting itself to migration (Spain = sociedad abierta; Spain = sociedad avanzada; Spain = sociedad generosa; Spain = sociedad plural; Spain = sociedad tolerante), and of having a special tradition to integrate migrants (Spain = cultura de integración).

The Spanish politicians use to highlight, as already mentioned above, the recent change from an emigration to an immigration country (Spain = hostsoc-from emigration to immigration country). Based on this assumption the PP points out that Spanish society first of all has to get used to the change immigration goes along with (Spain = hostsoc-society has to get used to migration) such as cultural change. Migration is defined in some statements as something that Spanish society suffers (Spain = hostsoc-sufrir ese fenómeno) and that is affecting the daily life (Spain = hostsoc-affects convivencia) and the social cohesion (Spain = hostsoc-affects social cohesion) of the host society, even creating social and security problems (Spain = hostsoc-social problems/problemas de orden público). An argument seldom used is the fear of rising unemployment rates linked to higher immigration (Spain = hostsoc-more unemployment). In contrast to that members of both political parties refer quite often to the fact that migration must be regulated and controlled when having in mind the limited capacity to receive immigrants and to integrate them into the Spanish labour market (Spain = hostsoc-capacidad de acogida limitada).

In two different circumstances the feelings of the Spanish society are addressed in political discourse. When debating the illegal border-crossings in Ceuta and Melilla the PP accuses the government of having created with their regularization campaign and the resulting "efecto llamada" (= attracting effect) a preoccupation in the Spanish society (Spain = hostsoc-preocupación/public opinion). They refer especially to a survey conducted by the CIS. Apart from that, Socialists facing the immigrants who desperately try to reach Spanish territory, speak about the compassion felt by the Spaniards for these people (Spain = hostsoc-compassion).

Migration policy is…/should be…

All statements and elements concerning the question of how to handle migration were subsumed under the category "Migration Policy". It can be divided roughly in five subcategories.

The first one summarizes all statements referring directly to the actors implicated in migration policy and the role they play or should play. On the level of external relations the actors mentioned are on the one hand the members of the European Union and on the other hand the countries of origin. With respect to the first the responsibility and obligation of Spain to cooperate and coordinate its migration policy with the other EU member states is highlighted (Migration Policy = Actors-EU -responsibility of Spain as member of the EU). Migration policy and measures should be multilateral not unilateral. One occasion when the PP accused the PSOE government to act unilaterally without having consulted the EU partners was the regularization process in the first half of 2005 (Migration Policy = Actors-EU-multilateral not unilateral Action). Due to the unique circumstances of migration to Spain and the growing migration pressure at the Spanish borders Spain is seen as one of the leading countries in setting the Agenda of EU migration policy (Migration Policy = Actors- EU-Spain is setting Agenda for migration issues). The Politicians of both parties demand further implication of the other EU members to collaborate in controlling the migration flows at the Spanish borders. It is seen to be a responsibility of all EU countries (Migration Policy = Actors-EU-responsibility EU for migration matters at Spanish borders), (Migration Policy = Actors-EU-common migration policy).

With respect to the relations between Spain and the countries of origin two different dimensions appear in political discourse. The first dimension includes security aspects, such as border control (Migration Policy = Actors-C.o.O.-Security issues). The second element mentioned is the cooperation in the socioeconomic development of these countries (Migration Policy = Actors-C.o.O.-Codesarrollo).

Not only the external dimensions of Spanish migration policy but also different domestic actors and their cooperation in migration matters are described. The Civil Society and NGOs are mentioned as important actors referring to migration policy (Migration Policy = Actors-C.S.-Cooperation with civil society/NGOs). Apart from that, politicians of both political parties demand more collaboration with the regional and local administrations (Migration Policy = Actors-CCAA-Collaboration Administrations), because they are the ones to translate into action measures promoting the integration of the immigrants (Migration Policy = Actors-CCAA- Integration policies). As already mentioned above, migration should be treated a policy field orientated towards consensus decision-making. All relevant actors should be included in the decision processes (Migration Policy = Actors-Actors consensus-pacto de Estado) and migration issues should not be subject of the fight between political parties (Migration Policy = Actors-no demagogy-no party politics).

A second subcategory of statements about migration policy includes the different elements or ingredients that are thought to be necessary to successfully deal with migration. Migration policy should correspond to international humanitarian standards (Migration Policy = Ingredients-humanitario). It should be sustainable (Migration Policy = Ingredients-sustainability), efficient (Migration Policy = Ingredients-efficiency) and over all not be left to chance (Migration Policy = Ingredients-planificación). Politicians claim that migration issues should be handled with strictness (estricta), rigour, determination, seriousness, clarity, transparency, consistency, sincerity, prudence, rationality, responsibility and solidarity.

Migration Policy = Action… is the third subcategory summarizing the statements about concrete measures in the field of migration policy. Due to the fact that the claim for action with respect to the dimensions Integration and Rights of migrants are quite diverse, both were subsumed under their own subcategory.

In general the claim is made that migration policy measures are or should be well planned and organized and not chaotic and arbitrary (Migration Policy = Action- políticas ordenadas vs. políticas desordenadas). The PSOE government emphasizes therefore that they want to organize the, until then, unorganized migration policy (Migration Policy = Action-poner orden donde había desorden). As one way to do so the reform of laws and institutions is seen. In the period of time analyzed here the reform debated most was the reform of the Organic Law 4/2000 in the year 2000, the Organic Law 8/2000. One of the main political aims of the governing PP is to allow only legal migration (Migration Policy = Action-allow only legal migration/labour migration). Following this the politicians declare war on the black economy (Migration Policy = Action-fight economía sumergida). As well they talk about fighting documentation fraud (Migration Policy = Action-fight fraud) and the exploitation of migrant workers (Migration Policy = Action-fight exploitation). The control of irregular immigration plays an important role in the discourse about migration (Migration Policy = Action- fight/control illegal migration). Rejecting a "policy of open doors" (Migration Policy = Action-no puertas abiertas) the strengthening of border controls is a frequent claim. Other measures to reduce irregular migration are to fight the mafias which traffic with humans (Migration Policy = Action-fight mafias/traffic in human beings) and to repatriate the migrants who have managed to reach Spanish territory without possessing valid documents. But the first thing that should be done when migrants manage to cross the borders by boat or by foot is to provide food, drink and medical service. Politicians demand that conditions of this primera acogida (= primary reception) should be improved.

Apart from these aspects concerning border control, measures considering domestic affairs are debated. The fight against racism, xenophobia, and discrimination (Migration Policy = Action-fight racism/xenophobia/discrimination) and the promotion of tolerance (Migration Policy = Action-promote tolerance) in society are two of them. The own emigration experience of the past should serve as a guideline how to treat immigrants today (Migration Policy = Action-take own emigration experience as guideline for treatment of immigrants now).

Thinking about how to integrate the newcomers into the host society is an important part of migration policy. Integration is mentioned as a general political aim. Migrants should be integrated and not excluded and discriminated. Often the term "integración social" (= social integration) is used as synonym to "integration". Different notions of the term integration can be found in the migration discourse. Integration is understood as the assimilation or adjustment of the migrants (Migration Policy = Integration-assimilation/adjustment by migrants) or, following the concept of multiculturalism, as protection of the cultural identity of migrants (Migration Policy = Integration-cultural identity/ multiculturalism) or in the sense of "Interculturalidad" as a process of reciprocal adjustment of migrants and host society (Migration Policy = Integration-Interculturalidad/adecuación cultural/mestizaje).

To be integrated into Spanish society migrants must have knowledge of values, norms and traditions of their host country and respect them (Migration Policy = Integration = knowledge of and respect for the Spanish values and norms). The local administrations should be provided with a sufficient budget for integration measures to avoid that the native population feels discriminated against (Migration Policy = Integration-sin que reste posibilidades ni recursos a los españoles = without taking possibilities and financial resources form the Spaniards). The two political parties seem to have very different assumptions about the relation between integration and the regular or irregular status of migrants. The PP highlights that only migrants already possessing documents should be actively integrated, which means the regular status is condition to be able to benefit from integration measures (Migration Policy = Integration = only legal migrants). On the other hand the PSOE draws the conclusion that full integration is only possible providing irregular migrants with documents (Migration Policy = Integration-darles papeles). The insertion into Spanish labour market, education and formation, especially language training are instruments thought of as being able to promote the integration of immigrants.

The issue of migrant Rights appears in different contexts. The claim to concede, respect and defend migrant rights has various connotations. In the context of the different regularization processes the concession of migrant rights was discussed (see Migration Policy = Rights-Regularización-Migration Policy = Rights- Regularización +). Another question posed by members of the PP, mentioned above, is if certain rights should be linked to the regular status of migrants (Migration Policy = Rights-derechos para los inmigrantes legales). That migrants have not just rights but also obligations, is a formula used quite frequently. The two major political parties agree that granting immigrants the political right to vote would not be appropriate. The option of giving them the right to vote at a local level is left open, at least by the PSOE.

Migrant rights are discussed also in the sense of requirements of Human Rights. The dignity of human beings and their respectful treatment are mentioned above all in the context of border crossings (Migration Policy = Rights-dignity/trato digno). The right to political asylum seems to play a minor role.

Political parties criticizing each other...

In migration discourse the politicians do not only refer to the subject itself but as it is quite common in political discourse, they criticize each other and the respective political measures. The statements of the PSOE about the politics of the PP government are summarized under the category GovPP = bad migration policy. On the other hand when the PP opposition criticizes the migration policy of the current PSOE government it falls under the category GovPSOE = bad migration policy. The controversies between the two major political parties focus basically on the important events during the analysed periods of time. The PP government faces hard criticism of the PSOE opposition with respect to the reform of the Organic Law 4/2000. The Socialists accuse the PP government in general of having broken the pact to found migration policy on the basis of a broad political consensus. In particular they criticize the restrictions of migrant rights in the new law, such as the right to join associations or trade unions and the differentiation made between regular and irregular migrants regarding these fundamental rights. Another very conflictive event was the regularization process of the PSOE government in the first half of 2005. The PP opposition accuses the Socialists to act against the jointly negotiated EU policies and to offend the other EU member states. Besides, according to the PP, the regularization process causes an "efecto llamada" (= attracting effect), attracting even more irregular immigrants, because they see a chance to get the necessary documents in a future regularization campaign. The Socialist government answers these accusations pointing to the regularization processes under the PP government, which in their opinion were uncontrolled and led to a criminalization of irregular immigrants in their aftermath. The present high number of irregular immigrants is therefore seen a result of the bad migration policy of the PP government. The regularization of 2005 changed this situation. The planning of the regularization process was based on a broad participation and consensus of different sectors of society, only the PP refused to cooperate and used migration issues for demagogy and electoral purposes. The occurrences in September/October 2005, when thousands of Sub-Saharans managed to climb the border fences of Ceuta and Melilla again led to a harsh debate about the causes of irregular immigration and about migration control. The PP argues that the observed phenomenon is a result of the "efecto llamada" which originates in the regularization campaign carried out a few months earlier and which produces a deep concern in the Spanish and European public. The PSOE replies that these people are pushed rather than pulled to Spain because of the desperate situation of poverty and hunger in their home countries. Further PP politicians accuse the government not to defend the Spanish interests against Moroccan territorial claims referring to the two disputed enclaves Ceuta and Melilla. In their reply, the Socialist side condemns this recurring on an antiquated discourse about the endangered territorial unity which no longer is questioned by anyone. As to the integration of immigrants the socialist government accuses the preceding PP government of having highlighted security issues and migration control and broadly ignored the integration of immigrants. The new government now sees to it and does spend money on measures for the social integration of migrants.

3.2 Catalonia

The political discourse about migration in Catalonia is in some dimensions similar to the one on the central state level, but mostly consists of different elements. This is due to the distribution of competences between the central state government and the regional government and the special role Catalonia plays as one of the "historical nationalities" within the Spanish state (see III.3).

Migration is...
Catalan politicians refer to at least two different forms of migration and their implications: On the one hand the interior migration from other Spanish regions, e.g. Andalusia, coming to Catalonia in the 1960s and 1970s and on the other hand the recent immigration of non-EU-citizens to Catalonia (Migration = interior vs. la nova immigració). The fact that Catalonia in comparison to other autonomous communities receives more migrants (Migration = characteristics-higher in Catalonia than in rest of Spain) is highlighted as the major char-

acteristic of the present immigration. It is also stressed that a growing number of migrants (Migration = characteristics-more migration/creixent) is distributed very unevenly within the region itself (Migration = characteristics-distribution). Besides that, it is described as a very heterogeneous and diverse immigration (Migration = diverse), culturally and with respect to the countries of origin.

All political parties state the importance of immigration as a subject for Catalan politics (Migration = priority subject), a complex and difficult issue (Migration = complex/dificil) which is a great challenge to handle (Migration = repte). In the context of illegal border crossing at the central state level the aspect of migration as human tragedy and drama is emphasized, similar to the central state discourse (Migration = drama/human tragedy).

Similarly to the discourse at the central state level, Catalan politicians name the causes of migration, meaning *pull* and *push factors*. As *pull factors* appear the demand for workforce of the Catalan labour market and the "efecte crida"[7] (Migration = Pull factors-...). The latter is mentioned by the CiU government which seems to have picked up the ideas of its informal coalition partner at the central state level, the PP. The bad economic situation and the demographic explosion in the countries of origin are, apart from the political reasons the *push factors* mentioned when talking about the migrants' motives to leave their countries of origin (Migration = Push factors-...).

There are positive and negative aspects attributed to immigration (Migration = positive and negative aspects). On the one hand immigration is seen as an opportunity for Catalonia (Migration = una oportunidad). Thus the political discourse positively highlights the importance of the economic, demographic and cultural contribution of the immigrants (Migration = economic contri-bution, =demographical contribution, = cultural contribution/diversity = rich-ness). On the other hand immigration is seen as being potentially conflictive. It could cause social conflicts, segregation and poverty (Migration = problem-social conflicts-segregación social/pobreza). It is seen both as a challenge and a threat to the persistence of Catalan identity (Migration = threat/challenge for Catalan identity). The latter is foremost an argument found in statements of CiU-members.

---

[7] The Catalan expression for "efecto llamada".

Migrants are…

As already shown at the central state level the neutral term "immigrant" is also in Catalonia substituted by various other words implying a certain definition how immigrants should be treated by the Catalan authorities.

The expression persones humanes (= human persons) is used like in central state migration discourse to stress that immigrants are human beings, to emphasize that they should be treated like human beings. Another way to speak of migrants without positive or negative connotations is to define them as gent vinguda de fora (= people coming from outside) or novinguts (= newcomers).

The replacement of the word immigrant with the terms Catalans nascuts fora del país (= Catalans born outside of the country), els nous catalans (= the new Catalans), los otros catalanes (= the other Catalans), nova població (= new population), nuevo ciudadano (= new citizen) implies the inclusion and integration of immigrants, the acceptance of them being a new part of the Catalan society. It is striking that only ERC, PSC and IC-V use these terms.

In accordance with the results of the analysis of central state migration discourse migrants are spoken of as victims. They are thought of as victims of the bad conditions of life in their countries of origin and therefore searching for a better life (Migrant = victim-of conditions of life C.o.O./searching for a better life). They are exploited by mafias trafficking with human beings and by employers (Migrant = victim-exploitation/mafias). Only rarely the persecution due to political reasons is mentioned (Migrant = victim-of persecution due to political reasons).

Catalonia is…

The political discourse about migration in Catalonia is very much characterized by self-reference to a distinctive collective identity. Elements of Catalan identity mentioned are foremost language and culture (Catalonia = Catalan identity-culture/…= Catalan identity-language). Besides that, the welfare state and the fact that Catalonia is a country of immigration (Catalonia = Catalan identity-país de acogida) and therefore heterogeneous and diverse are told to be features which have become inherent to Catalan identity over the years (Catalonia = Catalan identity-diversity). Identity building is described as a process of identity construction which needs to be discussed and promoted actively (Catalonia = describing identity building).

In relation and delimitation to the Spanish State and the central state government Catalonia is defined by all political parties as a nation (Catalonia =

Catalan identity- una nació). National identity appears in migration discourse roughly in two varieties. On the one hand nationalism is based on a civic concept of nation (Catalonia = nationalism-civic) and on the other hand ethnicity is the precondition for being Catalan (Catalonia = nationalism-ethnic).

In migration discourse the politicians often fall back upon the history of Catalonia (Catalonia = the past) to explain present or future developments. Under the Category Catalonia = the future all visions and projects for Catalonia's future were summarized.

Apart from that, Catalonia is described as an attractive country for migrants, among other things because of its economical progress. But like at the central state level politicians also state that it is a country which has a limited capacity to receive and integrate migrants (Catalonia = capacidad de acogida limitada).

Talking about Catalan values politicians mention democracy and democratic institutions, liberty, laicism in public affairs, equality in general and gender equality (Catalonia = Values -…).

It is remarkable how often the migration discourse itself is subject of the discussions about migration discourse (Catalonia = migration discourse).

Spain is…

In the Catalan migration discourse there are few references made to the Spanish context. Spain or the central state government are mentioned when talking about the definition of the Catalan nation as one among other Spanish nations (Spain = nació de nacions). In addition the question of the transfer of authorities which is dealt with in the chapter "migration policy…", the migration discourse at the central state level, particularly the affirmations of the PP government, are subject of Catalan criticism (Spain = migration Discourse).

Migration policy is…/should be…

Following the categorization of the material concerning the central state, statements and elements referring to the question of how to handle migration were subsumed under the category Migration Policy. The policy options are, for their part, organized in five subcategories:

1) Different actors are referred to when talking about migration in Catalonia. The EU appears in the context of the demand for a common migration policy of all EU-member states (Migration Policy = Actors-EU-common migration policy). Furthermore, Catalan politicians mention the cooperation with the countries of origin concerning development and security issues (Migration

Policy = Actors-C.o.O.-…). The collaboration with civil society associations and NGOs is highlighted especially when debating the integration of immigrants (Migration Policy = Actors-C.S.- collaboration with civil society/NGOs). Similar to the central state level, politicians at the Catalan level stress the importance of a broad consensus over migration policy measures (Migration Policy = Actors-actors consensus/pacto de estado. Utilizing migration issues for electoral purposes or demagogy is a practice rejected widely (Migration Policy = Actors-no demagogy-no party politics). An important aspect that appears when analyzing the political discourse about migration in Catalonia is the relation between the autonomous community Catalonia and the central state authorities. The predominant claim of Catalan politicians is the transfer of more competences and financial resources to the regional level (Migration Policy = Actors-CAT-E transfer of competences/…of money).

2) The subcategory Ingredients summarizes, as above, the view of the politicians about the characteristics of a successful migration policy. Due to the division of competences, the policy measures for the integration of the immigrants play a bigger role at the regional level. Therefore, the description of migration policy is often identical with integration policy. A formula which appears quite often is that migration policy should be integral. That means there should be no measures aimed solely at the immigrant population but measures must include the whole population. Apart from that migration policy is defined as transversal, i.e. the different departments of the *Generalitat* are responsible, each for a different sort of measures. Another claim, specific to the Catalan migration discourse, is that migration policy should follow the principle of proximity (Migration Policy = Ingredients-proximitat al territori). That means that measures should be implemented by the lowest local authority.

Besides these specific "ingredients", the Catalan politicians also enumerate elements similar to the central state discourse. According to that, migration policy should be e.g. responsible, coherent, efficient and progressive.

3) The categorization of the empirical material concerning the migration policy action showed that in the time period analysed two important central state initiatives were discussed also at the regional level: The reform of the *Ley de Extranjería* and the regularization process carried out by the PSOE government in the first half of 2005 (Migration Policy = Action-Ley de Extranjería/… Regularització). To improve the immigrants' situation politicians claim to prevent racism and xenophobia, to fight poverty, social exclusion and the mafias, and to weed out the black economy. The latter is connected substantially to

the demand for reducing irregular immigration (Migration Policy = Action-fight/reduce illegal immigration). A common formula is no puertas abiertas (= no open doors), or no papers per a tothom (= no documents for everybody). Migration flows should be controlled and illegal migrants repatriated. Apart from the irregular migration, regular migration is necessary, because the Catalan labour market necessarily demands work force (Migration Policy = Action-legal migration-demand of labour market). Therefore the CiU-government states that migrants should be selected according to labour market needs. Like in the migration discourse at the central state level, in Catalonia humanitarian aspects play a role too. Mainly the opposition parties ERC and IC-V claim that Catalonia should become a terra d'asil (= an Asylum country). An issue often discussed are the measures of the primera acollida (= first reception). Both opposition and government parties refer to the opportunity to learn from former immigration flows (Migration Policy = Action-lessons learnt from former immigration).

4) The fourth subcategory summarizes all migration policy actions which refer especially to the integration of immigrants. Here again, migration discourse reflects the division of competences between the regional and central state authorities. Issues concerning policy measures directed at the integration of immigrants are touched on more frequently by Catalan than by central state politicians. The different concepts and elements of integration, at this stage only listed and described in a simplified manner, will be analysed and explained in the following chapters, considering their context and underlying assumptions about the Catalan identity.

Primarily, integration policy measures appear in political discourse as part of the universal measures of social policy. General improvements in education, housing and health services are seen as the best way to integrate the newcomers. All political parties, but mostly in government position, stress the importance to preserve and protect the social cohesion and the daily peaceful living together (Migration Policy = Integration-preserve/protect social cohesion/convivencia). Often the causality between universal social policy measures and social cohesion is highlighted. Another element appearing quite often in migration discourse is the need to sensitize the Catalan population, by implementing measures of pedagogía ciudadana (= citizens pedagogy). On the other hand politicians claim to promote more participation of the immigrants themselves (…= Integration-promote migrant participation). Religion and religious diversity as a by-product of immigration is seen as a subject which is potentially conflictive and should therefore be handled as part of integration politics (Migration Policy = Integration-religion). A regular status and the incorporation into the Catalan labour market are seen as conditions for successful integration. All the measures enumerated above depend on the availability of sufficient financial resources. A frequent claim is therefore to increase the budget for the implementation of social policies (Migration Policy = Integration-increase budget).

How the integration process itself should look like is described in various, often interconnected ways. One is that integration is a mutual process of adjustment, a process where both parties learn from each other, a process that could be headed by the formula interculturalidad. Also appearing in the Catalan migration discourse is the claim for a specific Catalan way of integration, via catalana d'integració. From a more nationalist point of view the CiU sees a need to defend and protect Catalan identity. Catalan identity is presented as endangered (Migration Policy = Integration-defender/proteger identidad catalana). Therefore immigrants should learn Catalan, Catalan symbols, and values. The promotion of Catalan language and culture however is a topic that can be found on the agenda of all political parties in Catalonia (Migration Policy = Integration-promoting Catalan). Here statements tend to stress the obligation of immigrants to adjust to Catalan society. Looking at the statements about the integration of immigrants, the CiU emphasizes the fact that successful integration depends on the origin of immigrants (Migration Policy = Integration-depending on origin). Stressing the difference between Latin American and Moroccan immigrants, a different religion and language are seen as a difficulty for integration. Furthermore, the PSC, ERC and IC-V introduced a new concept of citizenship. The idea is to concede immigrants the status of being Catalan citizens including all rights and obligations (Migration Policy = Integration-concept of Ciutadania).

The results show that there are big differences between the different political parties when integration issues are discussed.

5) Similar to the central state level the talking about migrant rights is on the one hand linked to the debate about the reform of the Ley de Extranjería and on the other hand to the question of migrant integration. Criticizing the legislative reform all political parties in Catalonia, except the PPC, claim to concede, respect and defend migrant rights (Migration Policy = Rights-concede/respect/defend migrant rights). Immigrants should dispose of equal opportunities. All political parties refer to the human rights standards and demand that immigrants should live in condicions dignes. In relation to the integration of immigrants the formula that migrants should have rights and obligations is

common (Migration Policy = Rights-drets I deures). In the year 2002 parliament discussed a kind of contract (carta d'acollida) between the newcomers and the Catalan authorities defining these rights and obligations.

Political parties criticizing each other...

In migration discourse the politicians do not only refer to the subject matter itself, but they criticize each other and the respective political measures. The statements criticizing the Government of the CiU are summarized in the category "GovCiU=" and vice versa. The criticism versus the central state government of the PP was categorized with "GovfedPP =".As the criticism between the political parties centres on the identification with Catalonia and Catalan nationalism their analysis will be included in chapter VII about the frames of national identity in Catalan political discourse about migration.

4. ANALYSIS AND INTERPRETATION

As the research question, however, does not ask what politicians say about migration, but how they directly or indirectly refer to national identity talking about migration, the description of the political discourse on migration could only be a first step to facilitate further analysis. The second and more important step of the analysis thus was the interpretative reconstruction of frames of national identity.[8] Therefore, the previously classified empirical material was searched (per category or code) for definitions of distinctive features of a "We-group", and for boundaries constructed between a "We" and an "Other". The latter implicitly reflect definitions of the "We".[9]

Some of the resulting ascriptions or frames of national identity were found to embrace various sub-frames which correspond to the different dimensions and variations within a frame.[10] In chapter VI and VII the frames are presented

---

[8] For the detailed description and an example of a political frame analysis see Donati (2001): *Die Rahmenanalyse politischer Diskurse.*
[9] See the concept of "diskurssemantische Grundfigur das Eigene und das Fremde" of Busse (1997): Das Eigene und das Fremde. Annotationen zu Funktion und Wirkung einer diskurssemantischen Grundfigur, in Jung, Wengeler and Böke *Die Sprache des Migrationsdiskurses. Das Reden über "Ausländer" in Medien, Politik und Alltag,* Opladen: Westdeutscher Verlag, p. 21.
[10] For the division of *frames* into *sub-frames* see Gerhards and Rucht (1992): Mesomobilization: Organizing and Framing in Two Protest Campaigns in West Germany, *The American Journal of Sociology,* 98:3; Gerhards (2003): Diskursanalyse als systematische Inhaltsanalyse. Die öffentliche

and explained within their context, and subsumed under different areas of interest, such as "Economic development" or "Basic norms of the political system". All direct quotes of the analysed material and of the interviews were translated by the author from Spanish or Catalan into English. Documents are cited according to their denotation in the ATLAS.ti file. A complete list of all documents with the correspondent specifications can be found in the bibliography at the end.

Debatte über Abtreibungen in den USA und in der Bundesrepublik Deutschland im Vergleich, in Keller *et al. Handbuch Sozialwissenschaftliche Diskursanalyse. Band II: Forschungspraxis*, Opladen: Leske + Budrich; Gerhards and Rucht (2003): Öffentlichkeit, Akteure und Deutungsmuster: Die Debatte über Abtreibungen in Deutschland und den USA, in Gerhards *Die Vermessung kultureller Unterschiede*, Wiesbaden: Westdeutscher Verlag and Wessler (1999): *Öffentlichkeit als Prozeß. Deutungsstrukturen und Deutungswandel in der deutschen Drogenberichterstattung*, Opladen: Westdeutscher Verlag.

VI.
Central state discourse on national identity

The analysis of the political discourse on immigration and immigrant' integration on the central state level brought forward several elements or frames of national identity construction, described in the following.

1. THE CONSTRUCTION OF A COMMON PAST

As discussed in chapter II.1.2, a strategy to construct collective and especially national identity is to emphasize and remember a common past. By cultivating the memory of past events and narrating certain historical developments collective memory[1] and a historical continuity are constructed also in political discourse about migration.

At the central state level politicians of all political parties centre their affirmations on historical dimensions linked to migration issues. For the construction of a common past beyond these see chapter VI.2.

1.1 From an emigration to an immigration country

Most prominently they speak of Spain's past as an emigration country and the fundamental change in the 1990s from a country of emigration to a country of immigration. In view of the Spanish immigration rates (see IV.1), this explicit definition of Spain as an immigration country is not surprising and rather self-evident.

The temporal frame "from an emigration to an immigration country" was usually used as a medium to launch specific political ideas or to introduce the explanation of more specific issues, related to immigration.

Thus this specific frame could be found in technical descriptions such as the illustration of the changes in the migration balance and its effects on the demo-

---

[1] See Halbwachs (1992): *On Collective Memory.*

graphic development of Spanish society by the Spanish Minister for Labour and Social Issues Manuel Pimentel (PP) at the weekly given cabinet press conference in January 2000:

> "Until the mid-70s we do have a negative migration balance; it was us who left the country to look for work that the economic circumstances in our country could not provide at that moment and we had, nevertheless, a strong natural population growth because of the high birth rate. The years went by. Already in the years 1975-1979 we had a positive migration balance, basically because the emigrants who had gone abroad started to return to our country, and already at the beginning of the 1990s we started to adjust to more European circumstances, where the natural growth is insignificant, practically it is none, and the migration balance is the only thing that makes the population grow."[2]

In addition to these rather technical descriptions the frame of the recent change from a country of emigration to a country of immigration was used furthermore to promote political ideas or to justify political action or inaction as the extract of an interview by the Spanish President José María Aznar exemplifies. He reflected the difference between Spain and other European countries regarding the period of time that had gone by since migration balance had shifted to the immigration side:

> "One of the big differences in Spain –you have said it– is that, from being a country of emigrants we have passed to being a country where we have to worry about the problems which can cause us the reception of emigrants."[3]

However, not only the government made use of this kind of affirmations, also the Socialist opposition used it, but rather to criticise the PP government. In their evaluation of the Programa GRECO the PSOE accuses the government harshly of not having effectively acknowledged that Spain has become a country of immigration.[4] It further demands to design policy measures that rationalize the phenomenon.[5] Four years later the electoral manifesto of the PSOE in 2004

---

[2] P3: E-I-Gov-Portavoz-MTAS-Piqué-Pimentel-14-01-2000rtf.rtf-[Hasta mediados de los 70 tenem...] (25:25).
[3] P10: E-I-Gov-Presidente-Aznar-24-02-2000.rtf-[Una de las grandes diferencias...] (46:46).
[4] See P92: E-II-Opp-PSOE zum Plan Greco 27-12-2000.rtf-[reconocimiento de España como...] (27:27).
[5] See P92: E-II-Opp-PSOE zum Plan Greco 27-12-2000.rtf-[España por su nivel económico...] (41:41).

highlights the growing number of immigrants and states that the PP government had not adopted policy measures to integrate the immigrants into the labour market and into Spanish society:

> "We were a country of emigration and now we receive millions of immigrants without having a policy which would integrate them in the regular labour market and in an open and plural society."[6]

Against the background of this unique Spanish development from a country of emigration to a country of immigration politicians of both major political parties deduce a particular obligation towards today's immigrants. They underline an obligation to receive immigrants well, to be open to immigrants, to receive and to treat them like the expatriate Spaniards would have wanted to be treated by the countries they chose to emigrate to. In 2000, for instance, Aznar stated: "We have an obligation to be a tolerant, open people and to be capable of integrating them".[7] His Minister of Labour and Social Issues formulated it even more clearly in an interview given to the daily newspaper "El País" on February 23, 2000:

> "I do not want to make an economic analysis of the immigration phenomenon because that is unjust. The immigration phenomenon hast to be looked at with the same eyes that we would have liked to be looked at in the years when many Spaniards had to set out to other countries."[8]

As Spaniards emigrated in their majority or to Latin America or later to the Western European states these kinds of statements were directed particularly at those countries or the communities of Spanish origin residing in those countries as it is the case with an official speech Zapatero delivered at the occasion of his meeting the Spanish community in Argentina, during which he emphasized that Spain was an open, a constitutional, and a democratic country which was experiencing the reception of immigrants and which had the obligation to receive those well who work to build their future.[9]

---

[6] P97: E-III+IV-Gov-Auszüge aus Programa Electoral PSOE 2004.rtf-[Éramos un país de emigración y...] (101:101).
[7] P10: E-I-Gov-Presidente-Aznar-24-02-2000.rtf-[Ahora le voy a decir: nosotros...] (48:48).
[8] P8: E-I-Gov-MTAS-Aparicio-23-02-2000.rtf-[El fenómeno de la inmigración...] (46:46).
[9] See P54: E-III-Gov-Pres-Zapatero-25-01-2005.rtf-[una España abierta, desde una...] (24:24).

1.2 A tradition of cultural diversity

In discussions on migration policy another link between Spain's past and today's immigration is drawn. Politicians emphasize that cultural diversity is an element already based in the historical development of the country. Neither is cultural diversity new to the Spanish society, nor are immigration and the reception of foreigners. Spain and particularly the Canary Islands are thought to have a certain tradition of a "tierra de acogida" ("land of welcome") and of being open to external influences. This characteristic is described to have always formed part of its personality.[10]

In its chapter titled "El malestar de la cultura: una globalización regida por la dureza neoliberal" (The malaise of the culture: globalization ruled by neoliberal rigour), the Socialist electoral manifesto in 2004 criticizes how the PP government has handled cultural issues. One point of critique is that the PP has shown a "complete passivity with respect to the historic cultural diversity of our country".[11] The PSOE's electoral manifesto 2004 also states that the acceptance of new cultures resulting from recent migration movements is an expression of the "original pluri-cultural reality of Spain".[12]

However, these general affirmations remain vague regarding periods in Spain's history or regarding the origin of foreign cultural influences. Thus, hardly any explicit references to the roots of this cultural diversity could be found, apart from a speech which Zapatero delivered on the occasion of an official visit to Argentina in 2005. He then emphasized the historic link between Spain and Latin-America and referred to the mutual migration movements using the following words:

> "We have a history and, what is more important, a culture that has always been interlinked and enriched by reciprocal migratory flows. We are two open peoples who have known to live together and to enrich each other mutually."[13]

---

[10] See P18: Auszüge E-II-DSCongreso-CO_096-07-11-2000.rtf-[esos extranjeros que están red...] (280:296).

[11] See P97: E-III+IV-Gov-Auszüge aus Programa Electoral PSOE 2004.rtf-[Se muestra una absoluta pasivi...] (199:199).

[12] See P97: E-III+IV-Gov-Auszüge aus Programa Electoral PSOE 2004.rtf-[La realidad pluricultural orig...] (206:206).

[13] P53: E-III-Gov-Pres-Zapatero-25-01-2005-b.rtf-53:4 [Somos dos pueblos abiertos, qu...] (25:25).

These definitions of Spain being culturally diverse, implicitly negate the existence of cultural homogeneity, of Spanish culture as an essential, primordial element, and rather affirms a constructivist perspective of Spanish culture as an ever changing and re-constructed mélange of multiple influences.

2. BASIC NORMS OF THE POLITICAL SYSTEM

Discussing migration issues, politicians on the central state level define explicitly or implicitly what they understand to be basic principles and values of the Spanish nation.

2.1 The Spanish Constitution and democracy

The Spanish Constitution of 1978 is the fundamental and overarching framework that codifies the democratic system and its basic principles. As described above in chapter III.3 the constitutional consensus is the result of a pact between all political actors reached during the transition period. The democratic principle is thus the lowest common denominator of the Spanish political system.[14]

But not only of the Spanish system democracy is the supporting pillar, but of the European Union too, as Piqué, speaker of the PP government emphasized at the weekly press conference, in February 2000. According to him, Europe is founded on values that are based in democracy understood as the government of majority, but also on the respect of minority and human rights.[15] In the Programa GRECO the PP government indicated democracy as an objective which should be promoted and distributed. It denominated Europe and particularly Spain as the place where those persons who suffer from dictatorship, violation of their fundamental rights, persecution because they fight for democracy will find a "space of freedom".[16]

Five years later in 2005 on the occasion of his visit to Argentina, the Socialist President Zapatero described Spain as an open, a constitutional and a demo-

---

[14] See Winter (2004): Spaniens Intelektuelle: Eine neue Diskussionskultur und die Debatte um Identitäten und "Erinnerungsorte" (1976-2002), in Bernecker and Dirscherl *Spanien heute. Politik- Wirtschaft-Kultur*, Frankfurt a. M.: Vervuert Verlag, p. 648.

[15] See P2: E-I-Gov-Portavoz-Just-Piqué-Mariscal-11-02-2000rtf.rtf-[porque el proceso de construcc...] (38:38).

[16] See P99: E-PROGRAMA GRECO 30-03-2001.rtf-[La lucha por la democracia y p...] (114:114).

cratic country which was experiencing the reception of immigrants and which has the obligation to receive those well who work to build their future in Spain. Addressing the Spanish community in Argentina among whose members are many exiled persons who emigrated due to political persecution during Franco's authoritarian regime he focused on the democratic change Spain had undergone since those times. Not only was he addressing those Spaniards who emigrated to Argentina but also their descendents who often had decided to go back to Spain, especially after the grave economic crisis between 1998 and 2002.[17]

These statements are examples of how in migration discourse and political discourse in general of the common denominator of the Spanish political system, the democratic principle stipulated by the Constitution of 1978 is constantly reaffirmed. Implicitly this is also a reaffirmation of the membership in the "club" of western democracies.

2.2 Spain, "Staatsnation" or "Kulturnation"?

The importance that is attributed to the Constitution, its democratic principles and the resulting framework as the foundation of the Spanish political system in general also is reflected in the definition of what should be the basic elements for the integration of immigrants. It is thought to be indispensable that the Constitution and the Spanish laws are respected, regardless of the personal and cultural roots and traditions.[18] Nevertheless, the reference to the Constitution and the legal framework as an undisputable fundament of the Spanish political system and society can be based on different underlying assumptions. On the one hand, the Constitution and the resulting political system and legal framework are understood to be the constituting element of the nation which can be described with Meineckes concept of the *Staatsnation* (see ii.1.2). According to this, for all people living in this political nation, regardless of their cultural and ethnic origin the lowest common denominator is the Constitution and only the Constitution (see for concept of constitutional patriotism chapter ii.1.3). On the other hand, the Constitution is seen as an expression of the nation, defined culturally and historically, as a *Kulturnation*.

---

[17] See P54: E-III-Gov-Pres-Zapatero-25-01-2005.rtf-[una España abierta, desde una ...] (24:24).
[18] See P99: E-PROGRAMA GRECO 30-03-2001.rtf-[El marco de convivencia será l...] (101:101).

The discourse of the two major political parties moves between these two ideal types of a nation. However, the statements of politicians differ depending upon which political party they belong to and show a certain affinity to one or the other above described concepts.

Since the transition period, the Spanish left tends to focus on the constitutional and legal framework and underlines the concept of a political nation based on the common will to form a nation (see III.5.2). "In reality, what unifies a people is not race, not even language, nor religion, it is unified by the totality of its objectives and the totality of its hopes."[19] To this statement of a Socialist member of parliament can be added another one which the Spanish Minister of the Interior, Alonso Súarez made on the occasion of a parliamentary debate in 2005 which describes in a more detailed way what this assumption means for the interaction with immigrants:

> "our legal and constitutional framework determines the limits of our social living together, which means that of no foreigner a public or private behaviour can be required that goes beyond the norms, but on the other hand it determines that no custom or cultural identity can be beyond the respect for the system of values and constitutional rights that are required from all citizens."[20]

He emphasizes that foreigners can not be obliged to fulfil anything regarding his public behaviour that goes beyond the legal and constitutional norms. In accordance to that, a socialist member of parliament asked to give a definition of the Spanish collective identity answered the following:

> "The constitutional identity! I think that it is the constitutional identity. The constitutional identity which is founded primarily on the preservation of the democratic principle and the democratic principle means that it can be extended even to the concept of political participation to facilitate the integration of immigrants. It can be done. With difficulties, but it can be done. On the one hand that and on the other hand the preservation and the development of the Constitution itself. Which is the guarantee of the constitutional values and the fundamental rights and freedoms. That would be the collective identity of the Spanish people at this moment."[21]

---

[19] P20: Auszüge E-II-DSCongreso-PL_044-24-11-2000.rtf-[En realidad, lo que une a un p...] (1691:1696).

[20] P41: Auszüge E-III-DSCongreso-PL_071-23-02-2005.rtf-[determina que ninguna costumbr...] (733:736).

[21] E-1 Member of Parliament-PSOE, 2007.

In the same interview he explains how these rights and freedoms established in the Constitution derive from former constitutions and go back to the nineteenth century.[22]

On the other hand, in statements about the foundations of Spain, the PP also refers to the constitutional and legal framework but explicitly or implicitly includes pre-constitutional values and norms in their affirmations. The PP postulates in its electoral manifesto for 2004 that "the values and norms of the living together which our society and our constitutional and legal framework are based on"[23] must be accepted. According to that, today's political system is based on historically derived cultural and religious elements of Spanish identity. A conservative Member of Parliament confirmed this view saying "Yes. Our Constitution determines a series of things which reflect what defines Spain".[24] He further defines the Spanish identity as the sum of its laws and its history.[25] The former president and leader of the PP, Aznar expressed in his writings the belief of the Spanish Right in the historical continuity of the Spanish nation exemplarily.[26] According to him the roots and origins of present Spain go back to the times of the Catholic Kings, to the "Siglo de Oro" and the "Reconquista".

> "...a country which on a large scale has forged its personality during many years and many centuries; let's say in the Reconquista. For many centuries Spain has been a country whose border character has formed part of this personality. Today we are an external border of the European Union and we are also border, as we have always been, in relation to these African countries..."[27]

This statement for instance shows the historical determinism and the construction of the historic continuity of Spain being a border country. For the construction of a common past see also chapter VI.1.

---

[22] See E-1 Member of Parliament-PSOE, 2007.
[23] P98: E-III+IV-Opp-Auszüge aus Programa Electoral PP 2004.rtf-[los valores y las normas de co...] (23:23).
[24] E-2 Member of Parliament-PP, 2007.
[25] See E-2 Member of Parliament-PP, 2007.
[26] See for instance Aznar (2004): *Ocho Años de Gobierno. Una Visión Personal de España*, Barcelona: Planeta, pp. 91-93.
[27] P9: E-I-Gov-Presidente-Aznar-17-02-2000.rtf-[Nosotros estamos en la situaci...] (286:286).

2.3 Consensual decision-making

In addition to these general affirmations of the basic norms such as the constitution in migration debate politicians allude to a certain mode of democratic decision-making. In the field of migration the need for consensual/rational policy of all major actors within the Spanish state and society (political parties, Entrepreneurs, Trade Unions, NGOs, the Catholic Church) and thus a consensual mode of democratic decision-making is stressed by the different political actors. The formula of migration as a "cuestión de Estado" (State matter) and therefore the need to agree on a "pacto de Estado" (State pact), a pact between all political and social actors appears quite often in political statements about migration. The PP, for instance, stated in its manifesto for the elections in 2000 that "The immigration phenomenon requires a "política de Estado". We want to develop it with the maximum agreement of the political powers in Parliament".[28] Also the PSOE in government defined migration as a "cuestión de Estado", because it is an important and possibly controversial topic which requires consensus, not only within the Spanish State but also between the developed states of the international community.[29]

In various contexts the two major political parties have accused each other of having broken an existing consensus or of not being willing to reach a consensus on migration issues. For instance, after the reform of the Ley de Extranjería in 2000 (see chapter iv.1) the Socialist opposition harshly blamed the government of having missed again the opportunity to make a pact:

> "...the right has again refused the outstretched hand offered by the Socialist party with the proposal to achieve a state pact which would enable us to overcome the party confrontation in such a sensitive area as immigration."[30]

Five years later the Socialist party, by then in government responsibility, suggested that the PP should join the consensus on the regularization of irregular immigrants in 2005:

---

[28] P95: E-I+II-Gov-Auszüge aus Programa Electoral PP 2000.rtf-[El fenómeno de la inmigración ...] (35:35).

[29] See P39: Auszüge E-III-DSCongreso-PL_066-02-02-2005.rtf-[ahora se lo reitero desde el G...] (131:135).

[30] P14: E-II-Opp-SecrMigrPSOE-Rumi Ibanez-16-12-2000.rtf-[la derecha ha vuelto a desperd...] (7:7).

"I urge you to join this consensus that we have offered and that other speakers have accepted. It seems that you don't want to, perhaps because you desire to continue winning elections with laws that at the end withdraw rights."[31]

The Secretary of Organisation of the PSOE, Blanco, goes even further in his warnings and uses the picture of the "two Spains" to underline the importance of consensual policy-making. According to him elements of the "genetic code" of the Spanish democracy are "the value of consensus, the upholding of the dialogue no matter how big the discrepancies are, the will to construct the essential elements of living together jointly, and the healthy fear of confrontation and the reappearing of the two Spains".[32]

This shows that Spanish politicians explicitly define consensual decision-making to be still a fundamental principle of the Spanish democracy as it stems from the transitional pact between the right-wing forces close to the former regime and the left-wing opposition.

2.4 Meta-discourse

As a consequence of the claim to reach consensus in such an important policy field politicians of both, the PSOE and the PP demand that migration policy should not be an issue of party politics and electoral propaganda. Furthermore, it should not be an instrument of demagogy because there is a constant underlying danger to encourage negative feelings and xenophobic attitudes among the Spanish population. Migration is "a subject which should not be used for demagogy nor political opportunism, because it would mean playing with fire".[33] It is thus the "responsibility of everyone to consolidate a culture of tolerance".[34]

These statements show a particular sensitivity to the interaction of different discursive arenas. The influence media coverage and political discourse exert on the public opinion is itself an issue discussed among the political actors. It is hence discourse about discourse, respectively meta-discourse.

---

[31] P71: E-IV-DSCongreso-CO_377-28-09-2005.rtf-[Le reitero una vez más que ven...] (3596:3601).

[32] P56: E-III-Gov-SecrOrgPSOE-Blanco-24-01-2005.rtf-[Queremos recuperar la vigencia...] (5:5).

[33] P64: Auszüge E-IV-DSCongreso-CO_358-06-10-2005.rtf-[un tema con el que no se debe ...] (294:296).

[34] P21: Auszüge E-II-DSCongreso-PL_046-29-11-2000.rtf-[ya que es responsabilidad de t...] (68:70).

2.4.1 *Media coverage and public opinion*

In special circumstances such as the arrival of African immigrants at the Canary Islands or the mass intents to cross the fences of Ceuta and Melilla the national and European media focus on migration, particularly on illegal immigration. The following statement of the Socialist representative in Spanish Parliament, López Aguilar, shows that already in the year 2000 the political arena was aware of the crucial link between media coverage and public opinion:

> "It is evident that immigration is affecting all of Europe; it is evident that immigration strongly affects Italy, so exposed to the pressure on the part of the Balkan countries, with which it has borders or with the Mediterranean Sea; it is evident that within Spain it affects the whole national debate and it is sufficient to watch the coverage of the recent national developments that the media offer to understand to which point since March until now the problem not only has not disappeared, has not dissolved, but has maintained its virulence and has grown in the gaining of attention by the public opinion."[35]

However also the PP representatives are aware of the important influence media coverage has on the public opinion. A PP Member of Parliament mentions the public attention due to the events in 2005 in Ceuta and Melilla to accuse the government of not dealing well enough with immigration:

> "In our country an avalanche of immigrants is happening. All of Spain watches it almost live on television. Hundreds, thousands of illegal persons enter through our borders. We watch them how they organize in Morocco, how they enter, how they jump the fences. All of Spain watches on television and you deny it."[36]

2.4.2 *Political diction and public opinion*

In addition to the knowledge about the interaction of media and public opinion, Spanish politicians reflect in their statements about immigration the interaction between their own discourse and the public opinion. They are well conscious of how their discourse, particularly their diction, influences the public opinion on immigration and immigrants. The two major political parties thus seem to

---

[35] P18: Auszüge E-II-DSCongreso-CO_096-07-11-2000.rtf-[Es evidente que la inmigración…] (193:211).

[36] P68: Auszüge E-IV-DSCongreso-PL_118-05-10-2005.rtf-[Se está produciendo una avalan…] (419:424).

monitor each other critically regarding their discourse about migration issues and the effects this kind of discourse has on the public opinion.

In the context of the racist attacks in El Ejido[37] the PSOE-Opposition accuses the PP government of reinforcing xenophobic tendencies with their political discourse and of not having any coherent strategy to fight these sentiments. The PSOE therefore in their electoral programme includes claims to introduce measures of prevention and to promote tolerance and understanding:

> "An approach destined to express that the foreigners are invading us and that it has to be prevented is without doubt a pedagogy contrary to the need to fight xenophobia and racism, a monster that always is present, that can rise every moment, that has already risen very dangerously in our own country."[38]

On the other hand, PP representatives criticized sharply the regularization process starting in February 2005 and cited surveys[39] that demonstrate in their opinion an increasing preoccupation of the Spanish society with the immigration.[40] They accused the government to have made immigration seem problematic:

---

[37] In February 2000, after the murder of a young Spanish woman and the arrest of a Moroccan immigrant suspected of having stabbed her to death, racist riots erupted in El Ejido, a small fruit- and vegetable producing town in Andalusia. Three days running hundreds of Spaniards protested, shouting racist slogans and burning cars and shops belonging to North African immigrants who on their part armed themselves with rocks and clubs. In the aftermath, the local authorities and the police were accused of passivity and of having actually taken sides with the Spanish protesters.

[38] P20: Auszüge E-II-DSCongreso-PL_044-24-11-2000.rtf-[Un enfoque destinado a decir q...] (1512:1518).

[39] With respect to this question, political and social actors usually refer to the monthly repeated survey of CIS (Centro de Investigaciones Sociológicas) called "Barómetro" and particularly to the open question what the respondents rank as the three principal problems currently existing in Spain. In February 2005 when the above cited statement was made in congress, the three principal problems mentioned most were "unemployment" (58.8 per cent), "Terrorism, ETA" (46.1 per cent) and "Immigration" (21.8). 10 months before, in April 2004 and thus shortly after the terrorist attacks in Madrid and the general elections, the result was as follows: "Terrorism, ETA" (62.9 per cent), "Unemployment" (56.8 per cent), "Housing" (22 per cent) and "Immigration" (11.8 per cent). See Centro de Investigaciones Sociológicas (CIS), URL: http://www.cis.es.

[40] See P41: Auszüge E-III-DSCongreso-PL_071-23-02-2005.rtf-[Ustedes le han dado la vuelta ...] (312:315).

"What worries us most is that you have made immigration a problem, which it wasn't 10 months ago. Unfortunately, 10 months ago immigration was not considered to be a problem by the citizens."[41]

Nevertheless, representatives of the PSOE were convinced that there was no feeling of alarm in the Spanish public and that on the contrary the survey data showed that immigration was seen favourably as long as it is regular immigration:

"Consensual politics. We are willing. There is already a very broad consensus. The other day a national paper published an opinion poll which indicated that 70 per cent of the Spaniards favour that someone who has a job should dispose of a permit."[42]

Caldera, Minister for Labour and Social Affairs, neither perceived a particular concern, but he admitted that sometimes there could be ignorance about the phenomenon because it came so rapidly.[43]

Later that year, both, PP and PSOE discussed, in the context of the events at the border of Ceuta and Melilla, if immigration was perceived by the Spanish population as something to worry about or not. Again the PP accused the government of having raised concerns in the broad public. "You have caused that immigration is named as the third problem in the preoccupations of the Spaniards. Today, there are more than 1,100,000 people in an illegal situation in Spain."[44] Two weeks later a PP Member of Parliament stated that immigration was a very complex issue and that the Spanish citizens perceived it as such. He cited further that "it is the primary preoccupation, their primary priority among the current political problems".[45]

---

[41] P41: Auszüge E-III-DSCongreso-PL_071-23-02-2005.rtf-[Lo que más nos preocupa es que...] (300:304).

[42] P41: Auszüge E-III-DSCongreso-PL_071-23-02-2005.rtf-[Política de consenso. Tenemos ...] (755:759).

[43] See P25: E-III-Gov-MTAS-Caldera-02-01-2005.rtf-[yo creo que no hay inquietud...] (12:12).

[44] P66: Auszüge E-IV-DSCongreso-PL_112-21-09-2005.rtf-[Han hecho que la inmigración s...] (104:107).

[45] P64: Auszüge E-IV-DSCongreso-CO_358-06-10-2005.rtf-[Nos parece una materia muy com...] (729:732). The results of the CIS Barómetro for what is thought to be currently the three principal problems in Spain are for September 2005 "Unemployment" (53.0 per cent), "Terrorism" (34.2 per cent), "Immigration" (31.2 per cent) and for October the same year "Unemployment" (51.1 per cent), "Immigration" (37.4 per cent), "Terrorism" (25 per cent). See Centro de Investigaciones Sociológicas (CIS), URL: http://www.cis.es.

All the cited examples show a high degree of self-reflection on the part of Spanish politicians. This observation was confirmed in interviews with Members of the Spanish Parliament. A Socialist Congressman, for instance, explained:

> "A message has to be transmitted to the citizens of, let's say, how to acknowledge this new situation, the positive aspects and the uncertainties it arouses in us and which we have to overcome or try to solve. Therefore I believe that yes, it is true that this is a question that needs an intelligent discourse, not a demagogic discourse. This means, to use immigration for demagogy or campaigning is to generate a danger in the mind of the citizens that has short and long term effects."[46]

His colleague, a conservative Congressman, likewise emphasized the self-limitation in statements and affirmations about migration issues, because of the risk of encouraging xenophobic tendencies:

> "Therefore it is indeed true that a strong prevention exists, that we all restrain ourselves a little bit, we restrict ourselves, limit ourselves in the use of a series of facts, because if not it could generate, what is easily producible in Spain, an opinion contrary to immigration and to the foreign immigrant. It is very easy to make mischief and make the foreigners responsible for it. Therefore we limit ourselves much in our affirmations, because it is true that there have not been any conflicts in Spain, nor rejection, but if one of the major political parties –here the Socialist Party has 40 per cent and the Partido Popular the other 40 per cent and the remaining 20 are distributed between 50 political formations– if one of the two political parties led a xenophobic, racist discourse it would spark the public opinion."[47]

2.5 The rule of law

Two crucial issues discussed within the field of migration policy are the non-discrimination of immigrants regarding their rights and obligations and the respect for human rights. Although the former appears within the domestic arena and is closely linked to the integration policies and the latter forms part of the outwards-oriented debate about migration and border control, both issues are ascribed to be subject of the constitutional state. Politicians point out the rule of law as an essential element of a democratic state, and therefore an essential element of the Spanish democratic system.

---

[46] E-1 Member of Parliament-PSOE, 2007.
[47] E-2 Member of Parliament-PP, 2007.

The question of how to treat immigrants who already live in Spain but do not dispose of the necessary documents is very controversial between the two major political parties. The debate about the reform of the Ley de Extranjería in 2000 led to a political dispute about the rights of regular and irregular immigrants. The distinct positions of the two major political parties clashed when the PP majority changed the original version of the Ley de Extranjería LO 4/2000 into the LO 8/2000. The PP pushed through that only legal migrants enjoy certain rights and freedoms e.g. health care, education for their children, scholarships. A member of the PP group in parliament reproduced the official party line arguing that

"In our opinion, this seems injustice to us. If we suggest to give support for housing, health care, education, scholarships and, furthermore the possibility to get a regular situation in our country within two years, do you believe to encourage regular immigration like that?"[48]

In an official declaration, the PSOE opposition sharply criticized the limitations of the rights and freedoms of irregular immigrants, such as the freedom of assembly, of manifestation, of association, of strike, and of affiliation to a trade union and disclaimed the responsibility for the resulting legal text.[49] In an article Consuelo Rumí, today secretary for immigration issues in the Socialist government, expressed the fundamental beliefs of the Socialists in this matter:

"Because, at least from the position and values of the Socialists, the rights cannot be negotiated for other elements that we have suggested and that have been incorporated in the reform project. Their exercise has to be recognized independently of the nationality and the legal status of the citizens in correspondence with our constitutional state. They are therefore essential areas that cannot be derogated in the name of an ostensible rigidity that doesn't account for handling a phenomenon such as migration which requires intelligent and generous responses how they suit your institution and the challenge that advanced societies pose."[50]

---

[48] P20: Auszüge E-II-DSCongreso-PL_044-24-11-2000.rtf-[A nuestro entender, esto nos p...] (1808:1812).

[49] See P90: E-II-Opp-PSOE zum Ley de Extranjeria 24-11-2000.rtf-[Por lo que se refiere ahora al...] (16:16).

[50] P13: E-II-Opp-SecrMigrPSOE-Rumi Ibanez-08-12-2000.rtf-[Porque, al menos desde la posi...] (10:10).

She furthermore argued that in a democratic state you can not be ambiguous about rights, one day conceding them and refusing them the next day. This is not in accordance to the rule of law.[51] To "restrict the exercise of rights is unacceptable, because it affects essential elements of our constitutional state".[52] At this opportunity the PSOE also accused the PP government of criminalizing irregular immigrants.[53] A Socialist Member of Parliament thus highlights that "the irregular immigrants are not criminals they are persons who move to be able to work, to survive".[54]

Analysing the political discourse about migration control and particularly the control of the terrestrial borders the second issue linked to the constitutional state mentioned above, human rights, is striking. Explicit reference to the human rights, the respect of human dignity and the treatment of immigrants according to these internationally agreed values, such as the Universal Declaration of Human Rights[55] could be observed particularly in relation with migration control and security relevant issues, such as refusal, detention, and repatriation of illegal immigrants. Politicians referred to human rights especially in September and October 2005 when African immigrants, in their majority Sub-Saharans, managed to enter the two autonomous cities Ceuta and Melilla illegally crossing their border fences.

In September 2005 the Spanish government faced denunciations of human rights violations at the Spanish-Moroccan border of Ceuta and Melilla supposedly committed by Spanish and Moroccan security forces.[56] In reaction to that a representative of the PP in the Congress demands in the name of his parliamentary group

---

[51] See P20: Auszüge E-II-DSCongreso-PL_044-24-11-2000.rtf-[Ustedes se han mostrado ambigu...] (1263:1271); [El recorte de los derechos, la...] (1301:1307).

[52] P91: E-II-Opp-PSOE zum Ley Extranjeria 14-12-2000.rtf-[Sin embargo, la pretensión del...] (10:10).

[53] See P20: Auszüge E-II-DSCongreso-PL_044-24-11-2000.rtf - [En el fondo es una criminaliza...] (1655:1656).

[54] P20: Auszüge E-II-DSCongreso-PL_044-24-11-2000.rtf-[Los inmigrantes irregulares no...] (1656:1658).

[55] The Spanish Constitution mentions in Art. 10.2 the norms of the Universal Declaration of Human Rights and of further international agreements ratified in this field as fundamental and inviolable rights.

[56] See Amnesty International (2005): Spain/Morocco. Migrant rights between two fires, Public Statement, 03.10.2005, URL: http://www.amnesty.org/en/alfresco_asset/056ee2a3-a301-11dc-8d74-6f45f39984e5/eur410112005.en.pdf.

"the respect of human rights [...] That is the real collaboration that our parliamentary fraction wants to maintain with the Kingdom of Morocco, because Spain is a constitutional state in which the dignity of the people is sacred."[57]

Defending the government's reaction to the happenings in Ceuta and Melilla the Socialist Member of Parliament López Garrido rejects the request of the opposition to assign investigations of human rights violations at the border to an international commission with the remark that Spain is no banana republic but a democratic country with independent tribunals to oversee the compliance with the law.[58] He adds:

"That is why we cannot agree to your proposal of an international commission which does not correspond to the situation nor to the attributes of a member state of the European Union, and a democratic state, as is the Spanish state."[59]

A Socialist colleague speaks up in defence of the Spanish security forces, the Guardia Civil[60] emphasizing that "therefore it [Guardia Civil] is anxious for security and at the same time anxious to guarantee human rights in dealing with those security issues".[61] That means strict border controls, including repatriations and devolutions, yet in accordance with the respect for the human rights:

"As I say, every day immigrants are repatriated, although it is not said, every day repatriations are done in accordance to the established agreements, but always according to legality and according to the humanitarian assistance, and the respect of the human rights, not only with Morocco, but also with other countries with which this type of devolutions and repatriations are put into practice, too."[62]

---

[57] P71: E-IV-DSCongreso-CO_377-28-09-2005.rtf-[El respeto a los derechos huma...] (1793:1797).
[58] See P72: E-IV-DSCongreso-CO_383-10-10-2005.rtf - [En España existen leyes y trib...] (2413:2421).
[59] P72: E-IV-DSCongreso-CO_383-10-10-2005.rtf-[un Estado perteneciente a la U...] (3525:3527).
[60] The Guardia Civil (Civil Guard) is the Spanish gendarmery which has both military and civilian functions such as highway patrol, drugs and anti-smuggling operations, customs and ports of entry control, anti-terrorism, coast guard, etc.
[61] P71: E-IV-DSCongreso-CO_377-28-09-2005.rtf-[por lo tanto está obsesionado ...] (2704:2707).
[62] P64: Auszüge E-IV-DSCongreso-CO_358-06-10-2005.rtf-[Como digo, todos los días se r...] (803:819).

The conservative opposition claims the respect of the human rights and agrees with the government that "Spain is a constitutional state in which the human dignity is sacred".[63]

2.6 The principle of subsidiarity

In the political debate about the integration of immigrants, politicians at the central state level stressed the importance of the principle of subsidiarity, giving hence their support to the division of authority between the central state, the autonomous communities and the municipalities, as it is an expression of the decentralized state. Emphasizing the need for collaboration with the regional and local administrations regarding the integration of immigrants also implies an acknowledgment of their claim for broader political autonomy. Not surprisingly, the analysis showed that only Socialist politicians explicitly affirmed the principle of subsidiarity and thus showed their support to the authorities of the autonomous communities and the municipalities.[64] In its criticism of the Programa GRECO, the PSOE argued that "the policies to be conducted have to be implemented by the administrations and service-centers that are closest to the citizens and their problems".[65] A Socialist Member of Parliament too stressed that "the authority in integration matters are of the autonomous communities and municipalities"[66] yet that it is necessary to support their efforts and that hence the PSOE majority in Parliament has adopted the introduction of a state fund which is distributed to the regional and local administrations according to the number of immigrants they receive.[67]

---

[63] P71: E-IV-DSCongreso-CO_377-28-09-2005.rtf-[porque España es un Estado de...] (1796:1797).

[64] The principle of subsidiarity = the idea that a central authority should have a subsidiary function, performing only those tasks which cannot be implemented effectively at the regional or local level. It was introduced in the Treaty of Maastricht as a general principle for the EU.

[65] P92: E-II-Opp-PSOE zum Plan Greco 27-12-2000.rtf-[las políticas que se deben lle...] (51:51).

[66] P64: Auszüge E-IV-DSCongreso-CO_358-06-10-2005.rtf-[Quiero que quede claro que las...] (394:407).

[67] See Ministerio de Trabajo y Asuntos Sociales, Gabinete de Comunicación (2005): *Comunidades autónomas y ayuntamientos reciben 120 millones de euros para acogida e integración de los inmigrantes*, Nota de Prensa 18.04.2005, URL: http://www.tt.mtas.es/periodico.

3. Spain in relation to other states

In migration discourse various constellations of how politicians define Spain's position in relation to other states surface. This refers both to regional or multilateral and bilateral relations with other states.

3.1 Sovereignty and territorial integrity

Sovereignty and territorial integrity are fundamental conditions of a nation-state and its definition versus other nation-states. In the Spanish case, sovereignty over the urban enclaves, Ceuta and Melilla, surrounded by Moroccan territory, is still questioned by the Kingdom of Morocco.[68] After the Ceuta and Melilla incidents in 2005 a harsh and controversial debate about Morocco's posture and the reaction of the Spanish government unfolded. During a debate in the Congress, the conservative opposition brought up the issue of sovereignty over the two cities on the African continent. They accused the PSOE of not defending the "Spanishness" of Ceuta and Melilla and "that the whole citizenry has doubts if the government is rather defending the interests of the Spanish residents in Ceuta and Melilla or in its territories or if it is defending the interests of the neighbouring country".[69] In a TV talk show the PP leader Eduardo Zaplana also used the frame of Sovereignty and Spanish Unity to discredit the engagement of the PSOE government in a bilateral dialogue with the Moroccan government:

> "We have had a summit with the Moroccan president and President Zapatero has been incapable of defending the *Spanishness* of Ceuta and Melilla. They have talked about co-sovereignty, about possible formulas for the future and he has been incapable to say something as elementary as that Ceuta and Melilla are Spanish cities and that this question is not up for discussion. When the government of Morocco sees this debility in a government, sees this debility in its president, it will logically take charge."[70]

---

[68] See Nohlen and Hildenbrand (2005): *Spanien*, pp. 367-369; Mattes (1995): Postkoloniale Grenzprobleme im Maghreb, in Faath *Wuqûf 9. Beiträge zur Entwicklung von Staat und Gesellschaft in Nordafrika*, Hamburg: Hans Peter Mattes Verlag, pp. 146-148.

[69] P69: Auszüge E-IV-DSCongreso-PL_120-18-10-2005.rtf-[Después del tiempo que se llev...] (841:857).

[70] P62: E-IV-Opp-PP-Zaplana-05-10-2005.rtf-[Que hemos tenido una cumbre co...] (49:55).

Representatives of the PSOE responded to these statements with the statement that it wasn't necessary to reaffirm the "Spanishness" of Ceuta and Melilla because nobody ever had ever questioned it.[71] They accused the PP of using the old tenet of the Spanish right of the threatened sovereignty and unity of Spain for strategic purposes:

> "Since the constitutional pact there have been certain things that have not been challenged in this country, but for you everything is useful. You want to reopen debates that don't exist and you do it because it is profitable for your strategy, following the strategy of the ancient right. Note that in the year 1890 the government of Canóvas del Castillo already defended the *Spanishness* of the territories that were colonies and moreover the *Spanishness* of Ceuta and Melilla. Millán-Astray, Mola and Yagüe tempered their patriotic spirit in the years before the Spanish Civil War in the north of Africa and also defended the *Spanishness* in Ceuta and Melilla. Even Minister Castiella in the year 1963 presented a resolution to the United Nations affirming the *Spanishness* of Ceuta and Melilla. And I ask myself: What happens to the Spanish right, which 40, 50, 110 years later comes back to the same path to defend a Spanishness that no one is challenging at this moment?"[72]

Indeed, what surfaces in these fragments of the political discourse about illegal immigration into Ceuta and Melilla is the old and crucial ideological question of the territorial organization of the Spanish state, dividing the Spanish right and the Spanish left. In the cited statements of the PP representatives and the Socialist reaction it becomes clear that the reference to a threat to Spain's unity and sovereignty is a recurrent frame in the discourse of the Spanish right (see III.5.1). This becomes even clearer looking at what the former Minister of the Interior, Acebes, stated in the above mentioned parliamentary debate. He claims "a policy that believes that our strength and our progress, of all of us, lies in the unity; that defends firmly that Catalonia, the Basque Country and Ceuta and Melilla are Spain".[73] Here suddenly the two "insubordinate" autonomous regions Catalonia and the Basque Country are included in the debate. It is thus no longer a question of external relations with other states but rather an intermingling of external and internal affairs. This exemplifies once more that

---

[71] See P69: Auszüge E-IV-DSCongreso-PL_120-18-10-2005.rtf - [No necesitamos reafirmar la ci...] (1037:1039).

[72] P69: Auszüge E-IV-DSCongreso-PL_120-18-10-2005.rtf-[Desde el pacto constitucional...] (1039:1066).

[73] P68: Auszüge E-IV-DSCongreso-PL_118-05-10-2005.rtf-[una política que crea que nues...] (699:702).

in Spain territorial integrity is not only a subject of external relations but is also questioned and discussed internally.

3.2 Spain in relation to the European Union

As described in chapter III.3.1 Spanish identity has always been constructed against the background or in relation to other European states. However, the definition of how Spain and the other European states or the European Community related to each other has varied broadly over time. Spanish identity constructions have gone from Spain being abnormal or different from Western Europe to Spain being unchallengeable a part of the European Union. Today Spain is a member of the European Union and no politician in Spain would dare to question or criticize that. Nevertheless, depending on the actual situation and the subject discussed the relation between Spain and the European Union and the role Spain plays within the EU is looked at from different viewpoints and different aspects of this relation are highlighted.

Discussing migration issues, borders and boundaries appear to be fundamental. Defining both physical borderlines and abstract boundaries implies at the same time the assumption of what is on one side and what on the other side of it. Defining and naming borders and boundaries is thus part of the construction process of the collective identity, of the "self" and the "Other".[74] In migration discourse politicians on the central state level refer to geographically, economically or politically defined borders and give us an idea about how they position Spain within the defined physical spaces. In migration discourse, particularly when discussing the immigration from the African continent, politicians emphasize that the Spanish borders form the "external borders of the European Union" as well.[75] Furthermore, the specific geographic situation of the Canary Islands and the two Spanish enclaves, Ceuta and Melilla is highlighted.[76]

These statements implicitly contain the assertion that Spain forms part of the European Union. As Spain entered the European Community in 1986 this

---

[74] See Barth (1969): *Introduction.*

[75] P10: E-I-Gov-Presidente-Aznar-24-02-2000.rtf-[Los españoles tenemos que sabe...] (37:38).

[76] See for example: P18: Auszüge E-II-DSCongreso-CO_096-07-11-2000.rtf-[Canarias, como parte de España...] (98:107); P71: E-IV-DSCongreso-CO_377-28-09-2005.rtf-[Todos sabemos también que Ceut...] (179:185); P72: E-IV-DSCongreso-CO_383-10-10-2005.rtf-[Ceuta y Melilla forman parte m...] (594:597).

seems more than obvious. Nevertheless, Spanish politicians tend to continuously reaffirm Spain's belonging to Europe in their discourse about migration.[77]

Actually, when comparing the migration situation in Spain to the one in other EU countries, the PSOE government comes to the conclusion that Spain is not the only country of the EU facing migration pressure at their borders. The Southern European Countries such as Italy and Greece also have to deal with illegal immigration from African countries.[78]

> "Spain has an important border of the European Union in the south. It is not the only country that suffers from this problem, Italy has suffered from the massive avalanches of immigrants, Greece has suffered from them, and other countries that are not in Europe have suffered from them, and Spain has suffered from them, too."[79]

Therefore, migration is an issue to handle and to deal with jointly. Notwithstanding, the challenges related to migration to Spain do differ from the ones other European countries such as Germany, France and the UK face. The Plan GRECO explains for instance

> "that this phenomenon in Spain at the moment hasn't the same characteristics as in countries such as Germany, France or the UK, which have handled immigration for much longer and which places us in the privileged situation to take advantage of other experiences and to be able to tackle the planning of a state policy with the necessary instruments of planning, programming and coordination of all public powers in order to participate and promote the management of the phenomenon of the immigration in the European Union."[80]

Regarding Spain's position within the EU decision-making process itself, both, the PP and the PSOE, allude to their government as having managed to

---

[77] See P54: E-III-Gov-Pres-Zapatero-25-01-2005.rtf-[una España europea, pero ibero…] (24:24); P99: E-PROGRAMA GRECO 30-03-2001.rtf-[la inmigración como fenómeno d…] (16:16).

[78] See P18: Auszüge E-II-DSCongreso-CO_096-07-11-2000.rtf-[Es evidente que la inmigración…] (193:211).

[79] P72: E-IV-DSCongreso-CO_383-10-10-2005.rtf-[Estamos ante un problema de in…] (2427:2467).

[80] P99: E-PROGRAMA GRECO 30-03-2001.rtf-[que este fenómeno en España en…] (82:82).

play an important role and having set the agenda in the common EU migration policy.[81]

Apart from the already mentioned dimensions of Spain's relation to the other EU members, two different but not contradictory perspectives on the allocation of responsibility between Spain and the other EU countries could be found.

The first perspective focuses on the responsibility Spain has vis-à-vis the other EU members to control and handle illegal migration well. The PP formulated in its electoral manifesto of 2000 that the Spanish migration policy "should be a policy, congruent with the obligations and responsibilities that we have assumed within the European Union".[82]

The PSOE government, though less explicitly than the PP, bases its debate about border-control also on the responsibilities versus the European Union:

> "Schengen implies the urge to guarantee the uniform and rigorous control of our borders, because they are also borders of the European Union and we are bound by our commitments in Europe."[83]

In general, Spain, as member of the European Union and therefore part of the European Union's agreements should cooperate and arrange its migration policy measures with the other EU-states.

After the announcement of the regularization process in 2005 the opposition and other European countries accused the Spanish government to act unilaterally and not multilaterally as intended.[84] The PP blamed the PSOE government to have broken

---

[81] See P41: Auszüge E-III-DSCongreso-PL_071-23-02-2005.rtf-[porque además habíamos sido el...] (335:338); P40: Auszüge E-III-DSCongreso-PL_069-09-02-2005.rtf-[España no solo está coordinand...] (106:107).

[82] P95: E-I+II-Gov-Auszüge aus Programa Electoral PP 2000.rtf-[Debe ser una política congruen...] (35:35).

[83] P72: E-IV-DSCongreso-CO_383-10-10-2005.rtf-[Schengen, implican la necesida...] (617:621).

[84] There was indeed a negative reaction, at least on the German and the Dutch side criticising the lack of previous consultation. See Kleiner (2005): Von Spanien lernen. Legalisierung als Migrationspolitik, in *Blätter für deutsche und internationale Politik*, 6:2005.

"a European policy which from the beginning we have promoted as protagonists. While France, England, Germany and Italy are taking restrictive measures regarding the illegal immigration, Spain opens its doors."[85]

And warns further not to

"make policies of immigration contrary to what the Ministers of the European Union are saying, to apply them unilaterally and after doing so ask our European colleagues for help, the truth is, that this leaves us in an uncomfortable situation. Well, we will see what this will cost us and how much it will cost us."[86]

It must be kept in mind how much Spain has profited from its membership in the European Union in the last decades. Spain's positive performance within the EU is seen thus as a high priority subject for every Spanish government. Consequently it is a very strong and effective critique to state that the government acts against jointly agreed EU policy.

The second perspective in migration discourse is the claim that all countries of the European Union should account for what happens at the Spanish borders. As the Spanish borders are also the external borders of the EU, the other EU-member states have the responsibility to support Spanish efforts of migration control. Confronted with the illegal border-crossings in Ceuta and Melilla in autumn 2005 the governing Socialists demanded EU support: "It is therefore also a problem of, and of major importance to the European Union. These are its southern borders".[87] President Zapatero states that Spain can not handle this gigantic problem alone and that it must be handled by all Europe and all developed countries together.[88] He adds that "the regulation of the access conditions cannot be the exclusive responsibility of the ones who are next to the door".[89]

---

[85] P36:   E-III-Opp-SecrGenPP-Acebes-PortInmPSOE-Hernando-09-02-2005.rtf-[El   Gobierno ha roto una polít…] (17:17).

[86] P68:   Auszüge   E-IV-DSCongreso-PL_118-05-10-2005.rtf-[hacer   políticas   de   inmigración…] (1334:1340).

[87] P70:   Auszüge   E-IV-DSCongreso-PL_121-19-10-2005.rtf-[Por lo tanto, es un problema t…] (188:193).

[88] See P59:   E-IV-Gov-Presidente-Zapatero-15-10-2005-c.rtf-[España no es únicamente la que…] (123:123).

[89] P58: E-IV-Gov-Zapatero-26-10-2005.rtf-[La regulación de las condicion…] (7:7).

3.3 Spain in relation to Latin America

Spain's relation to Latin America has until today been determined by its colonial history on this continent. From this colonial past a special obligation and a special relation to Latin American countries is derived. In an official speech in January 2005 held on the occasion of his meeting the Spanish community in Argentina the socialist President Zapatero defines Spain as being both European and Ibero-American. The European Spain is contributing to this big project of unification, the European Union, a project which is working on such important things like the European Constitution. The first obligation he assigns to this European Spain is "to look at Ibero-America, to fight for Ibero-America, and feel its successes, because its progresses are Spanish progresses, too".[90]

However, not only the commitment towards Latin America appears in political discourse about migration also the idea of Spain being the intermediary between Europe and Latin America can be heard. Zapatero, for instance, stressed in an interview the advantages of Spain's close relation to the Latin American countries, namely that it strengthens the position of Spain in the world:

> "The relations with Venezuela, like with all Latin American countries, are crucial for Spain's position in the world. What makes us strong in the world is that we are a modern and democratic country, and that, furthermore, we have close to us six hundred million Ibero-Americans."[91]

4. ECONOMIC DEVELOPMENT

In the political discourse on central state level, migration is closely linked to the economic field, particularly the labour market. Two different frames in migration discourse about the country's economic situation can be found. The first results from the comparison with the economic strength or debility of other countries, the second from the preoccupation with the economic development Spain has undergone in the last decades.

---

[90] P54: E-III-Gov-Pres-Zapatero-25-01-2005.rtf-[una España abierta, desde una ...] (24:24).
[91] P59: E-IV-Gov-Presidente-Zapatero-15-10-2005-c.rtf-[A partir de que tuvimos la lib...].

4.1 Spain, a developed country and part of the first world

Apart from being described as the external borders of the European Union, the southern Spanish borders –the peninsular coastal borders, the coastal borders of the Canary Island, and the terrestrial borders of Ceuta and Melilla– are referred to as separating Africa from Europe, separating the poor from the rich. Secretary of State, Mr. Camacho Vizcaíno in a parliamentary debate in September 2005, for instance, characterized what was happening on the other side of the Spanish border as happening "on the other side of paradise".[92] Therewith he made explicit what many statements only convey implicitly, the dichotomy of "paradise" and "hell" with the Spanish border as separating "paradise" from "hell".

The descriptions of the poor African "Other" in central state discourse about irregular migration thus explicitly and implicitly express the self-definition of Spain as being on the "paradisical" –side of the border, on the rich side. They are a reaffirmation that the country pertains to the first world, to the community of developed countries.[93] As Suárez-Navaz formulates it:

> "The Spanish inclusion in the group of developed capitalist countries is creating both symbolic and material borders with a third world characterized by economic inequalities, high levels of poverty, and unstable political situations which allegedly 'promote' extremist social behaviour in the dominant discourse."[94]

The EU, and Spain as part of it, is presented as a "fortress"[95] of wealth and prosperity",[96] as the "major area of liberty, democracy, social progress" in the world of today which contains "some of the most powerful economies".[97]

---

[92] P71: E-IV-DSCongreso-CO_377-28-09-2005.rtf-[En esa configuración de la pol...] (2711:2721).

[93] See P18: Auszüge E-II-DSCongreso-CO_096-07-11-2000.rtf-[Canarias, como parte de España...] (98:107).

[94] Suárez-Navaz (1997): Political Economy of the mediterranean rebordering: New ethnicities, new citizenships, in *Stanford Humanities Review*, 1997:5.2, p. 179.

[95] The image of the "Fortress Europe" is also frequently applied in academic literature. In general it is used to describe the economic and political protectionism of the EU. Lately the term has regained importance in view of the desperate intents of North- and Sub-Saharan Africans to access the EU from the south via boat. See for instance Bendel (2005): Immigration Policy in the European Union: Still bringing up the walls for fortress Europe? in *Migration Letters*, 2:1.

[96] P18: Auszüge E-II-DSCongreso-CO_096-07-11-2000.rtf-[Canarias, como parte de España...] (98:107).

[97] P58: E-IV-Gov-Zapatero-26-10-2005.rtf-[la mayor área de libertad, dem...] (6:7).

As to statements about the boundary and deep divide the Spanish border symbolizes different variants could be found. On the one hand benevolent arguments about humanitarian aspects and consequences of the Spanish border being the border between rich and poor, on the other hand defensive reasoning about the challenges and the threat resulting from this specific geographic position were found in political discourse. Both are postulated in political discourse mainly with respect to the irregular immigrants who have reached the peninsular coasts or the Canary Islands by boat and the illegal border crossings in Ceuta and Melilla in 2005 (see chapter IV.2.1).

4.1.1 *Humanitarian reasoning*

Benevolent and rather rational explanations of the situation at the Spanish border are highly present in Socialist migration discourse, particularly when trying to use them from a governmental point of view to throw light on the incidents at the border fences of Ceuta and Melilla in autumn 2005. In a parliamentary debate Socialist Members of Parliament for instance state that "for many years the African countries have had a substantial economic difference compared to the countries of the first world".[98] Moreover, the southern border of Europe "is the border of the biggest economic disequilibrium in the world".[99] This significant difference between the per capita incomes of Spain and Morocco is said to be equivalent to a relation of fifteen to one.[100]

> "There is no other border in the world that would have such a big difference in income as the one that Ceuta and Melilla have with respect to Africa right now. There is a relation of 15 to 1 in the level of income. The border of Mexico with the United States has a relation of income of 5 to 1. In Ceuta and Melilla the relation is 15 to 1. Hence it can perfectly be explained."[101]

---

[98] P71: E-IV-DSCongreso-CO_377-28-09-2005.rtf-[Alguien puede decir que eso ya...] (2054:2063).

[99] P61: E-IV-Gov-SecrMovSocPSOE-Zerolo-23-10-2005.rtf-[la frontera sur de Europa, en...] (19:19).

[100] These numbers are affirmed one year later by the IMF's World Economic Outlook Database, September 2006 Edition, URL: http://www.imf.org/external/pubs/ft/weo/2006/02/data/index. aspx, [10.12.2007]. According to the IMF Morocco's nominal GDP per capita in 2006 was 1,712.506 US $, Spain's was 27,225.573 US $ which equals a relation of 16:1.

[101] P72: E-IV-DSCongreso-CO_383-10-10-2005.rtf-[No hay ninguna frontera en el...] (2450:2456).

The two autonomous cities, Ceuta and Melilla, are referred to as the "bottleneck" between Africa and Europe, between "their desperation and our opulence". The Minister of Interior, Alonso, interprets this as a sufficient explanation for the desperate behaviour of the immigrants climbing the fences and trying to reach Spanish soil.[102]

Apart from these explanations of the big economic differences on both sides of the European-African border and their effects, more detailed descriptions of the reality beyond the border could be found in migration discourse. The statements about the living conditions in Africa, for instance, draw a deplorable picture of poverty, hunger, war, despair, displacement and serve to explain why these people are prepared to take all risks to enter Europe, regardless under what conditions:

> "what a human disaster, it reflects the immeasurable magnitude of misery, of despair, of extermination in many cases, of wars and of displacement of populations in the major part of Africa and particularly in Sub-Saharan Africa."[103]

Particularly the situation in Sub-Saharan Africa is described as "the most desperate situation, from a humanitarian point of view, that our planet is suffering".[104]

Migrants, "Seres humanos" and victims

The humanitarian dimension of migration is stressed furthermore by the particular use of the term "seres humanos" (human beings). Migrants are explicitly referred to as human beings, especially when politicians talk about the immigrants trying desperately to cross the Spanish borders by boat or the fences of Ceuta and Melilla, and immigrants being victims of mafias and human trafficking. The term implicitly underlines the fact that they are human beings, not any impersonal objects. They have the same rights and dignity and should be treated in accordance to that. Pointing out the human nature can therefore be a possibility to generate sympathy and compassion in one's own society for the

---

[102] See P72: E-IV-DSCongreso-CO_383-10-10-2005.rtf-[en ese choque entre el desarro...] (250:259).

[103] P71: E-IV-DSCongreso-CO_377-28-09-2005.rtf-[que esta problemática, muy sim...] (166:179).

[104] P72: E-IV-DSCongreso-CO_383-10-10-2005.rtf-[países subsaharianos donde se...] (3586:3594).

desperate situation the immigrants try to escape Politicians of both major political parties allude explicitly to the humaneness of the immigrants. A PP Member of Parliament states that the task precisely is "to treat human beings like human beings".[105] In another parliamentary debate a Socialist Congressman claims "to contemplate the human beings like it should be done and to get them out of situations of exploitation".[106]

Migrants are presented as victims of mafias, victims of the desperate economic situation in their home countries, and sometimes also as victims of political persecution. Their suffering and hopeless situation is frequently described like in the following quotation of a PSOE Member of Congress:

> "The thousands of African citizens who travel thousands of kilometres risking their lives do not act in response of an 'efecto llamada' from this side of the border of Spain or the European Union; they arrive at the gates of Ceuta and Melilla, or they extradite themselves to the sea, to the mercy of an uncertain crossing, or they are trapped in the nets of scrupulous mafias for a very simple and at the same time terrible reason: because the conditions of war, misery, hunger [...] act on these men, women and children as a real, powerful and inevitable expulsion effect."[107]

The immigrants take a long and dangerous journey upon themselves to reach the "promised land". On that journey they accept a high risk and some even lose their lives.[108]

Migration is described by the PSOE government as a drama and a human tragedy. A Socialist Member of Parliament explains that "we face a problem —and I think that is how we all see it— that apart from being very bitter and very serious comprises a terrible human drama."[109] This is an "enormous human drama, implicit and explicit, of all and every single person who tries to access

---

[105] P68: Auszüge E-IV-DSCongreso-PL_118-05-10-2005.rtf-[si consiste precisamente en tr...] (184:188).

[106] P41: Auszüge E-III-DSCongreso-PL_071-23-02-2005.rtf-[de contemplar a los seres huma...] (557:559).

[107] P71: E-IV-DSCongreso-CO_377-28-09-2005.rtf-[Los millares de ciudadanos afr...] (185:196).

[108] See P71: E-IV-DSCongreso-CO_377-28-09-2005.rtf-[Europa y España deben ir a los...] (2371:2378).

[109] P68: Auszüge E-IV-DSCongreso-PL_118-05-10-2005.rtf-[que nos enfrentamos a un probl...] (1098:1103).

to our borders because of poverty, to look for a better life, to simply live",[110] according to another PSOE Member of Parliament.

Sympathy and compassion

The statements of Socialist politicians express sympathy and compassion for the desperate situation of the immigrants. On the one hand they describe their desperation and personal drama and on the other hand the feelings these stories and pictures cause in them and in the Spanish people who commiserate with the immigrants.

> "The deep sorrow and sadness we feel when we see that people who have often travelled hundreds of kilometres, sometimes thousands, through the north of Africa, Sub-Saharan Africa, escaping from poverty, from diseases, from internal conflicts, and the lack of perspectives in their countries of origin, have lost their lives in the immediate proximity of our borders."[111]

In the aftermath of a massive intent to climb the border fences of Ceuta which had caused many injured and even dead, Zapatero used the opportunity "to express my pain and to express what everybody feels after the events we witnessed yesterday in Ceuta, which have caused the loss of human lives".[112] Furthermore he described the increasing desperation "which from a human point of view is very painful".[113] In a subsequent statement Zapatero mentioned the feelings of the Spaniards when looking at the border fence, "a fence which tears us apart every time we see it".[114] A Socialist Member of Parliament describes that the conditions forced upon these persons as conditions "which cause gooseflesh in all of us who learn about them".[115] Even the idea of wanting to open the

---

[110] P68: Auszüge E-IV-DSCongreso-PL_118-05-10-2005.rtf-[del enorme drama humano, implí...] (1116:1119).

[111] P72: E-IV-DSCongreso-CO_383-10-10-2005.rtf-[que compartimos muy sinceramen...] (262:270).

[112] P82: E-IV-Gov-Zapatero-29-09-2005.rtf-[Y mis primeras palabras tienen...] (6:6).

[113] P82: E-IV-Gov-Zapatero-29-09-2005.rtf-[Quizás el incremento de la efi...] (59:59).

[114] P59: E-IV-Gov-Presidente-Zapatero-15-10-2005-c.rtf-59:25 [Para los inmigrantes que consi...] (112:112).

[115] P71: E-IV-DSCongreso-CO_377-28-09-2005.rtf-[En esa configuración de la pol...] (2711:2721).

borders "in view of the imminent, grave and intense human problems which surface at the borders of Melilla" appears in parliamentary debate.[116]

Spanish benevolence towards immigrants

The irregular immigrants are presented in migration discourse to be defenceless and vulnerable and must therefore be protected and helped.[117] There can be found statements which focus on Spain helping the poor and disadvantaged in their search for a better life. The politicians underline the benevolent attitude towards these "poor people" and towards the countries of origin. There are different kinds of policy measures to realise this. The Programa GRECO announces for instance that the persecuted and their families in Spain will find a space of freedom and opportunities for their future.[118] This refers to the political asylum "for those persons who are persecuted because of fighting for democracy and liberty in their countries of origin", and to the humanitarian asylum "for those who have to leave their homes because of warlike conflicts in which the civil population always is an innocent victim".[119] As the statement of a Socialist representative in Congress demonstrates, still in 2005 asylum is an issue to work at: "We think that it is necessary to continue expanding the protection of political refugees and of asylum-seekers, and that aspect can be approved".[120] (see III.2.2.2)

Another set of measures to help are the immediate life-saving measures for the stranded irregular immigrants. The PSOE government announced such measures in 2005:

> "...these persons will transitionally be provided with temporal accommodation, cloths, food and health care –I want to remind you that the Ministry of Health has an agreement with the Red Cross which attends the immigrants so that they are

---

[116] P71: E-IV-DSCongreso-CO_377-28-09-2005.rtf-[ante el inminente, grave e int...] (2410:2412).

[117] See P68: Auszüge E-IV-DSCongreso-PL_118-05-10-2005.rtf-[garantizando los derechos de t...] (567:569).

[118] P99: E-PROGRAMA GRECO 30-03-2001.rtf-[La lucha por la democracia y p...] (95:95); (114:114).

[119] P99: E-PROGRAMA GRECO 30-03-2001.rtf-[el asilo político para las per...] (105:105).

[120] P69: Auszüge E-IV-DSCongreso-PL_120-18-10-2005.rtf-[Nosotros creemos que es necesa...] (550:558).

not unprotected from a sanitary point of view–, as well as, apart from the health care provides basic information and orientation."[121]

Apart from these immediate measures in response to the entry of undocumented immigrants, development aid is thought to be an instrument to prevent migration by increasing the living standards in the countries of origin and thus fight the principal causes for migration.

The idea of "codesarrollo"

The concept of "codevelopment" links migration policy to the official development cooperation. Originally the concept was developed in France and introduced in the French development cooperation strategy.[122] Spanish politicians have also made use of the concept. Yet the term has been used to express different ideas, highlighting different aspects. The PSOE opposition defended for instance the above mentioned idea of preventing migration by developing the countries of origin: "We believe that the cooperation with these countries is an authentic preventive measure to reduce the flows of and the traffic with irregular immigrants".[123] In 2005 in view of the events in Ceuta and Melilla Zapatero picked up the idea of prevention by development cooperation and demanded that all countries of the EU and all developed countries should do something against the misery which leads people to desperately climb the fences of the two Spanish cities.[124]

The mutual character of "codevelopment" is underlined by those statements which promote migrants as actors of development, both in the receiving country and in the countries of origin. Already in 2001, the PP government put down in the Plan GRECO the idea that the immigrants contribute to the development

---

[121] P52: E-III-Gov-Vicpres-MTAS-Fernández...-Caldera-28-01-2005.rtf-[se proporcionará transitoriame...] (48:48).

[122] It was the French scholar Sami Naïr who coined the definition of codevelopment as being the idea of integrating immigration and development in a way that migration flows will be beneficial for as well the countries of origin as the receiving countries. It describes furthermore a consensual relationship between both sides. At the EU level, the concept of codevelopment was presented for the first time in 1999 in Tampere.

[123] P18: Auszüge E-II-DSCongreso-CO_096-07-11-2000.rtf-[Creemos que la cooperación con...] (441:447).

[124] See P82: E-IV-Gov-Zapatero-29-09-2005.rtf-[l compromiso es África y su mi...] (68:68).

of their countries of origin by sending money home.[125] It further supported the return to bring forward the development of their countries of origin:

> "The investment for the codevelopment of the countries of emigration has to be the key part of a global design of the government policies in the present legislature in which we have to encourage, among other things, the return of the emigrants to their countries of origin. Their better professional formation after having worked here will be an added value to their own munition which will enable them to contribute to the effort of development and growth of their own countries."[126]

The Socialist also announced in their electoral manifesto for 2004 the promotion of "codevelopment" projects including the immigrants as "agents of transformation, meaning immigrated persons who after being trained go back to their respective countries of origin and work there in the field of project development".[127]

4.1.2 *Defensive reasoning*

Both, humanitarian and defensive reasoning reflect the standpoint of the speakers, namely the rich, developed side of the Spanish-Moroccan border. Yet, unlike the above described humanitarian approach which implicitly affirms the differences and boundaries between rich and poor, expressing benevolence and compassion, defensive reasoning constructs a boundary by describing the irregular immigrants, the poor "Other" as a threat.

The following quotations of Spanish politicians about migration evoke negative connotations. They implicitly or explicitly picture migration as a potential threat to the Spanish society.

To "suffer" from migration

Politicians from both major political parties have used the verb "to suffer" in regard to migration movements. Extracts like "we have begun to suffer from this phenomenon not long ago",[128] or "this phenomenon of immigration, so

---

[125] See P99: E-PROGRAMA GRECO 30-03-2001.rtf-[al permitir la inmigración, ha...] (95:95).

[126] P59: E-IV-Gov-Presidente-Zapatero-15-10-2005-c.rtf-[si la Unión Europea y todos ju...] (110:110).

[127] P97: E-III+IV-Gov-Auszüge aus Programa Electoral PSOE 2004.rtf-[Un Gobierno socialista promove...] (16:16).

[128] P72: E-IV-DSCongreso-CO_383-10-10-2005.rtf-[Nosotros hemos empezado a sufr...] (2275:2283).

complex and wretched which we are suffering from and incurring"[129] express passivity and fatalism on the part of the speaker. Migration is presented as something that has to be taken as it is without having any possibility to regulate and influence it.

Migration, an invasion

When talking about migrants who cross the Spanish borders illegally, or in Ceuta and Melilla or at the Canary Islands, different metaphors and terms to describe these events are used which have the potential to evoke negative perceptions of threat and own helplessness. Representatives of both, the conservatives and the Socialists, fell back on the use on such ambivalent terms like "presión" (pressure), "avalancha" (avalanche) and "oleada" (wave). President Aznar, for instance, warned in 2000 "We are in the geographic situation in which we are, and we will have a very important migratory pressure from Africa".[130] A Socialist Member of Parliament spoke in 2005 of the migratory pressure that Sub-Saharans exert on the Spanish border.[131]

The use of the metaphor "oleada" underlines the impression of a threatening "invasion" even more. In 2000, the present Secretary for immigration and emigration Consuelo Rumí pictured the situation at the Spanish borders as "at the heat of the immigrant waves that push to access our country".[132] Acebes, Secretary General of the PP, also used the wave-metaphor arguing that "since the anouncement of the regularization a wave of immigrants has been rolling towards Spain by land, sea and air".[133]

Likewise the avalanche metaphor may evoke feelings of being overwhelmed by an enormous number of irregular African immigrants, although the real number is of no importance, compared to the number of irregular immigrants from Latin America entering via the Spanish airports (see IV.2.1). A PP Member of Parliament described the situation in Ceuta and Melilla in autumn 2005 using the avalanche metaphor to paint a picture of threat:

---

[129] P77: E-IV-Gov-Vicpres-Just-Fernández...-López-A.-07-10-2005.rtf-[en este fenómeno de la inmigra...] (63:63).

[130] P9: E-I-Gov-Presidente-Aznar-17-02-2000.rtf-[Nosotros estamos en la situaci...] (286:286).

[131] See P71: E-IV-DSCongreso-CO_377-28-09-2005.rtf-[Europa y España deben ir a los...] (2371:2378).

[132] P13: E-II-Opp-SecrMigrPSOE-Rumi Ibanez-08-12-2000.rtf-[La inmigración, como expresión...] (11:11).

[133] P36: E-III-Opp-SecrGenPP-Acebes-PortInmPSOE-Hernando-09-02-2005.rtf-[Desde el anuncio de la regula...] (11:11).

"In our country an avalanche of immigrants is happening. All of Spain watches it almost live on television. Hundreds, thousands of illegal persons enter through our borders. We watch them how they organize in Morocco, how they enter, how they jump the fences. All of Spain watches on television and you deny it."[134]

Also the PSOE made use of this metaphor, yet embedded in a less polemic and more technical rhetoric. The President of the PSOE, Chaves, for instance stated in an interview that "with the conviction that from the collaboration that exists between the Moroccan and the Spanish government at the end, in the short term, the necessary measures to avoid the avalanches of immigrants in the two cities will result".[135]

Migrants, sly dogs?

The PP opposition discourse about the border-crossings in Ceuta and Melilla in October 2005 describes the migrants as people who know very well how to "outwit" the Spanish authorities. The statements insinuate that the immigrants act on a kind of criminal energy, like a PP Member of Parliament argued that the immigrants "no longer queue up, but directly assault our borders".[136] The description of how the immigrants prepare to enter Spanish territory makes this even clearer:

"The immigrants stay in its territory, sometimes waiting for weeks and looking for the appropriate moment to attack the fences. Some are successful, and the ones who are not, wait again in Morocco for a better opportunity; for sure, not very hidden, because it is said to be a number of more than 1000 persons making ladders. Yesterday, they used 400 ladders of more than four metres in length."[137]

[134] P68: Auszüge E-IV-DSCongreso-PL_118-05-10-2005.rtf-[Se está produciendo una avalan...] (419:424).
[135] P60: E-IV-Gov-PresidentePSOE-Chaves-09-10-2005.rtf-[con la convicción de que de la...] (42:42).
[136] P68: Auszüge E-IV-DSCongreso-PL_118-05-10-2005.rtf-[récord, señor Caldera, en inmi...] (91:93).
[137] P67: Auszüge E-IV-DSCongreso-PL_115-28-09-2005.rtf-[auténticas avalanchas de inmig...] (62:77).

After passing the fences of Ceuta and Melilla they are said to go running "to the next police station so that they are defined as irregulars and that they are given an order of expulsion".[138]

Potential negative effects of immigration

In the political discourse on the central state level the idea of the potential threat that lies in immigration was underlined by PP representatives with the argument that immigration has the potential to cause problems within the Spanish society. President Aznar especially highlighted in 2000 the need of regulation to avoid future problems:

> "We, the Spaniards have to know that this process has to be done orderly and in collaboration between the different administrations, that norms cannot be adopted against the government for the sole reason of amusing oneself a bit and provoking a parliamentarian defeat, because that can cause more complications for the future, and that, the more we regulate these processes the more we guarantee our peaceful living together, our plurality and the rights of the immigrants, because the contrary could cause problems and could imply undesired conflicts."[139]

Without regulation and control immigration can have "very bad repercussions on the living together",[140] as stated by Acebes, Secretary General of the PP in 2005.

4.2 Spain's economic growth

Since the accession to the EU Spain has seen a considerable economic growth.[141] Today, Spain can present itself within the European Union as an equal with respect to its economic strength. In view of the Spanish past of economic backwardness, this seems to be a considerable source of collective self-confidence (see III.1).

The importance that is given to Spain's economic development and growth is reflected in utilitarian arguments about migration as an economic factor, pictur-

---

[138] P64: Auszüge E-IV-DSCongreso-CO_358-06-10-2005.rtf-[Lo que sí sé es que en este mo...] (718:724).

[139] P10: E-I-Gov-Presidente-Aznar-24-02-2000.rtf-[Los españoles tenemos que sabe...] (37:38).

[140] P35: E-III-Opp-SecrGenPP-Acebes-08-02-2005.rtf-[la entrada de inmigrantes tien...] (72:76).

[141] See Nohlen and Hildenbrand (2005): *Spanien*, pp. 21-31.

ing the immigrants foremost in their role as cheap labour supply. Spanish politicians on the one hand highlighted the advantages and contributions of regular migration and on the other hand the disadvantages of irregular migration.

Immigrants contributing to Spain's economic growth

As economic growth has lead to a lack of labour in certain sectors of the Spanish economy there is a strong labour market demand for foreign labour, mainly to do unqualified jobs (see IV.2.3) it is not surprising that politicians react to the public debate postulating utilitarian arguments in favour of immigration. The Conservatives stated in their electoral manifesto in 2000 that immigrants are needed "because of demographic and economic reasons".[142] Zapatero emphasized in 2005:

> "Those should have access who are able to work, that is good for the immigrant, good for the country where they come from, as they send remittances, and it is also good for our economy."[143]

In political statements about migration issues representatives of both political parties highlight the importance of the economic contribution of immigrant workers to the growing Spanish economy. Migration is presented as a desirable phenomenon which accounts for wealth and contributes to the growth of the country.[144] Alberto Ruíz Gallardón, Mayor of Madrid and member of the PP describes how immigration already has contributed to Spain's economic development:

> "...the immigration to Spain and to Madrid and we have to be very aware that this is no negative element, but an element that has allowed us to occupy the economic leadership of Madrid within Spain and the economic growth that Spain has at this moment. Neither of us, Madrid and Spain, would be as advanced as we are if during the last years many people who, through their effort, have developed our economy extraordinarily hadn't been incorporated. We should also be aware of the positive values and the positive contribution the immigration has accounted for our country, we should not describe everything in a negative manner, because if we do we will be terribly unjust. We owe a very important part of our prosperity to the

---

[142] P95: E-I+II-Gov-Auszüge aus Programa Electoral PP 2000.rtf-[En el próximo decenio España v...] (33:33).

[143] P26: E-III-Gov-Pres-Zapatero-14-02-2005.rtf-[Tienen que entrar aquellos que...] (134:134).

[144] See P20: Auszüge E-II-DSCongreso-PL_044-24-11-2000.rtf-[y además contemplando la inmig...] (1747:1751); P59: E-IV-Gov-Presidente-Zapatero-15-10-2005-c.rtf-[la inmigración, que nos está a...] (109:109).

work and effort of the immigrants. Secondly, the immigration is a phenomenon that requires responses, because new situations come up."[145]

Immigration of foreign workforce has become already an inherent element of the Spanish economy. Economic development can not be described anymore leaving aside migration issues.[146]

Closely linked to the acknowledgement of the economic contribution of immigrants are statements, highlighting their demographic contribution. Spain has currently one of the lowest birth-rates within the European Union. And the United Nations Population Division projects a further decrease in fertility for the future.[147] In 2000 the Minister for Labour and Social Affairs consequently observed that "the migratory balance is the only thing that makes the population increase".[148] A Socialist representative argues that immigration is needed not only to fill vacancies, but also for a sustainable system of pensions:

> "The European Union altogether as Spain in particular will need more and ever more foreign labour, not only to cover certain job positions but also to make the pension scheme sustainable in a society that ages and does not have enough demographic growth."[149]

Only regular immigrants wanted

Politicians of both political parties differentiate with respect to economic benefit between irregular and regular immigration advocating the latter.

As we have seen above, regular immigrants are welcome because regular immigration is "something that contributes to the economic development of the country".[150] The Spanish President Zapatero highlights "that the only possible

---

[145] P32: E-III-Opp-PP-Gallardón-28-02-2005.rtf-[la inmigración para España y p...] (350:362).

[146] The impact of immigration on the Spanish economy and labour market and vice versa has therefore been studied in various books and articles. See for instance Aparicio and Tornos (2000): *La inmigración y la economía española*, Madrid: Ministerio de Trabajo y Asuntos Sociales; Tornos, Aparicio Gómez and Fernández García (2004): *El Capital Humano de la inmigración*, Madrid: Ministerio de Trabajo y Asuntos Sociales.

[147] See United Nations Population Division: *Qinquennial estimates and projections, Birth rate, crude, per 1,000 population [code 13580]*, URL: http://unstats.un.org/pop/dVariables/DRetrieval.aspx, [20.12.2007].

[148] P 3: E-I-Gov-Portavoz-MTAS-Piqué-Pimentel-14-01-2000rtf.rtf-[y el saldo migratorio que es l...] (26:28).

[149] P57: E-IV-Gov-SecrRelIntPSOE-Jímenez-10-2005.rtf-[Tanto la Unión Europea en su c...] (79:84).

[150] P93: E-III-Opp-Comunicado PP 15-03-2005.rtf-[una inmigración legal y ordena...] (16:16).

immigration is legal immigration linked with jobs".[151] He underlines this statement proclaiming

> "that immigration can only be legal and orderly. We will keep up this principle so that immigrants can continue to come to our country to strengthen our economy and improve their expectations for their future lives."[152]

After winning the 2004 elections, the Socialists promoted a regularization process transferring immigrants residing in Spain yet not disposing of the necessary documentation, from an irregular into a regular status. Regularization of immigrants was on the one hand understood as an instrument to fight the black economy and exploitation of irregular immigrants, on the other hand as an instrument to include the migrant workers into the social security and tax system. The following statement of President Zapatero explaining the reasons for the regularization process, shows that the campaign was also based on the utilitarian idea that Spain could only benefit from regular immigrants:

> "It is evident. Immigration has to be linked to work, to the possibility of work, to the possibility to stay legally in another country, with rights, without the existence of a black economy, without the existence of fraud, because the whole citizenry wants the immigrants who are working to pay into the social security. As they earn here they have to pay into the social security which, furthermore, contributes to the strength of our pension scheme. And of course they want the employers engaging an immigrant to have them legally, and that this immigrant is granted workers' rights, and that this employer also pays into the social security. What we do is to introduce order where disorder has been, to bring to light and to regularize a legal situation."[153]

However, also regular immigration is only welcome within certain limits. The idea that Spain has limited capacities to receive immigrants, limited by labour-market needs, appeared, for instance in the statement of a PP Member of Parliament who argued that "in this first world not all of us fit in. I wish we would fit all in, but we don't".[154] Beyond this limit the immigrants are thought

---

[151] P82: E-IV-Gov-Zapatero-29-09-2005.rtf-[que la única inmigración posib...] (59:59).
[152] P81: E-IV-Gov-Zapatero-27-10-2005.rtf-[que la inmigración sólo podría...] (37:37).
[153] P26: E-III-Gov-Pres-Zapatero-14-02-2005.rtf-[Es evidente. Inmigración ha de...] (127:128).
[154] P68: Auszüge E-IV-DSCongreso-PL_118-05-10-2005.rtf-[En este primer mundo no cabemo...] (1081:1089).

to compete for job opportunities with the native population increasing the unemployment rate. A representative of the PP in parliament stated in 2000 that

> "from Spain's capacity of reception, which is obviously limited –that is why we cannot speak of open doors for immigration– on the basis that we have a social and occupational reality. We should not forget that."[155]

The necessity to consider the unemployed Spaniards in the calculation of the labour market needs for foreign workers is outlined furthermore in the Programa GRECO:

> "We cannot forget that Spain has its own unemployed citizens and two millions of emigrants, many of whom want to return to work in their country, a limited capacity of reception which should respond to a strict calculation of jobs that can be offered to the foreigners who emigrate due to economic reasons looking among us for opportunities they do not find in their own countries."[156]

Five years later, by then in the opposition, Conservatives still associate immigration and unemployment. The Secretary for Social Policy of the PP, Ana Pastor, accuses the government of producing more unemployment among immigrants due to the regularization under way:

> "When we had government responsibilities and led various regularizations, we achieved that there were people with jobs. I will give you a specification: today there are more unemployed immigrants than a year ago. What makes you talk about the search for opportunities when you only achieved that people come here and the maximum they can aspire to, is to work for 2 months in three years?"[157]

The utilitarian idea of admitting immigration only according to the real labour market needs and thus only admit immigrants that are useful for Spain is common in the discourse of PP representatives. In 2005 in an official declaration, for instance, the PP claimed to be realistic and to administer the migration

---

[155] P20: Auszüge E-II-DSCongreso-PL_044-24-11-2000.rtf-[de la capacidad de acogida que...] (1742:1747).

[156] P99: E-PROGRAMA GRECO 30-03-2001.rtf-[no podemos olvidar que España ...] (106:106).

[157] P37: E-III-Opp-SecrPolSocPP-Pastor-23-03-2005.rtf-[Cuando tuvimos responsabilidad...] (82:87).

flows with efficacy, adapted to the real capacity of reception and adapted to the labour market needs as well.[158]

However, not only the PP has used the argument of "Spain's limited capacities", also the PSOE, by then in government position, has picked it up. Caldera, Minister for Labour and Social Affairs predicted that there will be a moment in which the figures of immigrants will stabilize according to the demand of the Spanish labour market.[159] He went as far as to even define a particular limit for immigration:

"I think that it is reasonable to maintain a percentage between 8 per cent and 10 per cent of immigrants from the total of the population. A number, that considers the possibilities of integration and the functioning of our system."[160]

With respect to the regulation of immigration Zerolo, Secretary for Social Movements of the PSOE, emphasised in a statement that

"we are aware that the countries do not have an unlimited capacity to absorb all these people, that is why claims exist that this is done by controlled, modulated and tempered processes, and that is what we are doing."[161]

In comparison to the PP statements the Socialists do not make the link between labour market needs and the capacity to receive immigrants explicit. They speak for example of the necessity to have in mind the "social and economic situation of the country of reception"[162] or to control de entry of immigrants "according to our possibilities of accommodation".[163]

Politicians of both major political parties thus stress that in order to avoid immigrants becoming a burdening factor for the Spanish State, irregular immigration must be prevented and kept under tight control. Acebes, Secretary General of the PP, emphasizes that

---

[158] See P94: E-III-Opp-Comunicado PP sobre PolInmGov 08-02-2005.rtf-[Realismo: Gestionemos con efic...] (94:94).

[159] See P25: E-III-Gov-MTAS-Caldera-02-01-2005.rtf-[Los inmigrantes siguen siendo ...] (14:14).

[160] P25: E-III-Gov-MTAS-Caldera-02-01-2005.rtf-[Yo creo que lo razonable es qu...] (14:14).

[161] P61: E-IV-Gov-SecrMovSocPSOE-Zerolo-23-10-2005.rtf-[que somos conscientes de que l...] (15:15).

[162] P97: E-III+IV-Gov-Auszüge aus Programa Electoral PSOE 2004.rtf-[una gestión activa de los fluj...] (127:127).

[163] P56: E-III-Gov-SecrOrgPSOE-Blanco-24-01-2005.rtf-[El control de la entrada de in...] (5:5).

"there are two substantial and fundamental elements that we will put in action in the whole of Europe: generosity with legal immigration, but according to the possibilities to receive immigrants that Europe and each country have –our potentials of work, health care, education and housing– and to be firm as regards clandestine and illegal immigration".[164]

Likewise, a representative of the Socialist parliamentary group claims:

"...to fight against irregular immigration, to improve the mechanisms of canalisation of the legal immigration, to rationalize the quota of foreign labour, and to revise and improve the agreements of regulation and control of the migratory flows."[165]

Thus, both PP and PSOE in government emphasize the importance of migration control at the borders. President Aznar stresses, for instance, that "it is very important to pay the indicated attention to all questions related to border controls".[166] On the other side, Caldera, the Minister of Labour and Social Affairs of the PSOE government demands

"a new line of action that is to aim at the regular immigration with a serious and severe border control, because that is what guarantees the legality, along with the use of instruments to regulate the immigration with much more flexibility and efficacy."[167]

Regarding the control of irregular immigration special attention is paid to mafias and networks of human trafficking. Criminal organizations and mafias that traffic with humans and exploit immigrants must be fought.[168] Those immigrants who manage to enter Spanish territory illegally shall be repatriated immediately.[169] For details and data on repatriations see chapter III.2.2.1.

---

[164] P35:   E-III-Opp-SecrGenPP-Acebes-08-02-2005.rtf-[hay dos elementos sustanciales...] (37:41).

[165] P64: Auszüge E-IV-DSCongreso-CO_358-06-10-2005.rtf-[luchar contra la inmigración i...] (330:334).

[166] P 6: E-I-Gov-Pres-19-01-2000rtf.rtf-[Creemos que tenemos que ser mu...] (9:9).

[167] P25: E-III-Gov-MTAS-Caldera-02-01-2005.rtf-[una nueva línea de actuación...] (47:47).

[168] See P6: E-I-Gov-Pres-19-01-2000rtf.rtf-[Creemos que tenemos que ser mu...] (9:9).

[169] See P29: E-III-Gov-SecrInm-Rumi Ibanez-07-02-2005.rtf-[La lucha contra la inmigración...] (28:28); P42: Auszüge E-III-DSCongreso-PL_073-08-03-2005.rtf-[luchando contra la inmigración...] (2334:2336); P98: E-III+IV-Opp-Auszüge aus Programa Electoral PP 2004.rtf-[eguiremos avanzando en el refo...] (36:38).

5. SPAIN, AN IMMIGRATION COUNTRY

As elaborated in chapter VI.1, politicians frequently use a frame that describes the recent development of Spain from an emigration to an immigration country. This implies the self-definition of Spain as an immigration country and of the Spanish society as an immigrant receiving society. This acknowledgement of immigration as a part of everyday life is the prerequisite for a serious and effective integration policy towards the immigrants.

The concepts and ideas on part of the politicians about how to integrate immigrants into Spanish society reflect, moreover, which ones are thought to be the basic elements of the Spanish society. The self-definition of collective identity is thus inherent to the process of immigrant integration. Frequently politicians do refer to what is needed for successful integration and set up "guidelines" oriented on the self-conception of the Spanish society. The analysis of the political discourse about the integration of immigrants reveals thus how inclusive or exclusive the different conceptions of Spain and its collective identity are (see chapter II.1.3).

5.1 Advocating the integration of immigrants

Integration is something that both political parties or in opposition or with government responsibilities express as a general aim of their migration policy. It is presented as being a value *per se*, originating from the underlying assumption of the Spanish society as an open and tolerant society (see VI.1.2).

On the political agenda integration policy has become increasingly important since the Socialists took over government (see IV.2.4). Already in its opposition work the PSOE sharply criticised the PP government not to consider the integration of immigrants sufficiently. In a parliamentary debate a Socialist Representative thus claimed:

"More social integration because the basic philosophy of what the immigration policy in Spain needs today precisely is a policy of enrichment of diversity, of multiculturalism, to encourage that the Spanish community experiences the presence of the other, of the stranger as something good, as an extraordinary richness. More participation, because it is essential that the civil society, the NGOs, the trade unions and the employers have a say in migration policy."[170]

Five years later another Socialist Member of Parliament states in an ironic tone that finally the PP has included integration and not only security issues in their migration policy outline:

"It has taken you many years, but we have achieved that you approach a global perspective of security, that you speak of security not exclusively from a policing point of view, and that you also speak from a point of view of integration, coopera-tion and social policies. I believe that it makes us all happy that, although late, the political party you are representing arrives at social policies at some point."[171]

Furthermore, the PSOE criticized ex-post that the PP government had not invested in integration measures which the Socialist government in turn has done.[172]

The following statements show that the PP, though including integration into their political agenda, differentiates between regular and irregular im-migrants advocating only the integration of the former. Regarding the policy measures for the integration of immigrants the electoral manifesto for 2004 states "a policy that facilitates the integration of the immigrants that reside and work legally in our country".[173] Likewise a PP Member of Parliament argues:

"We are in favour of the integration of legal immigrants, considering our capac-ity of reception. We are in favour of the full integration of those persons who live among us, who have come to Spain to work, to contribute to improve our society with their effort, who have lived in Spain legally for years and want to build up their future among us."[174]

---

[170] P22: E-II-DSCongreso-CO_137-28-12-2000komplett.rtf-[Más integración social porque...] (1644:1653).

[171] P71: E-IV-DSCongreso-CO_377-28-09-2005.rtf-[Les ha costado muchos años, pe...] (3760:3768).

[172] See P41: Auszüge E-III-DSCongreso-PL_071-23-02-2005.rtf-[Cuando gobernaba el Partido Po...] (576:579).

[173] P98: E-III+IV-Opp-Auszüge aus Programa Electoral PP 2004.rtf-[una política que facilite la i...] (101:101).

[174] P42: Auszüge E-III-DSCongreso-PL_073-08-03-2005.rtf-[Nosotros estamos a favor de la...] (1643:1651).

According to that only regular immigrants that contribute with their work to Spain's economic wellbeing should be integrated, irregular immigrants are left aside.

Hence, there are differences between the PSOE and the PP as to how open and integrative they present the Spanish society.

Furthermore, politicians at the central state level define the Spanish society as open and integrative not only by postulating the general disposition to integrate immigrants, but also through statements pointing out that integration is no one-way-street but must be a mutual effort.

In the discourse of the PP, mainly in 2000, statements could be found that stressed the need to adapt to the growing number of immigrants. President Aznar, for instance, highlights that the Spanish society must accustom to the changes that immigration comes along with. He speaks of the fundamental change from being a country of emigration to being a country of immigration to which the Spanish society must get used to[175] and underlines that:

> "I want to tell you that we have to get used to it. That is why I so much insist that we should never look to the past. But even less now that we are in a country, in a new society, with new problems, and it is to these problems that we need to respond. The debate about the past is not at all useful; it is not at all useful that you speak to us about twenty years ago or about ten years ago, because we are in a completely different situation."[176]

In 2005 Piqué, an important figure within the PP leadership stated likewise that it was not the same to have to finance health care and education without immigrants than with them and he therefore sees an obligation on the part of the Spanish society to adapt to these changes.[177] These statements only refer to the changes in labour market, health care and education, etc., they do not mention the need to adapt to cultural diversity.

However, the idea of integration as a process of mutual cultural approximation can be found also in statements of representatives of both, the PSOE and the PP. Already in 2000 in its official declaration to the Programa GRECO,

---

[175] See P12: E-I-Gov-Presidente-Aznar-05-03-2000.rtf-[Pues hoy también el cambio fun...] (7:7).

[176] P12: E-I-Gov-Presidente-Aznar-05-03-2000.rtf-[Quiero deciros que tenemos que...] (9:9).

[177] See P34: E-III-Opp-PPC-Piqué-23-02-2005.rtf-[No es lo mismo tener que finan...] (302:303).

the PSOE spoke of "interculturalidad" and cultural diversity as principles that should guide integration policies.

> "The planning and development of integration policies for the immigrants that are staying in Spain: The integration as a synonym of normalization of the living together represents one of the elements that aim to be encouraged, through the modifications of the GPS. We understand that integration is possible and desirable based on the respect for cultural diversity and the acknowledgement of *intercultularidad* as a principle that guides the integration policies. One of the principle challenges of the program is to achieve that the immigrants and their families find a society inclined to the acceptation of the foreigners with normality. It is very important that the immigrants do not become another exluded and marginalized group.[178]

"Interculturalidad", in opposition to multiculturalist and assimilationist approaches[179] is the term used in Spain for the mutual cultural approximation between immigrants and receiving society as described in the following statement by Jiménez, Secretary for International Relations of the PSOE.

> "...it should take us to push a process of cultural adjustment that makes the integration of the immigrant population possible, something we should urgently set on the agenda. Integration needs time and a cultural evolution from those who come as well as from those that receive, but also effective public policies that educate for this encounter, to facilitate the mélange, to understand the richness that this process brings along. We need policies that preserve identity and favour plurality."[180]

---

[178] P92: E-II-Opp-PSOE zum Plan Greco 27-12-2000.rtf-[Diseño y desarrollo de polític...] (51:51).

[179] The definition of *assimilation* traces back to the American sociologists Park and Burgess as "a process of interpenetration and fusion in which persons and groups acquire the memories, sentiments, and attitudes of other persons or groups, and, by sharing their experience and history, are incorporated with them in a common cultural life". See Park and Burgess (1969): *Introduction to the Science of Sociology including the Original Index to Basic Sociological Concepts*, Chicago: University of Chicago Press, p. 735. France is often cited as example for a migration policy that aims at the assimilation of the immigrants. *Multiculturalism* on the other hand is a term that was first used in Canada to denominate a political programme that was directed at dealing with the culturally heterogeneous Canadian society emphasizing the protection of cultural diversity. Some European countries, such as the Netherlands, have also taken on this idea. For more details on past and recent debates about *multiculturalism* see Mintzel (1997): *Multikulturelle Gesellschaften in Europa und Nordamerika. Konzepte, Streitfragen, Analysen, Befunde*, Passau: Wissenschaftsverlag Rothe.

[180] P57: E-IV-Gov-SecrRelIntPSOE-Jímenez-10-2005.rtf-[nos debe llevar a impulsar un...] (87:95).

The idea is to incorporate the immigrants fully into "the social and cultural life of Spain, preserving freedom for their own cultural identity and for their traditions in a way that avoids uprooting".[181]

5.2 Requirements for the integration of immigrants

Apart from these vague statements about integration as a general aim, the analysis of the central state political discourse brought forward, what politicians define to be the basic elements of Spanish collective identity newcomers have to adjust to. As explained in chapter II.1.3 the requirements set up for immigrant integration reflect the underlying constructions of national identity. Those are either based on a rather civic or on a rather ethno-cultural conception of the nation.

Rights and obligations
In the political discourse about the integration of immigrants foremost appears the frame that immigrants have to respect the Spanish norms and values, more precisely the constitutional and legal framework. The emphasis that is given hereby to the political and legal community reflects a primarily civic conception of the Spanish nation (see also VI.2).

The PP government formulated, for instance, in the Programa GRECO:

"The framework for the living together would be the Constitution and the Spanish laws to which, with more or less effort, depending on their cultural roots, they have to adapt, which they have to respect and enjoy, in a democratic society in which respect, tolerance and equality are values we believe firmly in, which we teach to our children and young people and which we fight for in order that they are respected by everyone."[182]

According to the PP electoral manifesto, integration is thus only possible respecting the values and norms, the constitutional and legal framework as the fundament of the Spanish society and therefore the respect and the knowledge about these norms must be promoted.[183] In consequence, as a PP Member of

---

[181] P93: E-III-Opp-Comunicado PP 15-03-2005.rtf-[Queremos la integración de los...] (19:19).
[182] P99: E-PROGRAMA GRECO 30-03-2001.rtf-[El marco de convivencia será l...] (101:101).
[183] See P98: E-III+IV-Opp-Auszüge aus Programa Electoral PP 2004.rtf-[Los inmigrantes que vienen a v...] (23:23); (34:34).

174   MIGRATION AND THE CONSTRUCTION OF NATIONAL IDENTITY IN SPAIN

Parliament emphasizes, when "there is a conflict between the laws and norms, and the culture of the respective country of origin with Spain, the Spanish laws and norms prevail".[184]

Also the PSOE presented this idea. For instance in 2005 the Spanish Minister for Labour and Social Affairs, Caldera, emphasized:

> "There is a fundamental matter of fact: The immigrant should know that the values of the receiving society must be respected, especially the fundamental rights, the ones forming part of the backbone of our model of living together. Then, the integration of immigrants has to be encouraged respecting their culture, as long as it does not conflict with the fundamental values of the receiving society. The Spanish society can be proud of the way it has responded to this challenge. There have been a few outbursts of rejection, but fortunately they have been overcome."[185]

Furthermore, the dichotomy of immigrants having rights and obligations is a frequently used argument.[186] A PSOE Member of Parliament describes what he understands to be the obligations of immigrants:

> "…assuring that the immigrants who work enjoy their rights and fulfil their obligations: pay their taxes, pay into the social security, pay in, help to pay health care and education, like all the rest of the workers."[187]

The Programa GRECO even insinuates that only the one who is contributing to the social security system and paying his taxes is subject of fundamental and social rights and therefore forms part of the Spanish society.[188]

Language and religion
Language is another element that appears in the central state debate about the integration of immigrants. Yet it has not the same significance as in Catalan discourse.

r>

[184] E-2 Member of Parliament-PP, 2007.
[185] P25: E-III-Gov-MTAS-Caldera-02-01-2005.rtf-[Hay un hecho fundamental: el i…] (34:34).
[186] See P31: E-III-Gov-Vicepresidenta-Fernandez de la Vega-08-02-2005.rtf-[para que tengamos una inmigrac…] (9:9).
[187] P40: Auszüge E-III-DSCongreso-PL_069-09-02-2005.rtf-[asegurando que los inmigrantes…] (125:129).
[188] See P41: Auszüge E-III-DSCongreso-PL_071-23-02-2005.rtf-[El Gobierno está apoyando y ap…] (736:741).

Language skills and education are pointed out by the PSOE as being a vehicle for successful integration. The Minister for Labour and Social Affairs, Caldera, for instance, at the beginning of 2005 presented policy measures to support the learning of Castillian "which is fundamental".[189]

"The government supports and will support the promotion of education, the formation, those who help and facilitate the knowledge of these values and norms, along with the learning of Castilian and other official languages if necessary, as an integrating factor of the migration policy."[190]

This approach on part of the Socialists reflects the rather pragmatic view that language skills are useful. It cannot, however, be interpreted as the postulation of language as a criterion of belonging or not belonging to the Spanish "We-group".

There were found, however, a few references to language and religion in statements of PP representatives which point at an ethno-cultural definition of the Spanish nation. Affirmations that Latin Americans could be integrated more easily due to their linguistic, cultural and religious proximity can be explained, according to Flynn, with the underlying concern existing in Spain that non-European immigrants pose a challenge to the social cohesion and to the Spanish collective identity. Latin American immigrants seem to be a minor threat, because of their closer cultural, linguistic and religious affiliation.[191] President Aznar, for instance, implicitly referred to the differences between the Latin American immigration and the North African immigration and to the difficulties to integrate the latter:

"The problem is that we have to know that this is more difficult when we speak of different cultures. When the history is different, when the culture is different, when the roots are different, when the religion is different, all these questions that form part of the historic sediment lead to the need to be especially cautious with these factors."[192]

---

[189] P25: E-III-Gov-MTAS-Caldera-02-01-2005.rtf-[Cuando llegan los inmigrantes...] (32:32).
[190] P41: Auszüge E-III-DSCongreso-PL_071-23-02-2005.rtf-[El Gobierno está apoyando y ap...] (736:741).
[191] See Flynn (2001): *Constructed identities and Iberia*; Zapata-Barrero (2006b): *The Muslim community and Spanish tradition*.
[192] P10: E-I-Gov-Presidente-Aznar-24-02-2000.rtf-[El problema es que tenemos que...] (48:48).

A PP Member of Parliament got more explicit regarding the different starting points for immigrant integration:

> "Well, here in Spain we have lived very well in the last years and the major part of the Ibero-American immigrants integrate without any difficulty…their religion, their language, their last-names, their first-names, their history…[…]…they were part of Spain during four centuries…they integrate without any difficulty. Romanian groups having a Latin language and being Christians integrate without any difficulty. And where there are more problems is with Moroccan groups."[193]

5.3 Future expectations

The future expectations regarding immigration and integration expressed in political discourse show that immigration is included in the future vision of the Spanish state. The acknowledgement that "immigration will affect vitally the living together in the next decades"[194] and will change the Spanish society and create a new society is common. However, there are voices that demand that this change has to be guided and accompanied with political measures.[195]

Immigration and the integration of immigrants are generally expected to occur also in the future without major difficulties. A PP Member of Congress thinks that this will be the merit of the immigrants themselves. But, he uses again the argument already mentioned above in the previous chapter, of the different starting points for integration due to the different origins of the immigrants:

> "I think that in Spain integration will basically happen without difficulties. But not so much as a merit of the Spaniards but as of those who come. That means the fundamental nucleus of the legal immigration and the Latin Americans. Who already were Spaniards until Spain lost the colonies that it had a century ago. And therefore there are so many coincidences that the Ibero-Americans and also the Romanians will dilute between the Spaniards, and within one generation many of them will be indistinguishable, although they maintain their habits, their customs, but they will be indistinguishable. It may be that there will be more problems with those that have a very militant Muslim profile with different customs, with very

---

[193] E-2 Member of Parliament-PP, 2007.
[194] P7: E-I-Gov-MinInterior-MayorOreja-04-03-2000.rtf-[La inmigración va a afectar de…] (28:28).
[195] See P57: E-IV-Gov-SecrRelIntPSOE-Jímenez-10-2005.rtf-[Estamos en presencia de un aut…] (100:106).

different gastronomic habits, that is to say, of cooking, religious, linguistic habits. That means I only see difficulties in the integration of them if they…it depends substantially on them."[196]

A member of the PSOE parliamentary party in Congress agrees that there will be no major conflicts regarding the immigration, but he attributes that to Spain's past as an emigration country and to the personal experience of many Spaniards that went as emigrants to other countries and returned to their country. He thinks that in future it will depend on the politicians, on intellectuals and journalists:

"I believe that it is very difficult that in Spain we will have conflicts about immigration. Let's say that it is very difficult because of the type of immigration we have, because of our own experience and because of our own culture. It is very difficult. It will also strongly depend on the courage of the politicians and on the leadership of the politicians. It will also strongly depend on the role of the intellectuals, of the journalists."[197]

In addition to the emigration experience as a reason for the smooth immigration and integration process he lists "the tremendous vitality of the Spanish society", the economic growth and the consequential increase in labour.[198] Nevertheless, besides these optimistic notes he asks himself what would happen if there was an economic recession and high unemployment rates.[199] His colleague, also a PSOE member of Congress emphasizes that

"Spain is, in a process of, let's say, an expansive economy, of growth. We are growing 4 per cent which is more than double of the average of the countries of the European Union. Thus, this means that all the people who have come here have found a job quickly and have generated richness and are still generating richness. [...] Until when this will go on like that? Well, that is not known. According to how things go from an economic point of view, I believe that also immigration will depend a little on that. Today we can absorb the percentage of immigration that comes despite of the adopted measures, but the capacity of the Spanish society and of the Spanish economy to absorb is strong. However, when the economy is not that strong the capacity of absorption is less. And as the resources will be less, well,

---

[196] E-2 Member of Parliament-PP, 2007.
[197] E-4 Member of Parliament-PSOE, 2007.
[198] E-4 Member of Parliament-PSOE, 2007.
[199] See E-4 Member of Parliament-PSOE, 2007.

it will be more difficult to search for, let's say, solutions for the demand on social services. Then things can get much worse."[200]

Both political parties seem to share this assessment of the current and future situation. A PP Member of Parliament also asked for his future expectations stated that currently in Spain there were no problems because jobs are available for everybody. "The day when work is no longer available for everybody we'll discover if there are problems or not."[201]

Summarizing briefly the analysis of the political discourse on non-EU immigration at the central state level it can be stated that national identity is constructed by politicians neither using explicitly the terms nation, nationalism or national identity nor putting much emphasis on ethnic elements, but rather by identifying the Spanish State with collective categories such as immigration country, member of the industrialized world, member-state of the EU, democracy and democratic constitution, economic growth, etc.

---

[200] E-1 Member of Parliament-PSOE, 2007.
[201] E-2 Member of Parliament-PP, 2007.

VII.
Catalan discourse on national identity

The analysis of Catalan political discourse shows that political statements refer predominantly to Catalonia and to those topics of the political agenda being under the control of the *Generalitat*. Moreover, migration issues are discussed from the standpoint of Catalan minority nationalism and thus assuming the existence of a distinct Catalan national identity. The frames of Catalan national identity found in the political discourse are described in the following.

1. The construction of a common past

At the level of the Autonomous Community of Catalonia the analysis of the migration discourse brought forward general reference to Catalonia's past and more specific issue-related references to Catalonia's more recent past as an immigration country. This discursive construction of a common past, especially of historical continuity must be seen as forming part of a general strategy to construct Catalan national identity (see II.1.2).

1.1 The historic continuity of a distinct Catalan identity

The following statement is a good example of how collective memory of a common past and a distinct historical development of Catalan identity and autonomy are constructed by moderate nationalists who aim at strengthening the same. As described above in chapter III.6 this construction of historic continuity represents a central element of moderate nationalist ideology.

On occasion of the inauguration of the exhibition "Cataluña tierra de acogida", Jordi Pujol, President of the Generalitat, tried to provide answers to the question of where the roots and origins of Catalonia's current personality were to be found.

"A personality which is the fruit of diverse elements. For instance, in the case of Catalonia, what is the current personality of Catalonia fruit of? Well, in the first place of the contributions of the medieval times: territory, language, culture, proper institutions. The *Generalitat* we have re-established today is from the fourteenth century and therefore our current autonomy has a link to our medieval past, and it is neither solely fruit of the Constitution, nor of the Statute of Autonomy, nor of political decisions and pacts. It is something that comes from the profundities of history.

A second fundamental element was the industrial and economic revolution of the eighteenth and nineteenth century. Because of circumstances that probably were not our own merit, but perhaps fruit of coincidence, in the south of Europe, that means, south of Paris and of the Alps, the industrial revolution took place in two areas only: in the Lombardy and in Catalonia. Naturally, this created a very distinct type of society within the whole of Spain. And a Catalan mentality, a form of not being superficial.

Also in the twentieth century great demographic contributions of population that Catalonia has had from immigration – which has not been the only one it has had in the past – justify the title "Catalonia –Land of welcome". Fortunately, this contribution has incorporated itself well, thanks to all those who have been participating in the process."[1]

Pujol presented three major historical developments as being crucial for the formation of Catalan identity: The medieval predecessors of Catalan autonomy, the industrial and economic revolution concentrated within the Spanish state in Catalonia, and finally the various "waves" of immigration which have determined present Catalan identity.

In a first step he points out that such important characteristics of Catalan identity and autonomy like territory, language, culture and proper institutions can be traced back unto medieval times. Pujol highlights thus not only the long tradition of a distinct Catalan culture and language he also constructs a continuity regarding Catalan territory and political autonomy. Although, a real historic background to these affirmations exists, the manner in which the Catalan nationalists select only the suitable events in the far past, reproduce and interpret them can be described with Hobsbawms concept of invented traditions (see II.1.2). Thus, for instance certain political institutions at the Catalan level, such as the historic *Generalitat* did exist, but they cannot be compared with respect to their competence level and autonomy to modern political institutions.

---

[1] P57: CAT-Gov-Pres-Pujol 08-10-2002.rtf-[Una personalidad que es fruto...] (18:21).

A second element of Catalonia's past Pujol underlined to have contributed to build the present Catalan identity and to distinguish it from the rest of Spain is the industrial and economic revolution of the eighteenth and nineteenth century. This affirmation points to a typical frame of Catalan nationalist discourse which describes Catalonia as economically more developed and more progressive than the rest of Spain and the Catalans as hard-working and serious (see III.6.4).

In the same speech Pujol had earlier addressed the question of who identifies with this vision of a common past Catalan nationalism had constructed. He pointed out that Catalans did not identify with the same values of the past, nor with the same historic sense or version than other Spaniards. Also within Catalonia not everybody identified with the nationalist vision of the past, referring implicitly to the Castilian speaking Catalans originating from other parts of Spain. In spite of these different historic visions a common project, a common future must exist.[2] Therefore, Pujol added to his list the various immigration movements of the twentieth century as a third and more recent element that contributed to what Catalonia is today.

Although the majority of the people who migrated to Catalonia in the mentioned period of time were internal migrants, moving from other Spanish regions to Catalonia, they are commonly denominated by Catalan politicians, as above in the statement of PUJOL, as immigrants, and their movement as immigration. The usage of these terms underlines the idea that Catalonia is a distinct entity within Spain, enclosed by "borders", mainly denominated culturally and linguistically. Everybody crossing these imaginary borders becomes an immigrant, in spite of having the same nationality.

1.2 Catalonia, traditionally a country of immigration

A frequently used frame in the Catalan political discourse is to emphasize the history of immigrant reception and integration, and to highlight the positive contributions of these immigrants to the "common Catalan project".[3] Although there were previous immigration movements, the primary background for political statements about past immigration are the major migration movements

---

[2] P57: CAT-Gov-Pres-Pujol 08-10-2002.rtf-[Porque no todos en Cataluña, n...] (15:15).
[3] P57: CAT-Gov-Pres-Pujol 08-10-2002.rtf-[Porque no todos en Cataluña, n...] (15:15).

from other Spanish regions to Catalonia between the 1950s and the 1970s (see IV.3).

Catalonia is hence described in statements about migration as having a long history as a receiving country (país d'acollida).[4] Catalonia has always been a "welcome society", "a society who welcomed ideas, people, technology, mentalities, etc".[5] "The phenomenon of immigration is not new to Catalonia. In the course of our history we have historically been a receiving country for the immigration sector."[6] Such inclusive affirmations of a common past aim at promoting the identification of immigrants and their descendants with the idea of a distinct Catalan identity and the claim for autonomy as opposed to a centralist, homogenizing vision of the Spanish nation.

In its Plan of Immigration 2001-2004 the CiU government furthermore assigned Catalonia a particular tradition of immigrant integration:

> "Catalonia is the result of a permanent process of integration of people coming from other places. Our country has always received different people. We have a long tradition of integration. It is an open country where everybody has fitted in. Since medieval times, throughout the seventeenth century, and after that throughout the whole twentieth century, Catalonia has generally given the same response to the migration movements it has experienced: an attitude in favour of integration and living together."[7]

Piqué, leader of the Catalan PP (PPC), agreed on that:

> "Catalonia has been a country with an extraordinary capacity of integration of all its citizens, which many times came from abroad in considerable numbers, and it has had the capacity to integrate them, while at the same time maintaining its own nature and identity, but with a great capacity of integration and a constant attitude of solidarity. Catalonia has always shown solidarity and integration capacity."[8]

From this experience of having already received, and in their majority successfully integrated, such a high number of immigrants from other parts of

---

4   See P41: CAT-Gov-Conference Duran i Lleida CIU 15-11-2001.rtf-[Catalunya té una llarga històr...] (620:622).
5   P57: CAT-Gov-Pres-Pujol 08-10-2002.rtf-[que Cataluña ha tenido siempre...] (11:11).
6   P82: Auszüge-DSCP-P-010 15-03-2000.rtf-[el fenomen de la immigració no...] (296:317).
7   P38: pla Immigració 2001-2004.rtf-[La tradició integradora de Ca...] (224:259).
8   P3: CAT-Gov-Article-Entrevista Piqué PP 28-10-2003.rtf-[Cataluña ha sido un país con u...] (5:5).

Spain, politicians further deduce that this is a factor that facilitates the reception and integration of the current immigration from non-EU countries.[9]

The general conclusion that Catalonia has a long tradition of immigration and integration of immigrants also is reflected in more elaborate descriptions of the formation of the present collective identity of Catalonia. Not only is Catalonia described in these statements as having received generations of immigrants, but it is thought to be built upon their contributions.[10] This idea was also taken up in the latest Plan of Immigration of the *Generalitat*:

> "The Catalan Society has constructed itself through immigration. Our long history of migrations, as immigrants to this country and as emigrants to other places of the world, constitutes a basic element of what we share."[11]

To describe the construction and formation of what today constitutes the Catalan society, politicians used different metaphors.

The vision of the Catalan Socialists can be resumed with the words of a Socialist Member of Parliament comparing Catalonia to an onion.

> "Catalonia is a passageway, it is a well known land, historically, it is a land of successive arrivals of immigration. And which has known to integrate them, let's say, assuming the fact of different layers. Someone said to me some time ago that Catalonia was like an onion. That means it is constructing itself and was constructed based on different layers."[12]

Catalonia is thus seen to have formed "throughout the past of successive layers, which are twined around a nucleus holding together the whole".[13]

At the first sight only slightly different is how Pujol, the mastermind of the Catalan nationalist movement, describes the formation of Catalan identity. He compares Catalonia to a fruit tree which

> "can be refined, and it is often convenient to do so, and some of the best fruits that we have today result from the new parts. But the trunk has to exist, that is

---

[9] See Interviews: CAT-10 Member of Parliament-IC-V, 2005; CAT-2 Expert, 2005.

[10] See P34: CAT-Opp-Entrevista Montilla PSC 07-07-2002.rtf-[-Cataluña es una muestra de un...] (108:108).

[11] P39: Pla Immigració 2005-2008 I.rtf - 39:12 [La societat catalana s'ha cons...] (410:410).

[12] CAT-6 Member of Parliament-PSC, 2005.

[13] P79: Auszüge PSC Wahlprogramm Katalonien 2003.rtf-[Cataluña ha ido configurando s...] (4:8).

clear. Without it there would be no possibility of refining. There must be a trunk, roots, sap."[14]

The basic values of Catalan identity are thought to be the trunk of the fruit-tree. In the same speech, though, he later admits that this trunk also changes over time, because the different collective identities modify it.[15]

The heterogeneity and diversity of the Catalan society which are partly the result of past immigration movements are presented as an inherent element of the present Catalan identity. A Member of Parliament of the IC-V describes the process of identity-building and –changing as a "constant redefinition of the 'Catalanidad' through the integration of diversity".[16] The IC-V's electoral manifesto for 2003 also reflects the idea of an already diverse and heterogeneous Catalan society which is now incorporating new immigrants:

> "The enormous potential for emancipation which the new diversity means and the importance to incorporate the recognition of difference into our conception of the world must be stressed, since it is a basic dimension of pluralism and the concept of a just society in which every sector is hegemonic and everyone is equal. This diversity is pre-existent and anterior to the arrival of immigration. This diversity (of age, gender, social classes, interests, etc.) is substantial to the formation of contemporary urban-industrial societies characterized precisely by their heterogeneity."[17]

Diversity and heterogeneity as defining elements of Catalan identity are according to these statements not only defined culturally and ethnically, but also with respect to other dimensions, such as social classes, different generations, political interests.

> "The diversity of origins is only one of the elements of the heterogeneity of the Catalan society, composed of a great variety of collectives with different characteristics and different interests that constitute a framework in continuous transformation, crossed by socio-economic and highly marked inequalities."[18]

---

[14] P67: CAT-Gov-Pres-Pujol 27-07-2001.rtf-[Un frutal puede ser injertado…] (19:19).

[15] See P67: CAT-Gov-Pres-Pujol 27-07-2001.rtf-[Así pues, todos los que nos re…] (20:20).

[16] P82: Auszüge-DSCP-P-010 15-03-2000.rtf-[I, en tercer lloc, jo assenyal…] (78:85).

[17] P81: IC-V Wahlprogramm Katalonien -Propuestas Inm-2003.rtf-[Cal ressaltar l'enorme potenci…] (252:252).

[18] P89: Auszüge-DSCP-P-058 27-06-2001.rtf-[que avui s'aprovi un document …] (764:770).

Nevertheless, the different images used by Catalan politicians show that Catalan identity is always thought of having some common unchanging elements, which seems to be primarily the language. However, even language absorbs influences from other languages and develops.

Although admitting that collective identities change and absorb external influences the idea of preserving an own collective identity prevails in the Catalan political arena, particularly among the nationalist parties.

> "The Catalan people of today, is not the same as the Catalan people a hundred years ago. With so much immigration and so many changes, it is not the same. Of course it is not the same as the one in medieval times [...] but, at any rate, a historic continuity, which we can call the central theme of history and of what implies the values of identity, of reference, etc., obviously has to be maintained."[19]

The political objective of Catalan nationalists is thus to preserve and strengthen Catalan identity on the one hand and to integrate immigrants on the other hand. The Plan of Immigration of the CiU government proclaims that Catalonia has managed to do so, to integrate migrants of diverse origins preserving its own identity.[20] Pujol also presents it as a big merit of Catalonia to have preserved the cohesion of the Catalan people, the pacific living together and the good vicinity of six million Catalans and at last having preserved the basic Catalan identity.[21]

2. BASIC NORMS OF THE POLITICAL SYSTEM

Basically in Catalonia major variations in the political discourse about migration regarding the basic norms of the political system could not be observed, compared to central state discourse. As in general, the statements at the level of the autonomous communities focus primarily on the integration of immigrants.

---

[19] P67: CAT-Gov-Pres-Pujol 27-07-2001.rtf-[Así pues, todos los que nos re...] (20:20).
[20] P38: pla Immigració 2001-2004.rtf-[La tradició integradora de Ca...] (224:259).
[21] P63: CAT-Gov-Pres-Pujol 21-06-2001.rtf-[Sortosament, la societat catal...] (31:31).

2.1 Democratic values and human rights

In the integration debate Catalan politicians alluded to "valors democràtics", democratic values such as political pluralism, gender equality and the laicist state. The social, political, economic and cultural integration of immigrants requires the recognition of their rights and the demand to fulfil their obligations, and all that should happen within the "framework of values –political pluralism, laicity of the state, gender equality – which our society is build on".[22] It is understood to be an obligation of all political actors to object to every infraction "of a basic political culture and of shared principles which make us a unique people, after all a people which is organized democratically".[23]

Furthermore, the Immigration Plan 2005-2008 mentions the link between democratic legitimacy and the respect of the human rights concluding that every act of the Catalan authorities must be guided by the principles of human rights. It then lists the relevant international human rights agreements, such as the Universal Declaration of Human Rights.

> "The treatment of cultural diversity resulting from the migrations has to be incorporated in the values of justice and respect of the dignity of a person, as a nucleus of the democratic legitimacy and principal framework to guide the public interventions. The Human Rights are the core of the same legitimacy. The respect, the recognition, the guarantee to progressively extend the Human Rights as inexcusable principles, fundamental and universal, must guide the management of the accommodation process of the immigrated population in our society, beyond any strictly economic, political or cultural interpretation."[24]

2.2 Meta-discourse

In analogy to the central state migration discourse a specific feature of political culture is reflected also in Catalan migration discourse: The particular awareness of politicians about how they should treat migration issues in public (see chapter VI.2.4). However, only in statements of the opposition parties, PSC, ERC, IC-V, during the CiU government the meta-discursive frame of the impact political diction has on the public opinion was found. As immigration is, according to an IC-V Member of Parliament, the most important challenge for Catalonia

---

[22] P19: CAT-Opp-Article Montilla PSC 2002.rtf-[Una política de realidades pas…] (32:32).
[23] P86: Auszüge-DSCP-P-046 07-03-2001.rtf-[Ha de quedar clar que totes le…] (457:470).
[24] P39: Pla Immigració 2005-2008 I.rtf-[El tractament de la diversitat…] (476:488).

in the future politicians should talk about it with a "special sensitivity".[25] In view of what Marta Ferrusola, wife of Jordi Pujol, said in February 2002 about the immigrants, particularly of Muslim origin, and the threat they pose to Catalan society,[26] PSC leader Montilla claims that

> "the obligation of a responsible politician is to educate, exactly the opposite of what have done some people these days. When they say that the people have certain thoughts, we do not know if they think that the people think so or if the ones who think so are they themselves. It is a confusing attitude that aliments the worst passions. A politician may not be unguarded, but must be fierce in its rejection of opinions that could justify xenophobia."[27]

An IC-V Member of Parliament also sees the risk that lies in a certain negatively connoted political discourse about migration. He claims the need for an ethic codex for the treatment of immigration, because it could aliment xenophobic attitudes.[28]

It is "absurd to believe that Catalonia is immune to the phenomenon of racism that accompanies the migrations. It is a phenomenon potentially realizable in a society of our kind", an IC-V Member of Parliament argues. He further refers to the xenophobic tendencies that have existed against the Castilian-speaking immigration to Catalonia.[29]

Maragall explains how in the neighbourhoods of the former interior immigration hostile attitudes grew against the new immigration, because of situations of competence:

> "That means, when commentaries are made about the difficulties that the current arrival of the immigrants cause, it is somehow the intent to help resisting those who live in the neighbourhoods and who are immigrants of the first generation of the 60s who now see with despair that all the improvements they have achieved in their neighbourhood, with those schools that were miserable and now are decent schools, who now see that things are starting to get complicated. However, it is

---

[25] P83: Auszüge-DSCP-P-033 15-11-2000.rtf-[del fet que serà el repte més...] (15:18).

[26] See Joan Subirats (2002): *El 'éxito' de la (no) política de inmigración*, El País, 15.02.2002.

[27] P33: CAT-Opp-Entrevista Montilla La Vanguardia 05-03-2001.rtf-[Las opiniones de Heribert Bar...] (11:13); See also: P19: CAT-Opp-Article Montilla PSC 2002.rtf-[Si hay una actitud que acaba g...] (13:16).

[28] See P94: Auszüge-DSCP-P-088-089 29 u. 30-05-2002.rtf-[Per tant, jo crec que una de l...] (1264:1298).

[29] P86: Auszüge-DSCP-P-046 07-03-2001.rtf-[És igualment absurd creure's q...] (127:140).

not so clear that they are helping. This vision that the immigrants of the 60s have –who would, to start with, not say anymore that they are immigrants and they are totally right, they are true Catalans, citizens of Catalonia– , that they realize that now everything they have built up in 40 or 50 years, and particularly during the twenty years of democracy, could go to rack and ruin. This is the most dramatic and immoral what is happening in this country, because it happens before everyone's eyes and everybody is occupied discussing values and laws of aliens, but no one about how to solve the problems in the places where they actually happen. Therefore, the demoralisation of the population of these neighbourhoods is an immoral fact: they see how their lives are getting more complicated and that intolerance and brutal reactions are the only alternative in this situation where no solutions are provided. This is immoral and something we have to handle, all, jointly agreed."[30]

An ERC Member of Parliament emphasizes that in these problematic situations of competition and potential social conflict it is the responsibility of everyone, which kind of image of the immigrants is constructed in public discourse.[31]

3. CATALONIA, A NATION WITHIN THE SPANISH STATE

In general, political discourse in Catalonia continuously refers to the relation between the central state level and the autonomous community. Also in migration discourse, Catalonia is defined and positioned in reference to Spain or rather to the central state government and administration.

3.1 Catalonia, a part of the Spanish state

In the political discourse about immigration Catalan politicians refer explicitly to the Spanish state as a whole and not solely to the Catalan autonomous government and administration. Catalan politicians are thus actively involved in political debates reaching beyond the Catalan "borders". In issues concerning foreign policy or border control, Catalan politicians refer primarily to the policy options at the central state level, except from the areas of development

---

[30] P72: CAT-Opp-Speech Maragall PSC 06-09-2001.rtf-[És a dir, quan es fan comentar...] (47:47).
[31] See P84: Auszüge-DSCP-P-043 07-02-2001.rtf-[Moltes vegades, aquesta concen...] (234:245).

cooperation and of foreign cultural policy which are described below. Subjects, such as the common policy of the EU member states concerning immigration or the border control to the southern neighbours are discussed above from a central state perspective. To avoid redundancy, only the differences between the Catalan migration discourse and the central state migration discourse regarding the responsibilities of the central state level will be outlined in detail.

As we have seen before the new Ley de Extranjería and its reform in 2000 was an important issue at the central state level. It is thus not surprising that it was discussed controversially in Catalonia, too. The opposition parties PSC, ERC, IC-V sharply criticised the Law, because of the differentiation between the legal and illegal status of immigrants. A IC-V Member of the Catalan Parliament even speaks of juridical *apartheid*:

> "The Law on Aliens constitutes a veritable juridical *apartheid*. While the treasury department treats everybody equally, the Law on Aliens obliges to treat people different. How can we claim obligations, duties, integration, if we deny freedoms, elementary freedoms? How can we cement the construction of a country if we deny people's freedoms?"[32]

The PPC defended the Central government's law, and the CiU which was cooperating with the PP at the central state level at that time also supported it. A CiU Member of Parliament gives the following explanation for the support of the new law, although his party is not a hundred per cent convinced:

> "Well, it is also true that when a group positions itself in respect to a law at the end a global résumé has to be made and in our opinion the global résumé of this law is sufficiently positive to support it. By all means, it is as different as chalk and cheese from the law which was in effect in Spain during many years, and which is actually the law of the year '85, as you have just mentioned before. This new law, in which you have put much emphasis, is not only a law, let's say, of police measures, it is not only that, it's a law that has two major areas, two major parts: the first is the fundamental protection of the rights and freedoms of the immigrants, this is a substantial part of the law, and the other area is certainly the control and regulation of the migratory flows."[33]

---

[32] P89: Auszüge-DSCP-P-058 27-06-2001.rtf-[La Llei d'estrangeria constitu...] (149:154).
[33] P84: Auszüge-DSCP-P-043 07-02-2001.rtf-[Ara, també és veritat que quan...] (796:811).

Another important issue also discussed on the regional level were the different regularization processes of the PP government and the regularization in 2005 initiated by the PSOE government. The regularization processes were discussed in Catalonia regarding the effects for the Catalan society and the Catalan authorities.

The opposition parties thus criticized the regularization process initiated in 2000 by the central state government with respect to the lower numbers of immigrants given a regular status in Catalonia compared to other autonomous communities.[34] A PSC Member of Parliament concretely attacks the regional government, the *Generalitat,* for not being able to "profit from its good relations with the political party that supports the Central Government".[35] He accuses the CiU hence of not having defended well enough the regional interests in the past regularization process.

After the 2005 regularization process the accusations were exactly the other way round. Now the CiU criticized the PSOE and its federated Catalan partner, the PSC, and claimed that the Central government should have considered more the regional and local level when planning and organizing of the whole process.[36]

3.2 Catalonia, "una nació"

In the regional political debate about migration, moderate nationalist politicians define Catalonia in relation to Spain. According to their statements Catalonia is a nation within the Spanish state and Spain in turn a state consisting of different nations. A CiU Member of Parliament, for instance, emphasizes the national identity of Catalonia: "Our national identity as a people has always been linked to peace, to a public spirit, to the reception of others, to solidarity, and we want that to continue being so".[37] Apart from highlighting the distinctive national identity of Catalonia, an ERC Member of Parliament brings in another dimension when stating that "our country has a long history as a land of welcome for people coming from other places, with other cultures and languages. And it has

---

[34] See P84: Auszüge-DSCP-P-043 07-02-2001.rtf-[Per d'altra banda, una caracte...] (270:275).
[35] P84: Auszüge-DSCP-P-043 07-02-2001.rtf-[sinó perquè entenem que això c...] (461:474).
[36] See P104: Auszüge DSCP-P 047 12-05-2005.rtf-[Respecte al procés extraordina...] (69:85).
[37] P100: Auszüge DSCP-P 011 21-04-2004.rtf-[La nostra identitat nacional c...] (214:216).

more than any other nation of the Spanish State".[38] He thus implicitly presents Spain as a multi-national state and Catalonia as one of various nations within this state.

The specific elements that are thought to be the main distinctive features of the Catalan identity will be discussed in detail in chapter VII.5, presenting the ideas about the reception and integration of immigrants.

3.3 Catalonia and the central state administration

As in all debates about the relation of the regional and the central state administration, the negotiation of political responsibilities (see III.3) also plays a fundamental role in the field of immigration and integration policies. The Catalan side claims on the one hand to transfer responsibilities to the regional administration, on the other hand to transfer sufficient funds to finance the implementation of the transferred responsibilities, such as integration policy measures.

With respect to the first, Catalan politicians from all parties stress the need to have the responsibility to contract foreign workers in their home countries depending on the demand of the Catalan labour market. Artur Más, leader of the CiU, for instance, points out that

> "here we have a major loophole which we have not got tired of claiming again and again, and will continue to claim in the future, which is the capacity of the autonomous government, in our case the Government of Catalonia, to intervene in the control, the orientation, the selection, and the regulation of the foreign immigrants."[39]

The PSC also postulated in its electoral manifesto 2003 that the impact of immigration in the local sphere makes it necessary to insist on a broader and more effective participation in the definition of the annual quota for foreign labour.[40]

---

[38] P70: CAT-Opp-Conference Carod-Rovira ERC 04-06-2002.rtf-70:1 [el nostre país té,darrera seu....] (2:2).

[39] P 2: CAT-Gov-Article-Entrevista Artur Mas CiU 27-10-2003.rtf-[y en cambio aquí tenemos una g...] (20:21).

[40] See P79: Auszüge PSC Wahlprogramm Katalonien 2003.rtf-79:12 [La gestión de los flujos migra...] (64:74); see also: P85: Auszüge-DSCP-P-045 21-02-2001.rtf-85:12 [Els instem a negociar la fixac...] (498:502).

This claim goes along with the demand of the CiU government to transfer the responsibility to issue the residency and working permits for foreign workers to the regional administration, or at least the selection of immigrants for whom the central state administration then should issue the respective permits:

> "Ideally, the responsibility we want is that the *Generalitat*, by delegation of the central government, issues the residency and working permits. This would be the roof. Naturally, in the referential frame of state legislation. In the case that this was not possible we claim the Quebec model as a minimum which means that before the central government issues a residency and working permit, we have to have issued already a certificate of the selection of the respective immigrant. This obliges us to select in the countries of origin which we also want to do, and which the central government does not allow us to do."[41]

An ERC Member of Parliament justifies this claim basically with the subsidiarity principle.[42] According to him the *Generalitat* should assume the processing or the working permits, because this would mean less bureaucracy and therefore a more efficient and faster attention of the requests, and because it is closer to the population and thus knows better what the concrete needs and demands are.[43]

In addition to the discussion about the transfer of responsibilities, Catalan politicians also emphasize the need to transfer financial resources to carry out the integration policy measures which are part of the responsibilities already in the hands of the Autonomous Community and the tasks to be transferred in future.

> "It is evident that, to implement all that, considerable economic resources are needed. The investments necessary to apply the agreed policy measures have to be one of the principle priorities of all administrations in the coming years; moreover it has to be considered that the implemented actions will not be of immediate effect."[44]

---

[41] P23: CAT-Gov-Entrevista Artur Mas CIU El País 12-10-2003.rtf-[Idealmente, la competencia que...] (31:31).

[42] See footnote 64 in chapter VI.

[43] See P100: Auszüge DSCP-P 011 21-04-2004.rtf-[I també creiem que es fa neces...] (298:316).

[44] P119: Auszüge BOPC-197-18-06-2001 Document Comissió d'Estudi.rtf - 119:31 [És evident que, per a portar a...] (930:936). See also: P101: Auszüge DSCP-P 012 05-05-2004. rtf-[demanar, sol·licitar la transf...] (452:462).

Furthermore, Pujol asserts that, because of the fact that immigration for Catalonia is different than for Madrid or other autonomous communities –Catalonia has received until today higher numbers of immigrants– more money is needed to handle it.[45]

He even uses the general frame of an economic and financial discrimination against Catalonia saying that even the economic sector and the trade unions "publish document after document denouncing financial discrimination, a policy of economic concentration which harms Catalonia".[46]

3.4 Catalonia as an international actor

Although Catalonia is no independent state, Catalan authorities act in some circumstances directly on the international level and not as usual indirectly by influencing central state authorities. As mentioned above a typical field for regional government action is the cooperation with underdeveloped countries or regions. The aspect of development aid surfaces in migration discourse in combination with the reference to the limited responsibilities of the Catalan government. It is thus presented by the Catalan government as a regional aim to strengthen its own efforts in this policy field, for instance, in the "Pla d'Immigració 2001-2004", but also in other statements:

> "The government of the Generalitat has always put great importance to the Mediterranean policy. For various reasons, of identity and strategy…, but also because the immigration that comes to Catalonia is for the most part caused by underdevelopment of the southern coasts of the Mediterranean. We had most influence in that sense in the year 1995 with the Conference of Barcelona. Since then, due to various and very different reasons, it has to be recognized that there have not been many advances, nonetheless the *Generalitat* has kept the track, and within its responsibilities has continued to act. [...] We can point out that the *Generalitat* allots every year subsidies to the Catalan NGOs that execute programmes and projects both in the area of development cooperation as in the area of sensitization and awareness building in the Catalan society in favour of the developing countries. Some of the subsidised sensitization projects which the NGOs operate in Catalonia can refer indirectly or incidentally to questions related to the

---

[45] See P74: CAT-Opp-Speech Pujol CIU 10-11-2004.rtf-[En el cas de Catalunya el tema…] (432:438).

[46] P61: CAT-Gov-Pres-Pujol 17-09-2003.rtf-[Por otra parte los partidos qu…] (80:80).

issue of immigration, such as for example the intercultural dialogue, the culture of peace and the inter-religious dialogue."[47]

Apart from the reference to the EU Conference of Barcelona and the importance that is given to the Mediterranean policy there is a recurrent frame in the general Catalanist discourse describing Catalonia as a leading region within the "Europe of regions", thereby by-passing the Spanish central state level (see III.1.6).

4. ECONOMIC DEVELOPMENT

The economic progress, starting in Catalonia with the economic and industrial revolution in the eighteenth and nineteenth century, is mentioned in the nationalist discourse as an important element that distinguishes Catalonia from the rest of Spain.[48]

Apart from this historical perspective, Catalan politicians refer to the current economic situation, similar to the above discussed frames about Spain's economic development in central state migration discourse. In the Catalan debate, however, economic and labour market issues are discussed from a Catalan perspective and the frame of reference is Catalonia, not Spain as a whole.

4.1 Catalonia, economic progress and growth

Statements about the positive economic development in Catalonia are often made implicitly comparing it to the inferior economic performance of other Spanish regions. The emphasis Catalan politicians place on economic strength and everything associated with it can therefore be interpreted as a strategy to fortify the Catalan claims for more political autonomy.

In migration discourse Catalan politicians with different ideological backgrounds agree that Catalonia is an economically prosperous and progressive country and that this is an incitement for immigration. For instance the leader

---

[47] P38: pla Immigració 2001-2004.rtf-[però que també dóna resposta a...] (5366:5391). See also: P68: CAT-Gov-Speech Artur Mas CIU 21-10-2002.rtf-[la tercera i darrera via per e...] (92:99); P80: ERC Wahlprogramm-Migration Katalonien 2003.rtf-[Avançar cap a un món més just...] (280:281).

[48] For the detailed description of the *frame* that describes Catalonia as more developed and progressive than the rest of Spain see chapter VI.1.1.

of the Catalan PPC, Piqué, stated that "if we have immigration, and in considerable numbers, it is because we are an attractive country. On the contrary we would not have the capacity of attraction to immigrants".[49] Adela Ros (ERC), Secretary of the *Generalitat* responsible for immigration matters explained likewise in an interview:

> "That so many people are coming is because we are a rich society, with a strong economy to give opportunities to people. There is a positive reading: We have the immigrants we need and the richness to attract them."[50]

Catalonia is thus described, in analogy to Spain in central state migration discourse (see VI.4.I), as "the promised land", as the favourite destination of thousands of people who run away from the bad economic situation or from political repression in their countries of origin, and come with the hope for a better future.[51]

However, not only economic growth and progress are emphasized in the Catalan migration discourse, also the social progress and the importance of the social welfare state. President Maragall highlighted:

> "At the same time that Catalonia grows and prospers it is a country that progresses socially. We are not only speaking of a country that is situated, according to the economic parameters, well ahead of the European average. We are also speaking of a country that progresses in the social area, that has educational services, health care, social and cultural services more and more broadly and of a better quality; with a maximum rate of school attendance from four to sixteen years."[52]

His predecessor, Pujol, already in 2002 explained the link between Catalan nationalism and the welfare state. He outlines that Catalan nationalists not only have propagated linguistic and cultural topics, but have promoted the social welfare state since 1970 as one of their principle objectives.[53] Carod Rovira,

---

[49] P3: CAT-Gov-Article-Entrevista Piqué PP 28-10-2003.rtf-[Cierto es que si tenemos inmig...] (6:6).
[50] P22: CAT-Gov-Entrevista Adela Ros ERC 19-04-2004.rtf-[Si ve tanta gent és perquè som...] (29:29).
[51] See P71: CAT-Opp-Speech Carod-Rovira ERC 22-04-2003.rtf-[Les darreres dècades, potser e...] (5:5); P38: pla Immigració 2001-2004.rtf-[Les persones que vénen al nost...] (160:173).
[52] P51: CAT-Gov-Pres-Maragall PSC 18-10-2005.rtf-[I a la vegada que creix i pros...] (37:37).
[53] See P57: CAT-Gov-Pres-Pujol 08-10-2002.rtf-[Para ello tenemos que preserva...] (22:22).

leader of the ERC, by then opposition party, formulated the same idea describing Catalonia as a prosperous country which

> "should not only be the country of the Catalan language and culture, but also the country of welfare and of physical and democratic quality of life, the land of equality of opportunities, where, if you work, if you make some effort, if you risk something, you will prosper."[54]

In analogy to the central state discourse politicians on the regional level use the frame highlighting the economic contributions of immigrants. Immigration is presented, like above, as a desirable phenomenon which accounts for wealth and contributes to the economic growth of Catalonia. The Immigration Plan 2001-2004 lists the economic benefits immigration goes along with. Direct benefits, in terms of financial contributions are the immigrants' contributions to the Catalan income by means of their salaries, their retirement pensions, their fiscal obligations –such as paying taxes or paying into the social security.[55] Likewise the following Immigration Plan 2005-2008 argues that "the immigration is moreover a factor of enrichment, besides it generates and moves economic capital".[56]

Nevertheless, immigration must be regular immigration. Like at the central state level it is also consensus between the Catalan political parties that irregular immigration and the black economy must be eliminated and that mafias which traffic immigrants and exploit them as cheap labour must be fought. Maragall, for instance, stated that immigration was necessary, but the demand should never be so big that it ruled out a regular process.

> "To some extent yes. The offer of immigrants that want to come to Catalonia will increase. But the demand for immigrants on the part of Catalonia, which is inevitable and at the end convenient, shouldn't be as big that it does not allow an orderly reception of the immigrants we need, and who have to enjoy the rights, but they have to come legally and according to agreements. Let's say it clearly. The

---

[54] P71: CAT-Opp-Speech Carod-Rovira ERC 22-04-2003.rtf-[Si t'estimes el país on vius...] (32:32).
[55] See P38: pla Immigració 2001-2004.rtf-[Beneficis econòmics. Són de do...] (2156:2174).
[56] P39: Pla Immigració 2005-2008 I.rtf-[La immigració és a més un fact...] (93:93).

immigration is necessary, but without the control of flows and without legal documents it will provoke grave problems in the living together and in security."[57]

The economic and demographic contribution of immigrants is closely
linked. Hence, the demographic impact of immigration is also an argument
used in the Catalan migration discourse.

Unlike other Spanish regions, Catalonia looks back on a long tradition of
receiving interior migrants (see IV.3). It is thus not surprising that politicians at
the regional level refer to the demographic implications of the migratory flows
of the 1950s, 1960s, and 1970s. The Immigration Plan 2005-2008, for instance,
provides us with a summary of the demographic development in Catalonia:

> "The immigration movement was the fundament of the Catalan population growth
> in the first three quarters of the twentieth century. Only between the years 1950
> and 1975 a demographic balance of 1.5 million inhabitants is estimated, including
> the decade of the 60s as a period of maximum immigration. The intensity of those
> currents that originate almost completely from the rest of Spain and their con-
> centration in time and space had major repercussions. From a demographic point
> of view, the migratory contribution not only meant the growth of inhabitants in
> Catalonia, but also had a direct effect on the natural growth: The arrival of a young
> segment, in their zenith of fecundity, such as the immigrants of the 60s and early
> 70s, has translated into a major increase in the birth rate. The contribution coming
> from the rest of Spain decreased, so that the migratory balance fluctuated around
> nil between 1975 and 1995."[58]

The PPC draws to a large extent upon an electorate originating from the described interior migration.[59] Statements of PPC representatives therefore reflect
the importance of the demographic contribution of this part of the population
in Catalonia. A PPC Member of the Catalan Parliament stressed in 2000 that
without the contributions of immigrants, Catalonia wouldn't be the country of
three million and more citizens, but would have an over-aged population with

---

[57] P32: CAT-Opp-Entrevista Maragall PSC Tardor 2001.rtf-[En part sí. L'oferta d'immigra...]
(92:92).
[58] P39: Pla Immigració 2005-2008 I.rtf-[El moviment immigratori va ser...] (143:143).
[59] In a survey published in 2005 by the Institut de Ciències Polítiques i Socials 5 per cent of the
total respondents indicated to have voted for the PPC in the autonomic elections 2003: Of those
born in Catalonia it was only 4 per cent, of those born in Andalusia it was 7 per cent, of those
born in the "Rest of Spain" 12 per cent, and of foreigners 1 per cent. See Institut de Ciències
Polítiques i Socials (2005): *Sondeig d'Opinió. Catalunya*, Barcelona: ICPS, p. 132.

a lower level of social, economic and cultural development.[60] However, also the other political parties acknowledge the importance of the former immigration for Catalonia's demography. Pujol emphasized in a speech in 2004 that Catalonia would not have progressed like it has without the immigrants.[61]

Beside the affirmations considering past immigration movements, also the future demographic development is discussed. The Plan of Immigration 2001-2004 draws a pessimistic picture of the future without immigration. From 2010 on the Catalan economy would suffer from a lack of labour. According to that, 35,000 immigrants are necessary to avoid this situation.[62]

Despite of these numbers, moderate nationalists claim that the future population growth should not be based only on foreign immigration:

> "The demographic growth can not be based on foreign emigration only. Therefore, policy measures to increase the own birth rate must be introduced, based on the support of the families with small children or increasing the parental leave."[63]

5. CATALONIA, AN IMMIGRATION COUNTRY

As outlined above, Catalonia has explicitly been defined as an immigration country, not only since a few decades ago but throughout its long history. Catalan politicians include immigration into their narrative about the historic continuity of the Catalan nation, describing immigration as a characteristic factor in Catalonia's past and moreover as an inherent element of Catalan identity (see VII.1.2). The successful integration of immigrants into the Catalan society is hence a self-evident objective propagated over and over again in Catalan political discourse.[64] Immigration and integration policies are, furthermore, discussed more broadly on the regional than on the central state level, because,

---

[60] See P82: Auszüge-DSCP-P-010 15-03-2000.rtf-[el fenomen de la immigració no...] (296:317).
[61] See P74: CAT-Opp-Speech Pujol CIU 10-11-2004.rtf-[Sobre el tema de la immigració...] (304:347).
[62] See P38: pla Immigració 2001-2004.rtf-[Les xifres semblen contundent...] (792:803).
[63] P25: CAT-Gov-Entrevista Mas CIU El Pais 14-11-2003.rtf-[El crecimiento demográfico no ...] (59:59); See also P62: CAT-Gov-Pres-Pujol 18-09-2001.rtf-[Por lo tanto, nosotros, que en...] (37:37).
[64] Gil Araujo speaks of "public philosophies or theories of integration", see Gil Araujo (2007): *Las argucias de la integración. Construcción nacional y gobierno de lo social a través de las políticas de integración de inmigrantes. Los casos de Cataluña y Madrid*, Tésis Doctoral: Departamento de

following the principle of subsidiarity, they form part of the regional and local authorities' responsibilities. Catalonia is therefore again the primary reference frame and not Spain as a whole. A specific characteristic of the Catalan migration discourse is, moreover, that the reception and integration of the current immigration is always treated, as explained above, in the context of past immigration experiences, especially the Castilian-speaking "immigration" between the 1950s and 1970s.

5.1 Immigration, a challenge to Catalan identity

In spite of the many years that have gone by since Catalonia received considerable numbers of migrants from other Spanish regions the impact of the Castilian-speaking immigration is thus still a topic of the Catalan political discourse.[65]

Pujol, President of the *Generalitat*, remembered in a speech in 2004 the problems and risks the migration movements of the 1950s, 1960s, and 1970s implied:

"Who can deny that it brought serious problems? We remember so many neighbourhoods of barracks, so much marginalization, the 'Viviendes del Governador', and the deficiencies of all kind of communities which in a very short time span multiplied by two, by three, by five their population. Or by ten. We remember the mental shock that this situation represented to us. And that meant a risk for social fracture, of cultural confrontation, of linguistic tensions, of an exclusionary mentality on both sides."[66]

A statement of Carod Rovira, leader of the ERC, shows that the effects of the massive influx of Castilian-speaking migrants are still felt and must be dealt with.

"But we only have real possibilities to incorporate them fully into our national landscape if we already, and at once, prepare the circumstances so that this is made possible. At the same time, however, we have to lay the foundations for a new living together having solved before satisfyingly an issue still in parts pending. I refer

---

Cambio Social, Facultad de Ciencias Políticas y Sociología, Universidad de Complutense, Madrid, p. 265.

[65] See chapter II.2.3 for more details on the debate about "els altres catalans" in the 1960s and 1970s.

[66] P74: CAT-Opp-Speech Pujol CIU 10-11-2004.rtf-[Sobre el tema de la immigració...] (304: 347).

to the definitive inclusion of the former immigration of the post-war period, of the 50s, 60s, 70s, and of their descendants, without any subsidiary positions. I refer to imperious necessity of our people to win over, without any ambiguity, those 'altres catalans', as Candel said, those new Catalans that at home speak Castilian or Galician, for our national project. Because, without their participation, their implication, their protagonist role no true national project will be possible in our country."[67]

He further argues that those people, their children and grandchildren should finally be recognized as Catalans and no longer be marginalized. These citizens should no longer be called immigrants, because they'll continue to be immigrants throughout all their life time and even die being called immigrants.[68] The most important aim is therefore to promote the integration of the Castilian-speaking population, to include them into the Catalan nationalist project and hence try to avoid that a major part of the Catalan society opposes the idea of a distinct Catalan nation and identity. A representative of the CiU agrees with that vision of the current situation:

"There is a major part of this immigrant population that has integrated itself well and that therefore had the possibilities of economic advancement and possibilities to relate with the autochthonous culture, and these people, well, today form part and integrate themselves in this process of national freedom. And there is a part of the population, well, that has maintained its position, let's say, more in certain neighbourhoods, its language and so on. And I believe it is this population that at the moment has most difficulties and moreover, what to us seems perfectly logic and natural to understand, well, some historic positions of nationalism."[69]

The debate about the recent immigration from non-EU member states to Catalonia is crucially linked to these considerations about past migratory movements. Catalan politicians compare both migration movements highlighting the differences and the challenges the "new" immigration comes along with. The Plan of Immigration 2001-2004 states, for instance, that "it is no longer an internal immigration within a state having the same legislation, religious or

---

[67] P71: CAT-Opp-Speech Carod-Rovira ERC 22-04-2003.rtf-[Però només tindrem possibilita...] (6:6).
[68] See P71: CAT-Opp-Speech Carod-Rovira ERC 22-04-2003.rtf-[És hora ja de posar fi al disc...] (15:15).
[69] Interview: CAT-7 Representative CiU, 2005.

familiar affinities."[70] Also the subsequent Plan of Immigration 2005-2008 compares internal migration movements to the current non-EU immigration:

"In the past quarter of the century, the character of immigration has been very different. Even though many current migration processes have their roots in the past, there are new elements. As especially relevant for the demographic dynamic, the beginning of a new migration coming from abroad stands out."[71]

The latest immigration is described as being more complex, diverse and heterogeneous than the internal immigration in terms of origin, culture, language, customs, social class, etc.[72] Diversity and heterogeneity must be considered planning integration and social policy measures.[73] The integration of such a heterogeneous immigrant community is therefore presented as a complex task, even more so in view of the still unsettled differences with the prior interior Castilian-speaking migration.

The concern that non-Catalan-speaking immigration could possibly weaken what is defined as the Catalan identity appears hence also in statements about the recent immigration of very diverse origin. Pujol, for instance, points out that current immigration does not mean the same for Catalonia than for other autonomous communities, because in Catalonia it is much more important regarding its own collective personality.[74] Artur Mas, one of the CiU leaders, states that "the new African, Asian, Latin American and Eastern European immigration is at the same time an opportunity for the progress of the country and a threat to its identity".[75] A Catalan Member of Parliament even argues that the future of Catalonia as a nation and of its distinct identity could be in danger, because of immigration.[76] Pujol resumes these preoccupations in the following rhetorical questions:

---

[70] P38: pla Immigració 2001-2004.rtf-[Ja no és una immigració intern...] (5108: 5109).
[71] P39: Pla Immigració 2005-2008 I.rtf-[El caràcter de la immigració e...] (144: 145).
[72] See P89: Auszüge-DSCP-P-058 27-06-2001.rtf-[l'heterogeneïtat del que massa...] (383: 391).
[73] See P94: Auszüge-DSCP-P-088-089 29 u. 30-05-2002.rtf-[saber que no hi ha un únic per...] (2559: 2563).
[74] See P74: CAT-Opp-Speech Pujol CIU 10-11-2004.rtf [En el cas de Catalunya el tema...] (432:438).
[75] P68: CAT-Gov-Speech Artur Mas CIU 21-10-2002.rtf-[La nova immigració, africana...] (87:87).
[76] See P101: Auszüge DSCP-P 012 05-05-2004.rtf-[ens hi juguem el nostre futur...] (97:100).

"Now, for example, with the new immigration the question appears if we believe or if we do not believe in what we are. Is it worth to make an effort to keep on being what we are? Do we believe that Catalonia is valuable enough and of enough quality so that it is positive for the ones who come from abroad? So finally considering all that, is it worth defending the social model, the living together and the identity? Or do we want to be nothing? Do we want to be only a disintegrated group?"[77]

The fear of a disintegration of the Catalan society is formulated also by Socialist politicians presenting migration as a challenge or even a threat to social cohesion, whereas the term "social cohesion" implies the existence of a distinct Catalan "We-group". Catalonia does still exist because it has been able to preserve the community cohesion around a common national project.[78]

The recent immigration from non-EU-countries is thought to challenge the social cohesion, because it settles mostly in urban areas where the underprivileged Catalan population lives. This creates a high potential for social conflict, because the immigrants are perceived by many Catalans as competing with them for public services:

"The immigrated population –the regularized as well as the ones who are not– tends to concentrate intensely in certain neighbourhoods, villages and cities. This concentration makes the handling of this major social phenomenon, which especially affects the most underprivileged autochthonous citizens, very difficult. Furthermore, the presence of many tenthousands of people without documents plants a situation of risk to the welfare, the life-together, and the collective security."[79]

Many of the former interior migrants form also part of these lower classes and settle also in those urban areas where housing is not too expensive. As already mentioned, the "new" immigrants, underprivileged too, tend to settle in the same neighbourhoods. Maragall, PSC, describes the risk of social conflicts that lies in the competition between "old" and "new" immigrants:

"The non-EU immigration has sent a signal to our interior immigrants of the 1970s, in the sense that their conquests are precarious, they are more precarious than they thought them to be. The neighbourhoods of the former immigration

---

[77] P59: CAT-Gov-Pres-Pujol 10-09-2001.rtf-[Ara, per exemple, amb la nova…] (20:22).
[78] See Gil Araujo (2007): *Las argucias de la integración*, p. 219.
[79] P79: Auszüge PSC Wahlprogramm Katalonien 2003.rtf-[La población inmigrada –tanto…] (18:24).

today are the setting for the arrival of the non-EU immigrants. And suddenly the whole past of suffering is present again. The right, both from the Spanish as from the Catalan nationalism has understood that here is a tender spot and has in some moments (Law of Aliens, xenophobic declarations in Catalonia) become more extreme in their positions of rejection against the new."[80]

Likewise a PPC Member of Parliament highlighted that "it is not a problem of borders, it is not a problem of quota, it is a problem of social conflict". Furthermore, the Parliamentarian demanded action from the government which disposed of the necessary responsibilities to prevent the eruption of social conflicts due to situations of social competition.[81]

As on the central state level there are also statements of Catalan politicians that present immigration not only as a challenge but also allude to it as something threatening. Representatives of the Catalan section of the PP picked up the argument found in the central state discourse of the PP of the limited capacity to receive immigrants. In PPC's electoral manifesto for 2003 elections the party explains that "our capacity of reception is not unlimited" and claims "to adapt immigration to our real capacity of reception".[82]

Immigration is thus presented by Catalan politicians, particularly the Socialists as posing a threat to "social cohesion" if not handled well enough and predominantly by Catalan nationalists as posing a threat to "Catalan identity".

The statements describing immigration as a challenge are for the most part meant to emphasize the importance of an active integration policy. Two approaches to handle the challenges immigration comes along with could be found in Catalan political discourse about migration: on the one hand a social policy approach to deal with the challenges to social cohesion and Catalan civic identity and on the other hand a cultural policy approach dealing with the challenges immigration poses to the cultural elements of Catalan identity. Neither can they be attributed exclusively to a certain political spectrum or party, nor be separated totally from each other as they are finally based on the same underlying assumption of a distinct Catalan identity which must be preserved and strengthened. In chapter vii.5.2 and vii.5.3, the underlying concepts of Cata-

[80] P17: CAT-Opp-Article Maragall PSC 29-06-2001.rtf-[La inmigración extracomunitari...] (22:22).
[81] P94: Auszüge-DSCP-P-088-089 29 u. 30-05-2002.rtf-[no és un problema de fronteres...] (2386:2389).
[82] P77: Auszüge PP Wahlprogramm Katalonien 2003.rtf-[considera imprescindible respe...] (55:73).

lan national identity, including civic and cultural elements will be explained in detail.

5.2 The construction of cultural identity

Catalan politicians, particularly from a nationalist perspective (CiU and ERC) tend to link the debate about immigration and the integration of immigrants explicitly to the question of cultural national identity, as Adela Ros, Secretary for Immigration, points out.[83] As we have seen above, immigration is presented as a challenge and sometimes even as a threat to the distinct Catalan identity, defined as the collective identity based on a cultural foundation, which is first and foremost the Catalan language.

As a result it is thought to be necessary to protect and strengthen the elements defined to form the Catalan culture. Pujol, the mentor of Catalan moderate nationalism, argues that Catalonia, even more than other countries, has to consider its own national identity in view of the challenges immigration poses.[84] He claims that

> "The recipients have the right to see their identity guaranteed. Even including the pre-eminence of their identity. If not one day immigrants represent 80 per cent of the population, and the country has undergone an absolutely radical change, which is not the case now. If not, the right on its identity and even the pre-eminence of its identity should be guaranteed. They have the right."[85]

Therefore, Catalan nationalists propagate the defence and the fortification of "our way to be a collective, our identity". CiU leader, Artur Mas, considers this, however, in the long run to be a difficult project.[86]

In Catalan migration discourse many statements were found that reflect such an identity political approach vis-à-vis the immigration of non-Catalan speaking people. In the following, the predominant frames of the construction of a cultural Catalan identity, language and religion are presented.

---

[83] See P12: CAT-Gov-Artículo Adela Ros ERC 03-09-2004.rtf-[En Cataluña, el debate de la i...] (9:9).

[84] See P67: CAT-Gov-Pres-Pujol 27-07-2001.rtf-[Para ir un poco más allá en el...] (24:24).

[85] P56: CAT-Gov-Pres-Pujol 04-07-2000.rtf-[Los receptores tienen derecho...] (71:71).

[86] P2: CAT-Gov-Article-Entrevista Artur Mas CiU 27-10-2003.rtf-[a estos dos grandes objetivos...] (4:5).

5.2.1 *Language*

Pujol's famous definition that a Catalan is who lives and works in Catalonia and speaks Catalan is still an important guideline in immigration and integration policy. Carod Rovira, ERC-President, for instance, emphasizes that "in Madrid a Castilian-speaking Ecuadorian will always be an immigrant. Here, if he makes the step and speaks Catalan, he will be Catalan, he will be from here, will be seen like one of us".[87]

Language is widely accepted as the basic element of a distinctive Catalan identity (see III.6).[88] Catalonia is hence defined as the country where Catalan is spoken.[89] Not only for the nationalist parties, such as CiU and ERC, but also for the Catalan Socialists, language constitutes an essential element of Catalan collective identity. A PSC Member of Parliament argues that "We are defined by the will to form a community regardless from where you come. And as a nucleus, language".[90]

Catalan is presented by nationalists, in opposition to Castilian, as the traditional language. Pujol, for instance, argues that "today, with the new democratic Spanish Constitution the existence of two languages, Castilian and Catalan is recognized. Two official languages, nevertheless only one of them, Catalan qualifies as 'proper'".[91]

Artur Mas, his successor as president of the CiU, affirms likewise the status difference of Catalan in comparison to Castilian:

> "What happens is that the knowledge of Castilian, a common, a shared patrimony, even an ambit of universal interest for Catalonia should not be confounded with something that could alter the quintessence of a nation which is based on cultural characteristics, amongst them ones language. If anything makes us clearly different from a cultural point of view, it is our language. And therefore there can only be one."[92]

---

[87] P71: CAT-Opp-Speech Carod-Rovira ERC 22-04-2003.rtf-[A Madrid, un equatorià, parlan...] (25:25).

[88] See P74: CAT-Opp-Speech Pujol CIU 10-11-2004.rtf-[Atrevim-nos a fer una aproxima...] (392:412).

[89] See P15: CAT-Opp-Article-Entrevista Carod-rovira ERC 27-10-2003.rtf-[que Cataluña a de ser, evident...] (12:12).

[90] Interview: CAT-6 Member of Parliament-PSC, 2005.

[91] P63: CAT-Gov-Pres-Pujol 21-06-2001.rtf-[Sortosament, la societat catal...] (31:31).

[92] P2: CAT-Gov-Article-Entrevista Artur Mas CiU 27-10-2003.rtf-[Mas. Por la misma razón por la...] (52:53).

A CiU representative explained in an interview that Catalan, Castilian or Galician are all Spanish languages and could therefore be called Spanish. He suggests thus to conceptualize Spain detached from the historic image of Castile.[93]

Learning Catalan is thought to be the best way to integrate newcomers into the Catalan Society. It is presented as the "language of opportunities" which facilitates among other things the incorporation into the labour market. Carod Rovira, refers to the still existing imbalance in higher positions between Catalans with Catalan roots and Catalans with Castilian roots:

> "The sectors linked to this Castilian-speaking immigration from earlier decades were able to open up ways to personally prosper in different areas, but neither in the economy, nor in politics have they acquired a general status of power on the national level which could be clearly identified as such. Individual cases, we can all think of, are these: individuals, the example that can be related for their singularity which can not be extrapolated to a more general ambit as a social phenomenon. In Catalonia the power is still in the hands of those who always have had it. Some authochtonous sectors of the upper class, often related among each other with many family, friendship and other connections which are well distributed over almost the whole political party system."[94]

His fellow party member, Josep Bargalló thus claims to encourage the knowledge and the use of Catalan as a language that erases differences of origin and opens up opportunities.[95] According to a CiU Member of Parliament therefore "the Catalan way of integrating immigrants should be to promote programmes of reception geared to language abilities and to the knowledge about the Catalan society".[96]

Basically, this language oriented approach in integration policy has not changed much in the last two decades and must be seen in the context of linguistic "normalization" policy and thus the defence of Catalan identity versus Spanish identity (see chapter III.6.4 about the linguistic "normalization"). The following extract from the Plan of Immigration 2005-2008 shows the continu-

---

[93] See Interview: CAT-7 Representative-CiU, 2005.
[94] P71: CAT-Opp-Speech Carod-Rovira ERC 22-04-2003.rtf-[Els sectors vinculats a aquell...] (8:9).
[95] See P10: CAT-Gov-Article Josep Bargalló ERC 30-06-2005.rtf-[S'incentiva la participació i...] (14:14).
[96] P100: Auszüge DSCP-P 011 21-04-2004.rtf-100:4 [La via catalana per a la integ...] (49:58).

ity in the linguistic policy of the *Generalitat* regardless of the political party in government:

"Defence of the Catalan language and identity as the identity of the Catalan residents. Every policy of equality and of accommodation of the citizens residing in Catalonia is a linguistic policy. To assure the practice of the Catalan language as the proper vehicle of social, economic, political and cultural communication is one of the basic government objectives. That the language of daily use is Catalan can foster their integration. In the same way, it very much helps their institutional recognition that Catalan is the language of the immigrant associations, and their endeavour to enable immigration to make a positive contribution to normalization must be regarded as highly positive. Catalan has the opportunity to be the language of everyday communications for the new residents in Catalonia. It is a decisive moment. Already we count with thousands of new speakers of the proper language of Catalonia."[97]

The plan more or less implicitly presents the objective of linguistic "normalization", namely to qualify more and more people as Catalan-speakers and to strengthen the language community which at the same time means to strengthen Catalonia as a whole. That the Catalan language community needs to be strengthened unlike the Castilian-speaking community is, according to Pujol, indispensable because "a language that is spoken by four hundred million people is very different from a language that is spoken by ten million".[98] With respect to immigration, Carod Rovira states that "we have to win the new immigration for the Catalan language, as it is also a way to guarantee its future incrementing considerably the number of Catalan-speakers".[99]

5.2.2 *Religion*

In the last two decades of the Franco regime opposition grew under the auspices of parts of the Catholic Church in Catalonia. The most famous example is Jordi Pujol himself who started in the Catholic youth movement and became the mastermind of moderate nationalist ideology. Therefore the nationalist discourse of CiU still reflects this roots, and Christian tradition and origin, or more particularly the Catholic Church is seen as a crucial element of the formation

---

[97] P39: Pla Immigració 2005-2008 I.rtf-[Defensa de la llengua i identi...] (502:510).
[98] P60: CAT-Gov-Pres-Pujol 11-03-2002.rtf-[Som un país, primer, petit, qu...] (61:62).
[99] P4: CAT-Gov-Article Carod-Rovira ERC 20-01-2004.rtf-[Hem de guanyar la nova immigra...] (11:11).

of Catalan identity. Duran i Lleida, one of the CiU leaders, for instance, states: "Well, furthermore religion has shaped 2000 years of our history and, especially, the performance of the Catholic Church is indispensable for understanding our personality and our historic consciousness".[100]

Besides the particular Catholic tradition of Catalonia, Pujol joins the debate led by conservatives in different European countries about the Christian origin of the European Civilization when he argues that

"leaving aside the strictly religious issue and speaking of what there is –this is what does count for everyone–, that is the civilization of Christian origin, and all the European values are of Christian origin, and these are the values we think are important, don't you think?"[101]

As to the concrete immigration and integration policy Catalan politicians, particularly ERC representatives, on the one hand defend laicism with respect to all public affairs and on the other hand religious and cultural pluralism in the private sphere. Carod Rovira is convinced that

"The respect of laicism, its defence and its application, all this recognizing religious pluralism, is an indispensable requisite for the civil living together and our demo-cratic standard of living. Public education must be laicist education. One thing is the teaching of religious culture, positive and desirable for everybody, and another thing is catechesis, indoctrination, at the same hours others study ethics, as though it would was not a shared patrimony for everyone, believing or not. Religion thus, outside school hours, at home or in religious institutions."[102]

Therefore ERC has promoted in government the application of politics to deal with both, cultural pluralism and laicity within Catalan society.[103] In their electoral manifest for the elections of 2003 they explained the need to

"promote a pact for laicity with the religious denominations through the establish-ment of skeleton agreements between the Generalitat and the major religious com-

---

[100] P42: CAT-Gov-Conference Duran i Lleida CIU 25-10-2001.rtf-42:10 [Alhora, també el fet re-ligiós...] (225:236).

[101] P64: CAT-Gov-Pres-Pujol 22-06-2001.rtf-[Hi ha gent que diu: «Escolta...] (71:73).

[102] P70: CAT-Opp-Conference Carod-Rovira ERC 04-06-2002.rtf-[Tenint en compte que un de cad...] (37:41).

[103] See P10: CAT-Gov-Article Josep Bargalló ERC 30-06-2005.rtf-[S'incentiva la participació i...] (14:14).

munities during the next years to fix the religious rights and freedoms in Catalonia and to its limits."[104]

There is another argument linking the origin of immigrants and their potential for integration that reflects the importance of language and religious background as elements of a Catalan identity. In the central state migration discourse politicians argued that the integration of Latin Americans and Romanians was much easier due to their similar religious, cultural and linguistic background (see VI.5.2). In Catalan migration discourse this argument has varied slightly. Pujol resumed the particular situation in Catalonia in a speech in 2004: "On the other hand our immigration is more difficult to integrate, because it is partly Muslim, and partly because the South American immigration can not be integrated as easily as in the rest of the state".[105]

A few years earlier, Pujol had already explicated the difficulties he saw for the integration of Moroccan immigrants:

"If you speak with political and religious Moroccan leaders, you know perfectly well that many of them say: 'Listen, if integration means for you that our people pay Spanish tributes and taxes, it is fine with us. If integration means for you that our people intermarry with your people, no.' And this is what people tell you, I won't name them, who today and also in the past have been very important in Morocco, in politics and religion."[106]

However, in Catalonia also the integration of Latin Americans is seen as more problematic than in other parts of Spain. This is mainly because of the distinct language Catalonia has. A PSC Member of Parliament believes that in Catalonia therefore a certain attitude exists perceiving immigration, moreover the Latin American immigration, as a threat to Catalan identity.[107]

---

[104] P80: ERC Wahlprogramm-Migration Katalonien 2003.rtf-[Promoure un Pacte per a la laï...] (293:294); See also P94: Auszüge-DSCP-P-088-089 29 u. 30-05-2002.rtf-[És urgent, particularment, un...] (63:68).

[105] P74: CAT-Opp-Speech Pujol CIU 10-11-2004.rtf-[Però per Espanya el problema n...] (78:92).

[106] P74: CAT-Opp-Speech Pujol CIU 10-11-2004.rtf-[Però per Espanya el problema n...] (78:92).

[107] See Interview: CAT-6 Member of Parliament-PSC, 2005.

5.3 The construction of civic identity

Apart from the above described cultural elements, language and religion, Catalan national identity is defined in political discourse about immigration and immigrant integration as a civic national identity, and membership is not ascribed by means of ethnic origin. The official language use exemplifies this, as it is strikingly neutral and inclusive when it comes to immigrants. In the Catalan political migration discourse, immigrants are neutrally referred to as "people from abroad"[108] or "people who come from abroad"[109] or "newcomers".[110] Designations such as "Catalans born abroad",[111] "new Catalans",[112] "new population",[113] and "new citizens"[114] are examples for the inclusive diction in statements of Catalan politicians.

Another indication for a civic conception of the Catalan nation, particularly on part of the governing *Tripartit*, is that the integration of immigrants is primarily treated as a matter of social policy.

5.3.1 *The integration of immigrants, social policy*

Integration policy is described as to be bound to certain principles. The first principle should be to reach a maximum consensus of all political actors in the field of immigration and immigrant integration. Similar to the central state level also Catalan political parties claim the

> "need to work on the basis of a social and political consensus about the policies and actions that affect immigration, and not to make immigration an instrument of political confrontation nor of electoral campaigns thereby prejudicing living together. We believe that only like that we can work in favour of immigration and of social cohesion."[115]

---

[108] P4: CAT-Gov-Article Carod-Rovira ERC 20-01-2004.rtf-[Per aquest motiu, els nostres...] (9:9).

[109] P74: CAT-Opp-Speech Pujol CIU 10-11-2004.rtf-[Catalunya històricament ha est...] (17:19).

[110] P89: Auszüge-DSCP-P-058 27-06-2001.rtf-[la necessitat d'articular polí...] (98:99).

[111] P10: CAT-Gov-Article Josep Bargalló ERC 30-06-2005.rtf-[catalans nascuts fora del país...] (14:14).

[112] P10: CAT-Gov-Article Josep Bargalló ERC 30-06-2005.rtf-[els nous catalans] (14:14).

[113] P10: CAT-Gov-Article Josep Bargalló ERC 30-06-2005.rtf-[El Govern ha elaborat un Pla d...] (14:14).

[114] P12: CAT-Gov-Artículo Adela Ros ERC 03-09-2004.rtf-[nuevos ciudadanos] (9:9).

[115] P85: Auszüge-DSCP-P-045 21-02-2001.rtf-[necessitat de treballar des de...] (124:130).

A CiU Member of Parliament agrees with his PSC colleague and claims of the government to "make consensual politics to advance jointly in an area which is most important for the future of our nation."[116]

The second is the principle of subsidiarity or in Catalan "proximitat al territory" which describes the need to act as close to the population in need of administrational action as possible.

And the third principle is that integration policy is an integral and transversal policy field which means

> "not to integrate all immigration policies in a sole department, but, precisely try not to treat the services immigrants receive differently and therefore, to have integral policies from the different departments responsible for the respective policy fields within the *Generalitat*. This is exactly what the government of Catalonia does and, from the Department of the Presidency it coordinates the compound of those immigrant attending policies."[117]

The particular integration policy forms thus part of a broader social policy concept. This corresponds to the idea of avoiding a "system of parallel structures which could provoke and perpetuate situations of segregation". Immigrants are therefore attended within the framework of existing institutions, programmes and services.[118]

Immigration and immigrant integration are further transversal, crosscutting policy issues which include many different aspects. The Plan for Immigration 2001-2004, as well as the subsequent plan (2005-2008) thus postulated the cooperation and collaboration in immigration issues of various departments of the *Generalitat*, such as education, social services, housing, and health.[119] In 2000 the Secretary's office for Immigration was established, and later incorporated in the Department for Social Welfare, to coordinate the programmes and measures regarding immigration and immigrant integration.

As we have seen above, immigration is described as holding the potential for social conflicts, because the local population could perceive the newcomers as

---

[116] P100: Auszüge DSCP-P 011 21-04-2004.rtf-[hi hagués unes polítiques de c...] (19:24).
[117] P87: Auszüge-DSCP-P-050 19-04-2001.rtf-[no integrar totes les polítiqu...] (56:64).
[118] P96: Auszüge-DSCP-P-114 13-02-2003.rtf-[Tenim un model que no ha apost...] (852:857).
[119] See P38: pla Immigració 2001-2004.rtf-[Transversalitat (horitzontalit...] (5627:5632); P39: Pla Immigració 2005-2008 I.rtf-[11.El repte de la immigració h...] (534:534).

212   MIGRATION AND THE CONSTRUCTION OF NATIONAL IDENTITY IN SPAIN

a competition for public and social services. Besides, social segregation of immigrants is mentioned as having the potential to result in conflicts.[120]

To prevent such conflicts and the emergence of discord between immigrants and the local population, Catalan politicians therefore focus on social policy measures from which all people residing in Catalonia would benefit. As a IC-V Member of Parliament put it:

> "We therefore name things by using terms with which we are able to deal with the conflict from a perspective of social cohesion, because our society is plural and will be more and more plural, and that is why everyone who encourages fragmentations based on a perspective that primarily states that immigrants cause difficulties is redirecting the problem towards a malaise of our society that is not created by the immigrants."[121]

In its coalition agreement 2003 the *Tripartit* government has committed itself therefore to strengthen the social policy for everybody to improve the well-being and to assure the social cohesion avoiding all kind of discrimination that could result from a lack of resources in this area.[122] Josep Bargalló, ERC, explains this approach as "politics in favour of the quality of life for the vast majority, in favour of the equality of opportunities for everybody, in favour of the extension of the democratic rights and obligations for all citizens, without any discrimination".[123]

In consequence, it became necessary to provide more money for social policy measures. This is where the fund for integration the central state government has set up is able to make an important contribution to regional and local integration policy.[124]

Also the implication of NGOs, associations of the civil society and representatives of the immigrants themselves in the planning and implementation of integration policy is absolutely necessary. Both Plans for Immigration (2001-2004 and 2005-2008) and hence both, the CiU government and the PSC led

---

[120] See P1: CAT- Opp-Article Joan Saura 09-03-2001.rtf-[El problema de la ola migrator...] (11:11).

[121] P94: Auszüge-DSCP-P-088-089 29 u. 30-05-2002.rtf-[Plantegem les coses, per tant...] (1315:1323).

[122] See P37: Auszüge Koalitionsvertrag Tripartit 12-2003.rtf-[Reforçar les polítiques social...] (28:30).

[123] P 8: CAT-Gov-Article Josep Bargalló ERC 11-09-2004.rtf-[És a dir, polítiques a favor d...] (14:14).

[124] See chapter III.2.2.4.

government attribute importance to the collaboration and the contribution of all social and economic actors to respond to the challenges immigration goes along with.[125]

In concrete, two particular issues appear in the analysed statements: On the one hand the incorporation of immigrants into the Catalan labour market and on the other hand the promotion of immigrant participation.

Already in 2001 the parliamentary commission argued in its report that

"The occupational insertion is a key element for the integration. To have a paid job is the principal element for many for their integration into the community. Precarious situations generate instability of the person and of the society."[126]

The Plan for Immigration 2005-2008 refers likewise to the crucial role occupation plays in the process of integration as an important opportunity to participate in social life.[127]

It further aims at encouraging the participation of the immigrants themselves in "all aspects of the democratic processes and in the formulation of the policies and measures for their benefit".[128] Immigration participation is understood as an important part of the integration process. That is why

"the incorporation into the different spheres of society, into the institutions of participation and the normalization of the presence of immigrants in the media, in the public sphere and in Catalan institutions will be promoted. The participation of the citizens with foreign origin through the associations of groups with foreign origin as active agents should increase it."[129]

---

[125] See P38: pla Immigració 2001-2004.rtf-[Coresponsabilitat amb els agen...] (5638:5643), (5599:5602); P39: Pla Immigració 2005-2008 I.rtf-[Les actuacions del Govern no p...] (517:517).

[126] P119: Auszüge BOPC-197-18-06-2001 Document Comissió d'Estudi.rtf-[La inserció laboral és un elem...] (789:793).

[127] See P39: Pla Immigració 2005-2008 I.rtf-[L'ocupació constitueix una par...] (525:525); See also P12: CAT-Gov-Artículo Adela Ros ERC 03-09-2004.rtf-[Nuestros esfuerzos tienen que...] (12:12).

[128] P39: Pla Immigració 2005-2008 I.rtf-[10.La integració també és afav...] (533:533).

[129] P39: Pla Immigració 2005-2008 I.rtf-[10.La integració també és afav...] (533:533).

5.3.2 *Catalan citizenship and multiple identities*

Besides the social policy perspective, Catalan politicians emphasize other civic dimensions aiming at immigrants who identify with Catalonia and become Catalan citizens.

Like on the central state level also in Catalonia the argument of "rights and obligations" was discussed across political parties, however in reference to Catalonia and not to Spain as a whole (see VI.5.2). The discussion was guided by the reference to the constitutional and legal norms and explicitly calls for a mutual effort on both sides.

Most prominently CiU has claimed that immigrants must have rights and obligations, especially stressing the latter. In the context of the debate about the reform of the Law on Aliens on central state level, Pujol declared that it must not be forgotten to talk about obligations while discussing immigrants' rights:

> "I very much insist on rights, but we hardly speak of obligations, because it is of poor taste or it is not nice or unpopular. The generalized tendency of politicians to prevent these aspects impedes us to speak of obligations, but this is a big mistake we will pay for if we do not rectify it. It is necessary to speak of obligations of our people with respect to immigration, but also the other way round."[130]

A representative of the CiU in parliament explains what he thinks that immigrants are obliged to do, namely to respect the Catalan values, such as laicism, democracy, cultural pluralism, and gender equality.[131] Miret adds: "Compliance with the law within the framework of a democratic state".[132]

In 2002 the ERC, by then in opposition, introduced the law on the "Carta d'acolliment" (Letter of reception) in the Catalan Parliament.[133] The idea of this law was

> "to regulate the reception of newcomers to Catalonia with the purpose to inform them, consult and orient them about their rights and obligations, so that their

---

[130] P56: CAT-Gov-Pres-Pujol 04-07-2000.rtf-56:18 [Insisto mucho en los derechos...] (70:70).

[131] See P94: Auszüge-DSCP-P-088-089 29 u. 30-05-2002.rtf-[I aquí la gent del país en def...] (1705:1722).

[132] P18: CAT-Opp-Article Miret i Serra CIU 04-11-2005.rtf-[Compliment de la llei en el ma...] (7:7).

[133] See P120: Auszüge BOPC-368-10-12-2002 Carta d'acolliment.rtf-[ARTICLE 15. DRETS I DEURES DE ...] (452:475).

civic, occupational, social, cultural, and economic integration is protected and assisted by the public Catalan authorities."[134]

In statements of PSC politicians also the reference to rights and obligations was found, however, more balanced and stressing primarily the promotion of equality:

> "A discourse of progress has to reject all affirmations that state that the identity differences form a 'natural' and rigid line of separation between the people and it must postulate with determination the radical equality of all citizens in rights and obligations as an irrevocably principle."[135]

Integration is consequently defined in the Plan of Immigration 2005-2008 as a "bidirectional process, a dynamic and continuous mutual adjustment between the immigrants and autochthons".[136]

The target group of measures for a better integration of immigrants is hence not only the immigrant community itself but also the already established population. The positive aspects, such as their economic contribution should be highlighted and the customs and traditions should be explained to increase the acceptance of the immigrant population within the autochthonous population. Montilla, PSC leader, suggests

> "a policy based on reality means to educate in civic attitudes, in living together and in diversity all those who are already here and those who are coming, conscious that the immigration as old as history contributes to a major ethnic, cultural and religious diversity which we all together have to learn to deal with."[137]

The PSC led *Tripartit* has moreover introduced a new concept of citizenship with its Plan of Immigration 2005-2008. The idea is to treat immigrants as citizens of Catalonia with the same rights and obligations as all Catalan citizens. This new concept must be seen as the intent of inventing a Catalan citizenship in addition to Spanish citizenship. The former is open to all immigrants whereas

---

[134] P120: Auszüge BOPC-368-10-12-2002 Carta d'acolliment.rtf-[L'objecte d'aquesta llei és re...] (124:130).

[135] P79: Auszüge PSC Wahlprogramm Katalonien 2003.rtf-[Un discurso de progreso tiene...] (280:283).

[136] P39: Pla Immigració 2005-2008 I.rtf-[La integració és un procés bid...] (523:524).

[137] P19: CAT-Opp-Article Montilla PSC 2002.rtf-[Una política de realidades pas...] (38:38).

the latter is regulated by law and intrinsically tied to nationality. Contrary to the Spanish nationality that is given only to immigrants fulfilling certain requirements and in many cases not until they have resided legally for more than ten years in Spain, the Catalan citizenship requires only the inscription in the registers of the local authorities. This is sufficient, because "the inscription in the local registers expresses the will of the immigrant to settle in Catalonia and to share the existing public space without any distinction with its inhabitants already resident".[138] According to that, Catalan citizenship is linked to *de facto* residence and detached from the conventional sense of nationality. All this is developed from the norms of a public spirit which should be the "basic norm that orients the relations between people, no matter what their language of origin, their culture, religion and colour of skin might be".[139]

This conception of a Catalan citizenship picks up the idea of multiple identities which has been used frequently to describe the reality of a Catalonia where a high percentage of citizens stem from the Castilian-speaking immigration.

For instance, Carod Rovira, ERC, points out that individuals move within different collective identities depending on the situational context:

> "It is true that there are Catalans who are not at the same time Spanish but there are many who are, and there is no reason for them to stop being it. We cannot ask anyone to stop being what he used to be and to become or be a Catalan, and we therefore for the future will have to think of a country in which we live together, we that we are Catalans from a national point of view –and who do not claim any other adscription- with those who apart from their national condition as Catalans have others too."[140]

Although Carod Rovira doesn't explicitly cite them, he implicitly refers to the surveys where the people living in Catalonia were asked if they felt more Spanish, more Catalan, both equally or one or the other exclusively (see III.1.6.4).

The statement of Carod Rovira reflects furthermore that Catalan nationalists have understood that in view of the heterogeneous origins of people living in Catalonia the only way to defend and promote a distinct Catalan identity is to strengthen it while accepting the identification with multiple and nested col-

---

[138] P39: Pla Immigració 2005-2008 I.rtf-[En aquest context és important...] (418:462).
[139] See P39: Pla Immigració 2005-2008 I.rtf-[En aquest context és important...] (418:462).
[140] P15: CAT-Opp-Article-Entrevista Carod-rovira ERC 27-10-2003.rtf-[Esto implica seguramente cambi...] (13:13).

lective identities. It is thus not important that people identify exclusively with Catalan national identity, but that they identify with it at all.

5.4 Future expectations

Regarding Catalonia's future Catalan politicians wish for an open, plural society where equality of rights and obligations can be found. Defining the foundations of the new Statute of Autonomy, CiU, declares that "the final objective is a plural society, but sharing essential collective values".[141]

Likewise the PSC led government states in its Plan of Immigration 2005-2008 that

> "From now on we aspire a socially articulated society on the basis of the principle of equality, with a open and plural political and cultural project. It is an optimistic approach, which perceives the current migratory processes as a new opportunity to work on a Catalan society with future projection, stimulated by the tradition to receive immigrants."[142]

Piqué, leader of the Catalan PP, said in an interview that he wished Catalonia to recuperate a series of characteristics he believed it had lost over time. Catalonia should again be a pioneer, an advanced society open to the new, to external influences, prepared to take risks and to accept the opportunities modern and advanced societies have in the 21st century.[143] Similar to that, Duran i Lleida, CiU leader, claims that Catalonia shall become a leading region within Europe:

> "I imagine and wish a leading Catalonia to be a European point of reference. I know that we will not be a state despite of how much some try to confuse their electorate. Therefore, our leadership in the European Union cannot be so much political, but in the social ambit, in the field of education and formation, in the model of living together that synthesises identity and globalization as two sides of the same coin."[144]

---

[141] P36: Auszüge Bases per a un nou Estatut 04-2003.rtf-[L'objectif final est une socié...] (24:26).

[142] P39: Pla Immigració 2005-2008 I.rtf-39:15 [D'aquí que aspirem a una socie...] (413:413).

[143] See P3: CAT-Gov-Article-Entrevista Piqué PP 28-10-2003.rtf-[deseo una Cataluña que vuelva...] (3:3).

[144] P21: CAT-Gov-Entrevista Duran i Lleida CIU El País 12-11-2003.rtf-[Me imagino y deseo una Cataluñ...] (46:46).

In summary, the political discourse about migration and the integration of non-EU immigrants in Catalonia is dominated by the assumptions of a moderate nationalist ideology. It is therefore the Catalan society not the Spanish, politicians refer to when talking about the integration of immigrants. The Catalan nation is, moreover, defined as a civic nation with a strong cultural bias. To be more accurate, membership is defined in political discourse not by means of ethnic origin, but by means of civic elements and language knowledge. In the following chapter the results of the analysis of central state and Catalan discourse are presented with respect to the different constructions of national identity in Spain.

VIII.
Conclusions

The analysis of the political discourse on immigration and immigrant' integration on both, the central state and the Catalan level has shown that migration
discourse and the inner Spanish debate about the different national identities
are closely interlinked, both are processes of "multiculturalism".[1] The construction of national identity in Spain thus takes place within a complex context of
different "Others". From a central state perspective the peripheral nationalist
movements in the Basque Country, Galicia and Catalonia which struggle for
the recognition of their national identity and for broader autonomy are "Others". Vice versa the construction of a culturally homogeneous Spanish nation is
perceived by these movements as a threatening "Other". In addition, immigration from different Spanish regions became in Catalonia already in the first half
of the twentieth century and particularly from the 1950s onwards an "Other"
which challenged the distinct Catalan national identity and released a fundamental debate about how to best deal with it.

Spain as a whole has experienced within the last fifteen years a radical change
from an emigration to an immigration country adding non-EU-immigrants as
yet another group of "Others". In the previous chapters political discourse was
analysed in detail to find out how national identity is constructed on the side of
minority and majority nationalism in view of these "new Others". In the following the concrete categories of national identity constructed in discourse about
immigration and their implications for the relation between the central state
and the regional level will be resumed treating central state discourse and the
Catalan discourse as two sides of a coin. Due to the research question and the
consequential selection of the empirical material the results do not reflect every
facet of neither the Catalan nationalism nor of the constructions of Spanish national identity. However, they do reveal the main tendencies of the construction
of national identity in view of immigration from non-EU-citizens and enable

---

[1] See Zapata-Barrero (2005): *Inmigración en la España plural: un debate pendiente.*

to draw conclusions regarding possible changes in the construction of national identities in Spain.

1. The construction of national identity in Spain and Catalonia

1.1 Historical dimensions

The allusion to a common past and the construction of "collective memory" is presented in academic literature as playing an important role in nation-building processes. As a consequence of Spain's particular history of the Civil War, Francoist dictatorship, and the tacit agreement not to exploit these events of the twentieth century for political confrontation, forced the political actors to search for the fundaments of the Spanish nation either in the far (Reconquista, Catholic Kings) or in the recent past since democratisation (Constitution and "State of Autonomies"). At the central state level politicians seem to mostly avoid general references to the past. Considering the support Aznar and other PP leaders provide to a specific historical view that stresses the continuity from the Spain of the Catholic Kings, the "golden age", up to today, it is astonishing that in official political discourse about migration this is barely perceptible. Instead they focus on the historical development of immigration itself. Especially the recent transformation of Spain from an emigration to an immigration country is a recurrent frame.

Unlike central state politicians who refrained from historical references when talking about migration, Catalan political discourse included general references to the nation's historical development. The construction of historical continuity of a distinct Catalan culture and language and regarding the Catalan territory and autonomy is one of the basic pillars of Catalan nationalist ideology and is also reflected in migration discourse. Besides, immigration itself has become a constituting element of Catalan identity. At central state level the integration of immigrants emerged as a public issue not until 1994. In contrast, at the Catalan level internal migrations already at the beginning of the twentieth century provoked the first writings and discussions about the presence of non-Catalan-speaking migrants.[2] Today's hegemonic version of Catalan nationalism, forged essentially by Jordi Pujol, includes the various immigration movements of the past and highlights their contribution to the present Catalan identity. To

---

[2]   See Gil Araujo (2007): *Las argucias de la integración*, p. 265.

facilitate the identification with a Catalan identity, the Castilian-speaking immigrants and their history are made part of the constructions of a common past including all Catalans.[3] This strategy to include immigrants into the Catalan society through the discursive construction of a common past is most remarkable from a German point of view. Although Germany looks back on a history of more than 50 years of immigration there are hardly any intentions to narrate German history by incorporating immigration and the immigrant's perspective. By contrast, to the Catalan collective memory Catalonia is presented as being an attractive country where people have always been drawn to, a country of immigration.[4]

1.2 Principal categories

The above presented results of the discourse analysis have shown that when asking on central state level for the main features of present-day Spanish collective identity it all comes back to the principles of democracy and the "State of Autonomies" codified in the Spanish Constitution of 1978. The dark past of Civil War and dictatorship and the lack of dealing with it properly have made it difficult to construct common collective memory on the basis of historical developments and events. The democratic political system serves therefore as the only indefeasible common denominator between all political and societal actors. Its importance has been reaffirmed constantly no matter what political issue is concerned, and consensus was emphasized as the preferred mode of political decision-making. Nevertheless, there have been, on closer inspection, differences between the political parties in the valuation of the Constitution as an expression of the Spanish nation. The Left has tended to highlight the Constitution as the fundamental constituting element of the nation, as the expression of a political nation, of a "nation of will".[5] For the Spanish right, however, the Constitution is defined as the expression of a historically and culturally defined

---

[3] For further readings on memory and reconstruction of immigrant history see Motte and Ohliger (2004): *Geschichte und Gedächtnis in der Einwanderungsgesellschaft. Migration zwischen historischer Rekonstruktion und Erinnerungspolitik*, Essen: Klartext Verlag.

[4] The Catalan administrations support efforts to keep up the memory of previous immigration from other Spanish regions to Catalonia. A good example is the creation of the "Museum of the History of Catalan Immigration", including a Centre of documentation (see http://www.mhic.net).

[5] According to the concept of Meinecke: *Staatsnation*.

nation.[6] The first concept comprehends the possibility of the co-existence of various culturally defined nations under the roof of one political nation whereas the second concept does not differentiate between cultural and political nation and therefore rules out the idea of a multinational state.

When it comes to the definition of the fundamental principles of the political system, Catalan politicians define the Catalan nation as a part of a multinational Spanish state based on the democratic Constitution of 1978 which moreover codifies the system of the "State of Autonomies" and is therefore, beside the resulting Statute of Autonomy, the main reference regarding the claims for regional self-determination.

In addition to the strong commitment to democracy, in the last decades economic development and progress have played an important role in the definition of Spain and for its positioning in the international environment. Formerly exposed by its economic backwardness, compared to other European countries, Spain has caught up and is proud of belonging nowadays, as a member of the European Union, to the developed and industrialized world. Immigration was presented predominantly as having contributed crucially to this economic growth and well-being.

The same counts for the Catalan political discourse. Moreover, economic success and progress were presented by Catalan nationalists as elements which have distinguished Catalonia from the rest of Spain during many centuries; they still form part of the Catalan identity, and strengthen Catalonia's position within the Spanish State. Due to its good economic performance Catalonia is among the leading economic regions of the European Union, as Catalan politicians are not getting tired to point out.

Apart from that, the positive economic development is also the precondition for the welfare state approach (or social policy approach), the current Catalan government and the Spanish government under Zapatero are propagating as being the best way to integrate immigrants into the Spanish and Catalan society.

In the political discourse at the central state level immigration was treated generally in a rational and prosaic manner avoiding the definition of Spanish national identity by means of cultural or ethnic categories and thus avoiding the construction of a mystifying and romanticizing image of Spain –the latter exploited by the authoritarian regime for unifying purposes. Immigration was seen primarily as an economic and labour market issue. Even negative argu-

---

[6] According to the concept of Meinecke: *Kulturnation.*

ments such as Spain's limited capacity to receive immigrants refer to an economic context or to security issues rather than to a general fear of being dominated
by other religious, ethnic and cultural influences. Although these fears may exist
in parts of the Spanish population they were usually not expressed publicly by
politicians.

The general claims of mutual approximation between both immigrants and
receiving society and the adjustment of the immigrants to Spanish society are
neither accompanied by specifications to what immigrants should adjust to nor
what the basic elements of mutual approximation should be. As the concrete
policies and measures for the integration of immigrants lie within the autonomous communities' sphere of competence, central state discourse remains vague
about their actual aims. However, the importance that is given to the integration of immigrants into the Spanish society *per se* alludes to a strong underlying self-definition of Spain as an immigration country. The only condition of
integration mentioned for Spain as a whole was the respect for the fundamental
values and norms codified in the Spanish constitution and the legal system,
mentioned above. Although not explicitly defined as basic elements of Spanish national identity, language and religion are understood implicitly as important cultural elements with respect to immigrant integration, particularly in the
Spanish right. This can be deduced from the PP statements which highlight
the easier integration of Latin Americans due to their cultural, linguistic and
religious similarities.

In contrast to the central state political discourse the integration of immigrants and especially the search for concrete premises to successful integration
has been, due to the necessity to protect and strengthen a distinct Catalan identity, an issue of political discourse in Catalonia for many decades now. The
reference frame for the integration debate has always been the Catalan society,
not the Spanish society as a whole. Moreover, current non-EU immigration is
always treated against the background of the former inner-Spanish migration
movements and the changes they have implicated for Catalonia. The arguments
and ideas about how to integrate the immigrants and make them part of the
nationalist project of Catalonia have, in spite of the radical changes in migration
movements, remained more or less the same over the years. The Catalan language is still defined as the basic element of a distinctive Catalan national identity within a Spanish state and therefore the essential element for successful immigrant integration. Furthermore, Christian tradition and the Catholic Church
are underlined to have played a crucial role in the formation and protection

of Catalan identity, especially by CiU. However, Catalan politicians agree on laicism with respect to all public and administrational affairs and institutions. Besides these elements of cultural national identity, politicians, particularly of the PSC led *Tripartit*, also stressed the need to construct a civic Catalan national identity. The social policy approach towards the integration of immigrants and the idea of a Catalan citizenship irrespective of Spanish nationality and based on the assumption of the individual's identification with multiple collective identities are expressions of such a civic conception of the Catalan nation.

To sum up, the principal category on which Spanish national identity is constructed in central state discourse about immigration is the democratic political and legal system resulting from the Spanish Constitution of 1978. The outstanding category of national identity found in political statements about immigration in Catalonia is its language, Catalan. At both governmental levels economic growth and well-being have been used to stress the strong position regarding the corresponding "Others".

1.3 "In-group" versus "Out-group"

As explained above, national identity is constructed as an "In-group" a "We", distinguishing itself from an "Other", an "Out-group". Therefore the analysis aimed not only at detecting concrete categories of national-identity constructions but also at answering the question of who is presented at each level in discourse about migration as an "Other" and who belongs to the "We-group". This is of particular interest because long before immigration became an important "Other" in Spain, the peripheral nationalist movements already based their constructions of distinct national identities within a Spanish state delimiting from the idea of a unitary Spanish nation and vice versa the Spanish right has constructed the image of a homogeneous Spanish national culture wherein peripheral nationalist ideologies represented a threat to its unity and sovereignty.

The idea that the unitary Spanish nation is threatened externally by territorial claims on the part of the Moroccan government and internally by the claims of the nationalist movements for more political autonomy, also surfaces as a leitmotif in PP statements about immigration. The defence of "national unity" thus still constitutes a basic pillar in the ideology of the Spanish Right and the peripheral nationalist movements are still perceived predominantly as a threatening internal "Other". In contrast, the PSOE, based on its different concept of the Spanish nation, at the same time supported and promoted the "State of

Autonomies", renegotiating and extending various Statutes of Autonomy, most prominently the Catalan Statute and has treated therefore nationalist claims as part of a heterogeneous "We".

From the Catalan point of view there are some areas where Catalan political discourse refers explicitly to Catalonia as part of the Spanish state, for instance when it comes to the external relations with other states or legislative projects on the central state level. In these cases Catalonia is defined as forming part of the Spanish "We". Nevertheless, in the analysed statements about immigration the delimitation from Spain and the construction of a Catalan "In-group" prevailed. The main reference frame for political discourse about immigration is not Spain, but Catalonia, even for statements of PPC politicians. Catalonia is addressed as if it were a self-contained entity. The internal migrants moving to Catalonia from other Spanish regions have been labelled immigrants, as though they had to cross an international border between Spain and Catalonia. And indeed, according to moderate Catalan nationalist ideology, the boundaries between the Autonomous Community of Catalonia and the rest of the Spanish state symbolize the boundaries that delimit the Catalan nation. Besides, also in migration discourse, claims for more political and financial autonomy played an important role.

Apart from these inner-Spanish quarrels about national identity, both Spain and Catalonia frame their position in reference to other states in political discourse about immigration. As we have seen, Spanish collective identity has always been constructed against the background or in relation to other European countries and the European Union. Statements leave no doubt about the importance that is given in Spain to its membership of the EU and therefore of the western, industrialized world. A positive and strong performance within the EU has had high priority on Spain's political agenda. Not even Aznar's intents to strengthen the transatlantic relations could change that.[7] Furthermore, Spain is seen to have a special responsibility towards the Latin American countries, because of its long colonial history and consequently offers itself as mediator between the EU and Latin America.

The fact that Catalonia maintains international relations by-passing the foreign policy of the central state authorities is another indicator that it is conceived

---

[7] See Bernecker (2007): España y la Unión Europea: una relación cambiante, in Bernecker and Maihold *España: del consenso a la polarización. Cambios en la democracia española*, Madrid/Frankfurt a. M.: Iberoamericana/Vervuert.

as an autonomous cultural nation. In political discourse about migration development cooperation is mentioned as a typical field of such autonomous political action. The promotion of Catalan culture and language abroad or economic relations with different regions of the European Union are other examples.

From these variable definitions of "In-groups" versus "Out-groups", depending on the speakers perspective, most prominent has shown to be in political discourse about immigration the explicit or implicit delimitation of the Catalan "We" from the Spanish "Other".

Immigrants are also prospective "insiders" or "outsiders", yet internal ones. The next chapter shows how on each governmental level the "We" deals with the newcomers, these new "Others". This enables us to draw further conclusions regarding the underlying concept of the respective nation.

1.4 Civic or ethnic nation?

As described above, in the central state political discourse about immigration Spain was not found to be explicitly defined by the political actors as an ethnic or cultural homogeneous nation. However, the implicit affirmation of cultural elements such as language and Catholicism by PP politicians alludes to the construction of a unitary ethno-cultural Spanish nation in the tradition of the Spanish right. On the other hand, the demonstrative positive attitude towards immigration primarily linked to economic aspects and the reference to the already existing inner-Spanish diversity and heterogeneity, which is merely enriched by immigration and not a consequence of it, alludes to a civic concept of the Spanish nation. According to this, the positions of the two major political parties at the central state level still reflect the fundamental ideological differences existing historically between the Spanish right and the left described by Nuñez Seixas.[8] Although both refer to the Spanish Constitution when asked for the fundamental elements of the Spanish nation and thus reconfirm the democratic pact, it becomes clear only at second glance that the two political parties act on different assumptions regarding the Constitution. Nevertheless, in public discourse about immigration the two major political opponents fall back on the consensual element, the Constitution of 1978 and remain vague regarding any further definition of national identity.

---

[8]   See Nuñez Seixas (2001): *What is Spanish nationalism today?*

In contrast, at the Catalan level national identity is expressed and construct-ed explicitly, also in political discourse about migration. The discourse of all political parties, except the regional section of the PP, reflects moderate Catalan nationalist ideas as they have been forged by Jordi Pujol, the former CiU leader and long standing president of the *Generalitat*. This hegemonic version of Cata-lan nationalism defends a predominantly civic conception of a distinct Catalan nation, although with strong emphasis on the preservation and promotion of the Catalan language. The famous word of Pujol that Catalan is who lives and works in Catalonia and speaks Catalan appeared in variations in the discourse of all major Catalan political parties. Their discourse differed though with respect to the importance they lay on language skills and to the question if those are conceived as an exclusive condition for the "membership" of the Catalan "In-group" or simply as a preferable and helpful vehicle for integration.[9]

The initiative of the PSC led *Tripartit* to introduce a new concept of a Cata-lan citizenship, based on the assumption that the receiving state is not always equivalent with the receiving society,[10] is again an expression of a civic concep-tion of national identity, internally inclusive and externally delimiting.

Catalan politicians thus pursue a strategy of inclusion of the immigrants into the Catalan "In-group" in order to strengthen the own claims for a distinct Catalan nation, opposite to the idea of a unitary Spanish nation. Nevertheless, the identification of individuals with the Catalan national identity is conceived as forming part of a set of multiple identifications with various "We-groups", that is to say, of the individuals' "nested identities".[11] The dominant construc-tion of Catalan national identity is thus characterized by the inclusion of in-ternal difference and diversity. Openness and heterogeneity are even defined as constituting elements of Catalan versus Spanish national identity. Assmann and Friese describe such cases when identity is no longer the opposite of otherness, but otherness thought of as an element of collective identity, as a "practice of difference".[12]

---

[9] See Flora (2000): *Stein Rokkan. Staat, Nation und Demokratie in Europa. Die Theorie Stein Rokkans*, Frankfurt a. M.: Suhrkamp, p. 255 for language as a criterium for "membership" in a group.

[10] Zapata-Barrero (2005): *Inmigración en la España plural: un debate pendiente*.

[11] See Díez Medrano and Gutiérrez (2001): Nested identities: national and European identity in Spain, in *Ethnic and Racial Studies*, 42:5.

[12] See Assmann and Friese (1999): Einleitung, in Assmann and Friese *Identitäten. Erinnerung, Geschichte, Identität*, Frankfurt a. M.: Suhrkamp, p. 23.

2. Changes in migration discourse and the construction of national identity?

The comparison of the results presented above for the central state level with the study Triandafyllidou conducted in the first half of the 1990s reveals surprising similarities. Surprising, because the migratory situation at that time was very different from the current migration movements. The total number of foreigners living in Spain in those years was still quite low. Moreover, a high percentage of the immigrants were EU citizens, in many cases pensioners who, no longer economically active, enjoyed their retirement in the warm South (see IV.1). Nevertheless, some of Triandafyllidou's findings from her quantitative analysis of press articles and her qualitative analysis of interviews point in the same direction as the findings of the here presented study conducted a decade later.

In the quantitative part Triandafyllidou detects for instance the specific perception of a link between the country's emigration past and its recent experience as an immigrant receiving country. The emigration history of Spain is seen, according to her analysis, as a part of its identity, which reflects the cultural and national diversity characterising this collective identity.[13] With respect to Spain's relations to other states, she also confirms a strong Eurocentric tendency in press discourse and the delimitation from the Southern neighbours and home countries of immigrants by putting special emphasis on its EC-membership.[14] Furthermore, Spaniards are found to have a relatively open and positive attitude towards the immigrants. Triandafyllidou spots two contrasting normative discourses: a humanistic, solidarity approach which emphasises the contribution of the immigrants to the receiving society and a nationalistic discourse which legitimizes discrimination and unequal treatment. These two discourses seem to be linked in a moderate law-and-order approach which demands more effective immigration policy and control and the integration of immigrants. In the Spanish case humanism and solidarity within the own society are accentuated and xenophobic attitudes denied. The "We-group" is presented as tolerant and people with racist or xenophobic attitudes are defined as marginal to the host

---

[13] See Triandafyllidou (2001): *Immigrants and National Identity in Europe*, p. 114.
[14] See Ibid., p. 112-126.

society, or even as outsiders.[15] This positive "In-group" representation is in fact a typical feature of political discourse about minorities.[16]

In analogy to the social policy approach here found primarily in Catalan political discourse, Triandafyllidou states that

> "conflict between immigrants and the domestic population is attributed to the circumstances under which contact takes place. More specifically, the massive arrival of immigrants to a small town or village, their concentration in decaying inner-city neighbourhoods, their poverty and the fact that they tend to live in overcrowded apartments are identified as the main factors that lead to xenophobia and racism."[17]

Regarding the explicit definition of specific elements of a Spanish national identity the findings of the analysis of the press discourse correspond to the ones presented here earlier, that is to say, the almost complete absence of references to language, culture or national identity which "shows that the idea has been abandoned that a set of personality features characterises all Spaniards and is part of Spanish identity".[18] However, Triandafyllidou's analysis of the interviews also show that those immigrants originating from countries linked to Spain through specific historic ties and therefore sharing the Spanish linguistic and cultural tradition, namely the Latin American countries, are perceived as easier to integrate. Spanish law also gives them priority regarding the conditions for naturalisation. Contrary to that, the author detects that "Moroccans are perceived as the "Other" par excellence", but, as suggested by the interviewees, this attitude depends more on social and cultural differences than on nationality or history.[19]

Triandafyllidou finally concludes that

> "Spaniards have been able to take advantage of their 'national' experience of being a multinational state characterised by linguistic and cultural difference. The cultural diversity of immigrants is therefore not seen as an insurmountable obstacle to integration. Moreover, the legacy of the Franco regime makes Spaniards par-

---

[15] See Ibid., p. 127.
[16] See van Dijk (1993): *Elite Discourse and Racism*, London/New Delhi: Sage Publications, pp. 72-76.
[17] Triandafyllidou (2001): *Immigrants and National Identity in Europe*, p. 131.
[18] Ibid., p. 111.
[19] Ibid., p. 125.

ticularly sensitive to issues of rights and democracy (even though representatives of the public administration did express the odd nationalist voice among Spanish interviewees, as if they still subscribed to the conservative tradition in Spanish politics.)"[20]

Although these findings reflect predominantly the ideological fundaments of the left recognizing the multinational character of Spain, the author suggest with her explanatory note in parenthesis that Spanish nationalism in the tradition of the Spanish right still exists.

The comparison of the results of Triandafyllidou with the results here presented shows that the basic frames in discourse about migration have not changed despite the changes in migration numbers and countries of origin. The augmentation of immigration from non-EU countries does not alter the discursive construction of an "Other", the mere presence of Latin Americans or Moroccans in Spain was sufficient to provoke the presented reactions. Furthermore, the basic definition of the Spanish nation, on the one hand as a political nation including different cultural nations, on the other hand as a unitary cultural nation has not changed considerably either over the last ten years. These fundamental ideological differences between the Spanish left and the Spanish right that emerged throughout the nineteenth century, however, were silenced as far as possible in public discourse by the transitional pact and the constitutional consensus. It is surprising that after three decades of democracy in Spain the considerations of the transition period are still valid even to the point that the two major political parties shy away from open political conflict and postulate consensual decisions as the preferred mode of policy-making. The here presented results of the analysis of political discourse about migration at the central state level show a constant demand for political consensus in this field and an extra cautious treatment of issues concerning immigration. Politicians of both major political parties highlight the importance of consensual decision-making, thus of a political pact in such an important policy field as migration policy is considered to be.

Migration policy should furthermore not be exploited in the parties' struggle for political power. This is reflected in what was called above "meta-discourse". Politicians seem to be well conscious of the influence political discourse has on public opinion and that therefore using immigration and especially negative im-

---

[20] Ibid., pp. 137-138.

ages of immigrants for political purposes means to encourage negative and even xenophobic attitudes among the Spanish population.

During the 1990s the consensus in migration policy not to use immigration as an issue to mobilize the electorate still existed.[21] Kreienbrink assumes that this was the case because in those years the phenomenon immigration still had not reached the level it has reached in the first years of the new millennium.[22] The solo attempt of the PP to reform the new Aliens act in 2000 meant, according to him, the breaking of this consensus. In the period here analysed between 2000 and 2005 the two major political parties accuse each other of having broken the pact and at the same time stress how important such a consensual decision-making would be.

Nevertheless, Spanish political discourse about immigration remained, in comparison to other European countries, rather rational. The mutual control not to exploit immigration for political purposes was on the whole kept up. The awareness of how dangerous a demagogic handling of immigration issues is and how it could evoke negative feelings or even xenophobic tendencies within Spanish and Catalan society is a peculiarity of central-state and Catalan political discourse. Comparing it for instance to the German political discourse where immigration and asylum issues have been used in the past by politicians of both major political parties to obtain votes by deliberately adding fuel to the fears of the German population, this cautious treatment is even more striking.

3. Recent development and outlook

Recent developments, however, strengthen the impression that the consensual phase in Spanish politics is over and that little by little polarization between the two major political actors, PP and PSOE, takes hold. Bernecker and Maihold even speak of cracks and abysses in the Spanish society that have opened as a consequence of the electoral results of March 14, 2004. "Society is experiencing a level of continuous political polarization that does not allow comparison to the times of consensus resulting from the transition to democracy."[23] The polarization has surfaced already in various areas of Spanish politics, for instance in the differences of foreign policy priorities. On the one hand Aznar's government

---

[21] See Kreienbrink (2007): *Inmigración e integración social*, p. 242.
[22] See Ibid., p. 239.
[23] Bernecker and Maihold (2007): *Presentación: Consenso y polarización en España*, p. 7.

has promoted the alliance with the USA and supported the war with Iraq. On the other hand the government of Zapatero withdrew the Spanish troops from Iraq and sought again the close relations with the European partners, especially France and Germany.[24] The recent and very controversial debate about the Ley de Memoria Histórica (Law of Historical Memory)[25] and the virulence of the underlying general question of how to deal with the past provides more evidence of an increasing public polarization within Spanish politics and society.[26] The controversies about how to handle ETA have also considerably deepened the political polarization between PP and PSOE. During Aznar's government fighting ETA terrorism acted as a cohesive element.[27] The affirmations of PP government accusing ETA of the terrorist attacks on March 11, in spite of being aware that evidence suggested an Islamist background, revolved the outcome of the elections held four days later. PSOE assumed government, and since then the treatment of ETA is an issue of continuous political quarrels. In the Conservatives' discourse ETA terrorism is also used as an argument to picture the threat of disintegration of the Spanish nation if the regions are given more political and financial autonomy.[28] The PP has centred its political activity in the defence of Spanish unity and has given up its former approach to extent the party's influence at the regional level, especially in Catalonia, the Basque Country and Galicia.[29] In contrast, the PSOE under Zapatero has supported the claims of the autonomous communities for new statutes of autonomy and for an extension of their political and financial autonomy.

No important political issues will be exempt from this increasing political polarization,[30] not even such a sensitive issue as it is immigration. As explained above, migration discourse was still quite rational in the analysed period of time. However, there are first hints that this is changing recently. The PP, for instance,

---

[24] See Gratius (2007): *España y sus relaciones con las Américas: entre continuidad y ruptura.*

[25] Finally, after two years of harsh debate the "Law of Historical Memory" (Ley de Memoria Histórica) was passed October 31, 2007. Most important, the new Law is an official condemnation of Francoism, it furthermore recognizes the victims of the Civil War and the Francoist regime and declares all imprisonments and executions because of political, ideological and religious reasons as illegitimate, and it obliges the municipalities to withdraw all Francoist symbols and monuments. The PP criticised the law as being unnecessary and only reopening wounds.

[26] See Reig Tapia (2007): *El debate sobre el pasado y su importancia para el presente.*

[27] See Bernecker and Maihold (2007): *Presentación: Consenso y polarización en España*, p. 12.

[28] See *Mees (2007): El debate sobre nación y Estado en España: viejos retos, nuevas posibilidades*, p. 307.

[29] See Ibid., p. 310.

[30] See Bernecker and Maihold (2007): *Presentación: Consenso y polarización en España*, p. 7.

already in the regional and municipal elections in May 2007 used immigrants as scapegoats for local problems. Moreover, the extreme right has won more seats than ever since the transition to democracy, in city councils in Catalonia with an explicitly xenophobic campaign.[31] In addition to ETA and the inner-Spanish debate about national identities, immigration was one of the main issues in the campaign for the 2008 parliamentary elections. The PP wanted power back and did not shrink from deepening the polarization of the Spanish society and from exploiting sensitive issues like immigration. However, how much electoral arguments about immigration influence the Spanish population and encourage negative attitudes versus immigrants depends decisively on the economic development of the country. As long as the economic benefits of immigration prevailed and as long as there was a strong demand for foreign labour, public discourse about migration was dominated by the positive aspects.[32] But in view of the recent economic recession and the rising unemployment figures among natives and immigrants this might change. The first reactions of the PSOE government advert to a more restrictive approach in future immigration policies. Already in March 2008 the Spanish Minister for Economy, Pedro Solbes has declared that there will be less demand for foreign labour in coming years. Moreover, the government is continuously strengthening the border controls to fight irregular immigration and it considers the expansion of the already existing programms for voluntary return and the restriction of the provisions for family reunification. Nevertheless, immigration to Spain will beyond doubt continue in the near future. Integration policy will continue to be of major importance both for central state government and for the autonomous and local authorities, especially with regard to education matters and the second and third generation.[33]

---

[31] The xenophobic "Plataforma de Catalunya" could pocket seventeen seats in municipal councils (compared to 4 in the elections of 2003). See El País (2007c): *La irrupción de los 'micropartidos'*, 29.05.2007.

[32] See Interviews: E-1 Member of Parliament-PSOE, 2007; E-2 Member of Parliament-PP, 2007; E-4 Member of Parliament-PSOE, 2007.

[33] Kreienbrink (2008): *Länderprofil Spanien*, p. 9.

Bibliography

I. LITERATURE

ABRAMS, Dominic and Michael A. HOGG (1990): An Introduction to the social identity approach, in Dominic ABRAMS and Michael A. HOGG *Social Identity Theory. Constructive and Critical Advances*, New York/London: Harvester Wheatsheaf, 1-9.

AGRELA, Belén (2002): La política de inmigración en España: reflexiones sobre la emergencia del discurso de la diferencia cultural, in *Migraciones Internacionales*, 1:2, 93-121.

ALTER, Peter (1985): *Nationalismus*, Frankfurt a. M.: Suhrkamp.

AMNESTY INTERNATIONAL (2005): *Spain/Morocco. Migrant rights between two fires*, Public Statement, 03.10.2005, URL: http://www.amnesty.org/en/alfresco_asset/056ee2a3-a301-11dc-8d74-6f45f39984e5/eur410112005.en.pdf, [09.02.2007].

ANDERSON, Benedict (1983): *Imagined Communities. Reflections on the Origin and Spread of Nationalism*, London/New York: Verso.

ANGERMÜLLER, Johannes (2001): Einleitung: Diskursanalyse. Strömungen, Tendenzen, Perspektiven, in Johannes ANGERMÜLLER, Katharina BUNZMANN and Martin NONHOFF *Diskursanalyse: Theorien, Methoden, Anwendungen*, Hamburg: Argument Verlag, 7-22.

ANGERMÜLLER, Johannes (2005): Sozialwissenschaftliche Diskursanalyse als interpretative Analytik, in Reiner KELLER *et al. Die diskursive Konstruktion von Wirklichkeit. Zum Verhältnis von Wissenssoziologie und Diskursforschung*, Konstanz: UVK Verlagsgesellschaft, 23-47.

APARICIO, Rosa and Andrés TORNOS (2000): *La inmigración y la economía española*, Madrid: Ministerio de Trabajo y Asuntos Sociales.

ARANGO, Joaquin and Maia JACHIMOWICZ (2005): *Regularizing Immigrants in Spain: A New Approach*, in Migration Information Source, URL: http://www.migrationinformation.org, [26.05.2006].

ARMSTRONG, John (1995): Towards a Theory of Nationalism: Consensus and Dissensus, in Sukumar PERIWAL *Notions of Nationalism*, Budapest/London/New York: Central European University Press, 34-43.

ASSMANN, Aleida and Heidrun FRIESE (1999): Einleitung, in Aleida ASSMANN and Heidrun FRIESE *Identitäten. Erinnerung, Geschichte, Identität*, Frankfurt a. M.: Suhrkamp, 11-23.

AUBARELL, Gemma, Xavier ARAGALL and Jordi PADILLA (2003): *Gestionar la diversitat. Reflexions i experiències sobre les polítiques d´immigració a Catalunya*, Barcelona: Institut Europeu de la Mediterrània.

AZNAR, José María (2004): *Ocho Años de Gobierno. Una Visión Personal de España*, Barcelona: Planeta.

BALCELLS, Albert (1996): *Catalan Nationalism. Past and Present*, Houndmills, Basingstoke, Hampshire: MacMillan Press.

BALCELLS, Albert (2004): *Breve historia del nacionalismo catalán*, Madrid: Alianza Editorial.

BALDWIN-EDWARDS, Martin (2004): *The Changing Mosaic of Mediterranean Migrations*, in Migration Information Source, URL: http://www.migrationinformation.org, [27.01.2004].

BARNARD, Frederick M. (2003): *Herder on Nationality, Humanity, and History*, London/Ithaca: McGill-Queen's University Press/Montreal & Kingston.

BARNARD, Frederick M. (1965): *Herder's Social and Political Thought. From Enlightment to Nationalism*, Oxford: Clarendon Press.

BARTH, Frederik (1969): Introduction, in Frederik BARTH *Ethnic Groups and Boundaries. The Social Organization of Cultural Difference*, London: George Allen & Unwin, 9-38.

BAUMER, Andreas (2001): Jenseits der Pyrenäen: Parteiensysteme und gesellschaftliche Konflikte in Spanien und Portugal, in Ulrich EITH and Gerd MIELKE *Gesellschaftliche Konflikte und Parteiensysteme*, Opladen: Westdeutscher Verlag, 141-156.

BEHR, Hartmut (1998): *Zuwanderung im Nationalstaat. Formen der Eigen- und Fremdbestimmung in den USA, der Bundesrepublik, Deutschland und Frankreich*, Opladen: Leske + Budrich.

BENDEL, Petra (2005): Immigration Policy in the European Union: Still bringing up the walls for fortress Europe?, in *Migration Letters*, 2:1.

BENDIX, Reinhard (1996): Strukturgeschichtliche Voraussetzungen der nationalen und kulturellen Identität in der Neuzeit, in Bernhard GIESEN *Nationale und kulturelle Identität. Studien zur Entwicklung des kollektiven Bewußtseins in der Neuzeit*, Frankfurt a. M.: Suhrkamp, 39-55.

BERAMENDI, Justo G. (2000): Identity, Ethnicity, and the State in Spain: 19th and 20th Centuries, in William SAFRAN and Ramón MÁIZ *Identity and Territorial Autonomy in Plural Societies*, London/Portland, OR.: Frank Cass, 79-100.

BERGER, Peter L. and Thomas LUCKMANN (2001): *Die gesellschaftliche Konstruktion der Wirklichkeit. Eine Theorie der Wissenssoziologie?* Frankfurt a. M.: Fischer Taschenbuch Verlag.

BERNECKER, Walther (2007): España y la Unión Europea: una relación cambiante, in Walther BERNECKER and Günther MAIHOLD *España: del consenso a la polarización. Cambios en la democracia española*, Madrid/Frankfurt a. M.: Iberoamericana/Vervuert, 45-69.

BERNECKER, Walther and Sören BRINKMANN (2004): Spaniens schwierige Identität. Geschichte und Politik zur Jahrtausendwende, in Walther BERNECKER and Klaus DIRSCHERL *Spanien heute. Politik-Wirtschaft-Kultur*, Frankfurt a. M.: Vervuert Verlag, 123-144.

BERNECKER, Walther, Torsten ESSER and Peter A. KRAUS (2007): *Eine kleine Geschichte Kataloniens*, Frankfurt a. M.: Suhrkamp.

BERNECKER, Walther and Günther MAIHOLD (2007): Presentación: Consenso y polarización en España, in Walther BERNECKER and Günther MAIHOLD *España: del consenso a la polarización. Cambios en la democracia española*, Madrid/Frankfurt a. M.: Iberoamericana/Vervuert, 7-18.

BILLIG, Michael (1995): *Banal Nationalism*, London/New Delhi: Sage Publications.

BIRSL, Ursula *et al.* (2003): *Migration und Interkulturalität in Großbritannien, Deutschland und Spanien. Fallstudien aus der Arbeitswelt*, Opladen: Leske + Budrich.

BLANCO FERNÁNDEZ DE VALDERRAMA, Cristina (1993): The New Hosts: The Case of Spain, in *International Migration Review*, 27:1, 169-181.

BOYD, Carolyn P. (1997): *Historia Patria. Politics, History, and National Identity in Spain, 1875-1975*, Princeton, New Jersey: Princeton University Press.

BREUILLY, John (1994): *Nationalism and the State*, Chicago: The University of Chicago Press.

BRINCK, Renate (1995): *Regionalistische Bewegungen zwischen internationaler Integration und regionaler Eigenständigkeit: Baskenland und Katalonien*, Hamburg: Lit-Verlag.

BUSSE, Dietrich (1997): Das Eigene und das Fremde. Annotationen zu Funktion und Wirkung einer diskurssemantischen Grundfigur, in Matthias JUNG, Martin WENGELER and Karin BÖKE *Die Sprache des Migrationsdiskurses. Das Reden über „Ausländer" in Medien, Politik und Alltag*, Opladen: Westdeutscher Verlag, 17-35.

CACHÓN RODRÍGUEZ, Lorenzo (2003): La Inmigración en España: Los desafíos de la construcción de una nueva sociedad, in *Migraciones*, 2003:14, 219-304.

CALHOUN, Craig (1994): Social Theory and the Poltics of Identity, in Craig CALHOUN *Social Theory and the Politics of Identity*, Cambridge, M. A.: Blackwell Publishers, 9-36.

CANDEL, Francesc (1965): *Els altres catalans*, Barcelona: edicions 62.

CARIUS, Björn (2004): Im "berechtigten Eigeninteresse". Die Konstruktion nationaler Identität, in Siegfried JÄGER and Franz JANUSCHEK *Gefühlte Geschichte und Kämpfe um Identität*, Münster: Unrast-Verlag, 105-132.

CARLING, Jorgen (2007b): Migration Control and Migrant Fatalities at the Spanish-African Borders, in *International Migration Review*, 41:2, 316-343.

CENTRE D'ESTUDIS JORDI PUJOL, URL: http://www.jordipujol.cat, [23.01.2007].

CENTRO DE INVESTIGACIONES SOCIOLÓGICAS (CIS), URL: http://www.cis.es, [23.01.2007].

CHARRO BAENA, Pilar and José M.ª RUIZ DE HUIDOBRO DE CARLOS (2000): La Ley Orgánica 4/2000: Análisis técnico-jurídico de sus principales novedades, in *Migraciones*, 2000:7, 7-56.

CHILTON, Paul and Christina SCHÄFFNER (1997): Discourse and Politics, in Teun A. VAN DIJK *Discourse as Social Interaction. Discourse Studies: A Multidisciplinary Introduction. Volume II*, London/Thousand Oaks/New Delhi: Sage Publications, 206-230.

COHEN, A.P. (1985): *The Symbolic Construction of Community*, London/New York: Routledge.

COLOMER, Josep M. (1998): The Spanish "State of Autonomies": Non-Institutional Federalism, *West European Politics*, 21:4, 40-52.

CONGRESO DE LOS DIPUTADOS: *Constitución Española*, URL: http://www.congreso.es/funciones/constitucion/const_espa_texto.pdf, [19.02.2007].

CONSEJO ECONÓMICO Y SOCIAL (2004): *La inmigración y el mercado de trabajo en España*, Madrid: Consejo Económico y Social.

CONVERSI, Daniele (1997): *The Basques, the Catalans and Spain*, London: Hurst & Company.

CORDES, Sandra und KLEINER-LIEBAU, Désirée (forthcoming): Der spanische Senat - Wandel territorialer Repräsentation zwischen dezentralem Einheitsstaat und Föderalstaat, in Gisela RIESCHER, Sabine RUSS and Christoph HAAS *Zweite Kammern*, München/Wien: R. Oldenbourg Verlag.

CÓRDOBA (2006): *La ola de cayucos en el 2006 deja 800 cadáveres en el Atlántico*, 28.12.2006, URL: http://www.diariocordoba.com, [26.11.2007].

CORKILL, David (1996): Multiple National Identities, Immigration and Racism in Spain and Portugal, in Brian JENKINS and A. S. SPYROS *Nation & Identity in Contemporary Europe*, London: Routledge, 155-171.

CORREDERA GARCÍA, María Paz (1994): La política de "extranjería" en España, in Jesús CONTRERAS *Los retos de la Inmigración. Racismo y pluriculturalidad*, Madrid: Talasa, 121-144.

DAHINDEN, Urs (2006): *Framing. Eine integrative Theorie der Massenkommunikation*, Konstanz: UVK Verlagsgesellschaft.

DÄUBLE, Helmut (2000): *Auf dem Weg zum Bundesrepublikaner. Einwanderung- kollektive Identität-politische Bildung*, Schwalbach/Ts.: Wochenschau Verlag.

DÍEZ MEDRANO, Juan (1995): *Divided Nations. Class, Politics, and Nationalism in the Basque Country and Catalonia*, Ithaca/London: Cornell University Press.

DÍEZ MEDRANO, Juan and Paula GUTIÉRREZ (2001): Nested identities: national and European identity in Spain, in *Ethnic and Racial Studies*, 42:5, 753-778.

DONATI, Paolo R. (2001): Die Rahmenanalyse politischer Diskurse, in Reiner KELLER *et al. Handbuch Sozialwissenschaftliche Diskursanalyse. Band 1: Theorien und Methoden*, Opladen: Leske + Budrich, 145-175.

DOUGLASS, William A. *et al.* (1999): *Basque Politics and Nationalism on the Eve of the Millenium*, Reno: University of Nevada.

EISENSTADT, Shmuel Noah (1996): Die Konstruktion nationaler Identitäten in vergleichender Perspektive, in Bernhard GIESEN *Nationale und kulturelle Identität. Studien zur Entwicklung des kollektiven Bewußtseins in der Neuzeit*, Frankfurt a. M.: Suhrkamp, 21-38.

EL PAÍS (2004a): *Las Reformas estatuarias que proyecto cada autonomía*, 24.05.2004.

EL PAÍS (2004b): *Los inmigrantes con contrato podrán solicitar la regularización a partir del 31 de enero*, 14.12.2004, p. 32.

EL PAÍS (2005a): *"Ésta es la última oportunidad para los empresarios que contratan a 'sin papeles'"*, Interview with Consuelo Rumí, 07.02.2005, p. 22.

EL PAÍS (2005b): *La Reforma del Estatuto Catalán. Comparación del Texto vigente y del proyecto*, 14.10.2005.

EL PAÍS (2007a): *La llegada de inmigrantes por mar cae und 55% tras el refuerzo de controles fronterizos*, 08.08.2007, p. 19.

EL PAÍS (2007b): *Malí firma el martes un acuerdo con España que incluye repatriaciones*, 20.01.2007, URL: http://www.elpais.com, [26.01.2007].

EL PAÍS (2007c): *La irrupción de los 'micropartidos'*, 29.05.2007.

ELPAIS.COM (2004): *Cuatro estatutos y 40 leyes*, 02.01.2007, URL: http://www.elpais.com, [04.01.2007].

ELPAIS.ES (2005): *El Gobierno aprueba 120 millones para el fondo de ayuda para la integración de inmigrantes*, 20.05.2005, URL: http://www.elpais.es, [23.05.2005].

ELPAIS.ES (2006): *Moratinos dona 10 millones a Guinea-Conakry y Gambia a cambio de acuerdos de repatriación*, 10.10.2006, URL: http://www.elpais.es, [13.10.2006].

EL PERIÓDICO (2005): *La tanca de Melilla pateix el pitjor assalt de la història*, 28.09.2005, p. 34.

ELMUNDO.ES (2006): *Resultados Referendum Estatuto Catalán 18 Junio 2006*, URL: http://www.elmundo.es/especiales/2006/06/estatuto-catalan/resultados/globales/09/, [20.02.2007].

ENTMAN, Robert M. (1993): Framing: Toward Clarification of a Fractured Paradigm, in *Journal of Communication*, 43:4, 51-58.

ESSER, Torsten (2007): Diguem yes! Vom Protestlied zum Mestizo-Sound. Musik in Katalonien, in Torsten ESSER and Tilbert D. STEGMANN *Kataloniens Rückkehr nach Europa 1976-2006*, Berlin: Lit Verlag, 181-204.

ESTRUCH, Joan (1991): Die Soziale Konstruktion von nationalen Identitäten. Das Beispiel von Katalonien als Nation im spanischen Staat, in Erich FRÖSCHL, Maria MESNER and Uri RA'ANAN *Staat und Nation in multi-ethnischen Gesellschaften*, Wien: Passagen Verlag, 265-275.

FAIRCLOUGH, Norman (1992): *Critical language awareness*, London: Longman.

FAIRCLOUGH, Norman and Ruth WODAK (1997): Critical Discourse Analysis, in Teun A. VAN DIJK *Discourse as Social Interaction. Discourse Studies: A Multidisciplinary Introduction. Volume II*, London/Thousand Oaks/New Delhi: Sage Publications, 258-284.

FERRERES I CALVO, Ernest and Jordi LLORENS I VILLA (1992): *Història de Catalunya*, Barcelona: Grup Promotor.

FLORA, Peter (2000): *Stein Rokkan. Staat, Nation und Demokratie in Europa. Die Theorie Stein Rokkans*, Frankfurt a. M.: Suhrkamp.

FLYNN, M. K. (2001): Constructed identities and Iberia, in *Ethnic and Racial Studies*, 24:5, 703-718.

FOUCAULT, Michel (1973): *Archäologie des Wissens*, Frankfurt a. M.: Suhrkamp.

FOUR MOTORS FOR EUROPE, URL: http://62.101.84.82/4motori.nsf/framesweb/index, [19.02.2007].

FOX, Inman (1997): *La invención de España. Nacionalismo liberal e identidad nacional*, Madrid: Ediciones Cátedra.

FRADERA, Josep M. (2001): El proyecto español de los catalanes: tres momentos y un epílogo, in Antonio MORALES MOYA *Nacionalismos e imagen de España*, Madrid: Sociedad Estatal España Neuvo Milenio, 21-36.

FRANCO, Dolores (1980): *España como Preocupación. Antología*, Barcelona: Editorial Argos Vergara.

FUSI AIZPURÚA, Juan Pablo (1990): Centre and Periphery 1900-1936: National Integration and Regional Nationalisms Reconsidered, in Frances LANNON and Paul PRESTON *Élites and Power in Twentieth-Century Spain*, Oxford: Clarendon Press, 33-44.

FUSI AIZPÚRUA, Juan Pablo (2000): *España. La evolución de la identidad nacional*, Madrid: Ediciones Temas de Hoy.

GEDDES, Andrew (2003): *The Politics of migration and immigration in Europe*, London/ Thousand Oaks/New Delhi: Sage Publications.

GEE, James Paul (1999): *An Introduction to Discourse Analysis. Theory and Method*, London/New York: Routledge.

GENERALITAT DE CATALUNYA: *Estatut d'autonomia de 1979*, http://www.gencat.cat/generalitat/cat/estatut1979/index.htm, Art. 9, [19.02.2007].

GERGEN, Thomas (2000): *Sprachengesetzgebung in Katalonien. Die Debatte um die "Llei de Política Lingüística" vom 7. Januar 1998*, Tübingen: Max Niemeyer Verlag.

GERHARDS, Jürgen (2003): Diskursanalyse als systematische Inhaltsanalyse. Die öffentliche Debatte über Abtreibungen in den USA und in der Bundesrepublik Deutschland im Vergleich, in Reiner KELLER *et al. Handbuch Sozialwissenschaftliche Diskursanalyse. Band II: Forschungspraxis*, Opladen: Leske + Budrich, 299-324.

GERHARDS, Jürgen and Dieter RUCHT (1992): Mesomobilization: Organizing and Framing in Two Protest Campaigns in West Germany, in *The American Journal of Sociology*, 98:3, 555-596.

GERHARDS, Jürgen and Dieter RUCHT (2003): Öffentlichkeit, Akteure und Deutungsmuster: Die Debatte über Abtreibungen in Deutschland und den USA, in Jürgen GERHARDS *Die Vermessung kultureller Unterschiede*, Wiesbaden: Westdeutscher Verlag, 165-188.

GIL ARAUJO, Sandra (2007): *Las argucias de la integración. Construcción nacional y gobierno de lo social a través de las políticas de integración de inmigrantes. Los casos de Cataluña y Madrid*, PhD Thesis, Departmento de Cambio Social, Facultad de Ciencias Políticas y Sociología, Universidad Complutense de Madrid.

GILLESPIE, Richard (1989): *The Spanish Socialist Party. A History of Factionalism*, Oxford: Clarendon Press.

GONZÁLEZ ENCINAR, José Juan (1992): Ein assymetrischer Bundesstaat, in Dieter NOHLEN and José Juan GONZÁLEZ ENCINAR *Der Staat der autonomen Gemeinschaften in Spanien*, Opladen: Leske + Budrich, 217-230.

GRAHAM, Robert (1984): *Spain. Change of a Nation*, London: Michael Joseph.

GRATIUS, Susanne (2007): España y sus relaciones con las Américas: entre continuidad y ruptura, in Walther BERNECKER and Günther MAIHOLD *España: del consenso a la polarización. Cambios en la democracia española*, Madrid/Frankfurt a. M.: Iberoamericana/Vervuert, 97-116.

GUIBERNAU, Montserrat (1997): Nations without states: Catalonia, a case study, in Montserrat GUIBERNAU and John REX *The Ethnicity Reader. Nationalism, Multiculturalism and Migration*, Oxford: Blackwell Publishers, 133-154.

GUIBERNAU, Montserrat (2002): *El nacionalisme català. Franquisme, trancisió i democràcia*, Barcelona: Pòrtic.

GUIBERNAU, Montserrat (2006): National identity, devolution and secession in Canada, Britain and Spain, in *Nations and Nationalism*, 12:1, 51-76.

GUIBERNAU, Montserrat (2007): *The Identity of Nations*, Cambridge: Polity Press.

GUIBERNAU, Montserrat and John HUTCHINSON (2004): History and National Destiny, in *Nations and Nationalism*, 10:1/2, 1-8.

HABERMAS, Jürgen (1992): Anerkennungskämpfe im demokratischen Rechtsstaat, in Charles TAYLOR *Multikulturalismus und die Politik der Anerkennung*, Frankfurt a. M.: Fischer Verlag, 147-196.

HALBWACHS, Maurice (1992): *On Collective Memory*, Chicago/London: The University of Chicago Press.

HALL, Stuart (1992): "The west and the rest", in Stuart HALL and Bernhard GIEBEN, *Formations of modernity*, Cambridge, Polity Press/The Open University, 275-320.

HALL, Stuart (1996): Introduction: Who Needs "Identity"? in Stuart HALL and Paul DU GAY *Questions of Cultural Identity*, London: Sage Publications, 1-17.

HALL, Stuart (2001a): Foucault: Power, Knowledge and Discourse, in Margaret WETHERELL, Stephanie TAYLOR and Simeon J. YATES *Discourse Theory and Practice. A Reader*, London/Thousand Oaks/New Delhi: Sage Publications, 72-81.

HALL, Stuart (2001b): The Spectacle of the Other, in Margaret WETHERELL, Stephanie TAYLOR and Simeon J. YATES *Discourse Theory and Practice. A Reader*, London/Thousand Oaks/New Delhi: Sage Publications, 324-344.

HASTINGS, Adrian (1997): *The Construction of Nationhood. Ethnicity, Religion and Nationalism*, Cambridge: Cambridge University Press.

HECKMANN, Friedrich (2003): From Ethnic Nation to Universalistic Immigrant Integration: Germany, in Friedrich HECKMANN and Dominique SCHNAPPER *The Integration of Immigrants in European Societies. National Differences and Trends of Convergence*, Stuttgart: Lucius & Lucius, 45-78.

HELL, Matthias (2005): *Einwanderungsland Deutschland? Die Zuwanderungsdiskussion 1998-2002*, Wiesbaden: VS Verlag für Sozialwissenschaften.

HILDENBRAND, Andreas (1993): Das Regionalismusproblem, in Walther L. BERNECKER and Carlos COLLADO SEIDEL *Spanien nach Franco. Der Übergang von der Diktatur zur Demokratie 1975-1982*, München: R.Oldenbourg Verlag, 104-126.

HOBSBAWM, Eric (1983): Introduction: Inventing Traditions, in Eric HOBSBAWN and Terence RANGER *The Invention of Tradition*, Cambridge: Cambridge University Press, 1-14.

HÖHNE, Thomas (2001): "Alles konstruiert, oder was?" Über den Zusammenhang von Konstruktivismus und empirischer Forschung, in Johannes ANGERMÜLLER, Katharina BUNZMANN and Martin NONHOFF *Diskursanalyse: Theorien, Methoden, Anwendungen*, Hamburg: Argument Verlag, 23-34.

HUNTOON, Laura (1998): Immigration to Spain: Implications for a Unified European Union Immigration Policy, in *International Migration Review*, 32:2, 423-450.

HUTCHINSON, John (1987): *The Dynamics of Cultural Nationalism. The Gaelic Revival and the Creation of the Irish Nation State*, London: Allen & Unwin.

HUTCHINSON, John and Anthony D. SMITH (1994): *Nationalism*, Oxford/New York: Oxford University Press.

IMF's WORLD ECONOMIC OUTLOOK DATABASE, September 2006 Edition, URL: http://www.imf.org/external/pubs/ft/weo/2006/02/data/index.aspx, [10.12.2007].

INSTITUT DE CIÈNCIES POLÍTIQUES I SOCIALS (2005): *Sondeig d'Opinió. Catalunya*, Barcelona: ICPS, p. 132.

JÄGER, Margarete (2003): Die Kritik am Patriarchat im Einwanderungsdiskurs. Analyse einer Diskursverschränkung, in Reiner KELLER *et al. Handbuch Sozialwissenschaftliche Diskursanalyse. Band II: Forschungspraxis*, Opladen: Leske + Budrich, 421-438.

JÄGER, Siegfried (1993): *Brandsätze. Rassismus im Alltag*, Duisburg: Diss.

JÄGER, Siegfried and Jürgen LINK (1993): Die vierte Gewalt. Rassismus und die Medien. Einleitung, in Siegfried JÄGER and Jürgen LINK *Die vierte Gewalt und die Medien. Rassismus und die Medien*, Duisburg: Diss, 7-20.

JOST, Stefan (1994): *Die politische Mitte Spaniens. Von der Unión de Centro Democrático zum Partido Popular*, Frankfurt a. M.: Peter Lang.

JULIÁ, Santos (1990): The Ideological Conversion of the Leaders of the PSOE, 1976-1979, in Frances LANNON and Paul PRESTON *Élites and Power in Twentieth-Century Spain*, Oxford: Clarendon Press, 269-285.

JULIÁ, Santos (2004): *Historias de las dos Españas*, Madrid: Taurus.

JUNG, Matthias, Martin WENGELER and Karin BÖKE (eds.) (1997): *Die Sprache des Migrationsdiskurses. Das Reden über "Ausländer" in Medien, Politik und Alltag*, Opladen: Westdeutscher Verlag.

KEATING, Michael (1993): Spain. Peripheral nationalism and state response, in Craig McGARTY and Brendan O'LEARY *The Politics of Ethnic Conflict Regulation. Case Studies of Protracted Ethnic Conflicts*, London/New York: Routledge, 204-225.

KEATING, Michael (1996): *Nations against the State. The New Politics of Nationalism in Quebec, Catalonia and Scotland*, London: MacMillan Press.

KELLER, Reiner (1997): Diskursanalyse, in Ronald HITZLER and Anne HONER *Sozialwissenschaftliche Hermeneutik*, Opladen: Leske + Budrich, 309-333.

KELLER, Reiner (2004): *Diskursforschung. Eine Einführung für Sozialwissen-schaftlerInnen*, Wiesbaden: VS Verlag für Sozialwissenschaften.

KELLER, Reiner (2005a): Wissenssoziologische Diskursanalyse als interpretative Analytik, in Reiner KELLER et al. *Die diskursive Konstruktion von Wirklichkeit. Zum Verhältnis von Wissenssoziologie und Diskursforschung*, Konstanz: UVK Verlagsgesellschaft, 49-75.

KELLER, Reiner (2005b): *Wissenssoziologische Diskursanalyse. Grundlegung eines Forschungsprogramms*, Wiesbaden: VS Verlag für Sozialwissenschaften.

KELLER, Reiner et al. (eds.) (2005): *Die diskursive Konstruktion von Wirklichkeit. Zum Verhältnis von Wissenssoziologie und Diskursforschung*, Konstanz: UVK Verlagsgesellschaft.

KERCHNER, Brigitte (2006): Diskursanalyse in der Politikwissenschaft. Ein Forschungsüberblick, in Brigitte KERCHNER and Silke SCHNEIDER *Foucault. Diskursanalyse der Politik. Eine Einführung*, Wiesbaden: VS Verlag für Sozialwissenschaften, 33-67.

KLEINER, Désirée (2005): Von Spanien lernen. Legalisierung als Migrationspolitik, in *Blätter für deutsche und internationale Politik*, 2005:6, 735-740.

KOLAKOWSKI, Leszek (1995): Über kollektive Identität, in Krzysztof MICHALSKI *Identität im Wandel. Castelgandolfo-Gespräche 1995*, Stuttgart: Klett-Cotta, 47-60.

KOWERT, Paul (1998): Agent versus Structure in the Construction of National Identity, in Vendulka KUBÁLKOVÁ, Nicholas ONUF and Paul KOWERT *International Relations in a Constructed World*, New York/London: M. E. Sharpe, 101-122.

KRAUS, Peter A. (1996): *Nationalismus und Demokratie. Politik im spanischen Staat der Autonomen Gemeinschaften*, Wiesbaden: Deutscher Universitäts Verlag.

KREIENBRINK, Axel (2004): *Einwanderungsland Spanien. Migrationspolitik zwischen Europäisierung und nationalen Interessen*, Frankfurt a. M./London: IKO-Verlag für Interkulturelle Kommunikation.

KREIENBRINK, Axel (2006): Länderprofil Spanien, in Focus Migration, Hamburgisches Weltwirtschaftsinstitut.

KREIENBRINK, Axel (2008): Länderprofil Spanien, in Focus Migration, Hamburgisches Weltwirtschaftsinstitut.

KREIENBRINK, Axel (2007): Inmigración e integración social de los inmigrantes en España entre consenso y enfrentamiento político, in Walther BERNECKER and Günther MAIHOLD *España: del consenso a la polarización. Cambios en la democracia española*, Madrid/Frankfurt a. M.: Iberoamericana/Vervuert, 239-264.

KUNZE, Rolf-Ulrich (2005): *Nation und Nationalismus*, Dortmund: Wissenschaftliche Buchgesellschaft.

LEMBERG, Eugen (1964): *Nationalismus II. Soziologie und politische Pädagogik*, Reinbek: Rowohlt Taschenbuch Verlag.

LEY ORGÁNICA 7/1985, de 1 de Julio, sobre derechos y libertades de los extranjeros en España, URL: http://extranjeros.mtas.es/es/normativa_jurisprudencia/nacional/ley7_1985. pdf, [19.02.2007].

LEY ORGÁNICA 4/2000, de 11 de enero, sobre derechos y libertades de los extranjeros en España y su integración social, Boletín Oficial de Estado Nr. 10, 12.03.2000, URL: http://extranjeros.mtas.es/es/normativa_jurisprudencia/nacional/leyorganica_ dchos_libertades.pdf, [19.02.2007].

LEY ORGÁNICA 8/2000, de 22 de diciembre, de reforma de la Ley Orgánica 4/2000, de 11 de enero, sobre derechos y libertades de los extranjeros en España y su integración social, Boletín Oficial de Estado Nr. 307, 23.12.2000, URL: http://extranjeros.mtas.es/es/ normativa_jurisprudencia/nacional/ley_organica_8-2000.pdf, [19.02.2007].

LLOBERA, Josep R. (1996): *The Role of Historical Memory in (Ethno)Nation-Building*, London: University of London.

LOSADA, Antón (2000): National Identity and Self-government: The Galician Case, in William SAFRAN and Ramón MÁIZ *Identity and Territorial Autonomy in Plural Societies*, London/Portland, OR.: Frank Cass, 142-163.

MAIHOLD, Günther and Andreas MAURER (2005): Neue Impulse aus Europas Süden. Spanien und Portugal stärken ihre Initiative im europäischen Einigungsprozess, in *SWP-Aktuell*, 2005:13, 1-8.

MATOUSCHEK, Bernd (1997): Soziodiskursive Analyse öffentlicher Migrationsdebatten in Österreich. Zu Theorie, Methodik und Ergebnissen einer diskurstheoretischen Untersuchung, in Matthias JUNG, Martin WENGELER and Karin BÖKE *Die Sprache des Migrationsdiskurses. Das Reden über "Ausländer" in Medien, Politik und Alltag*, Opladen: Westdeutscher Verlag, 106-120.

MATOUSCHEK, Bernd, Ruth WODAK and Franz JANUSCHEK (1995): *Notwendige Maßnahmen gegen Fremde? Genese und Formen von rassistischen Diskursen der Differenz*, Wien: Passagen-Verlag.

MATTES, Hanspeter (1995): Postkoloniale Grenzprobleme im Maghreb, in Sigrid FAATH *Wuqûf 9. Beiträge zur Entwicklung von Staat und Gesellschaft in Nordafrika*, Hamburg: Hans Peter Mattes Verlag, 139-174.

McRoberts, Kenneth (2001): *Catalonia. Nation Building without a State*, Oxford: Oxford University Press.

Mees, Ludger (2007): El debate sobre nación y Estado en España: viejos retos, nuevas posibilidades, in Walther Bernecker and Günther Maihold *España: del consenso a la polarización. Cambios en la democracia española*, Madrid/Frankfurt a. M.: Iberoamericana/Vervuert, 297-315.

Meinecke, Friedrich (1908): *Weltbürgertum und Nationalstaat. Studien zur Genesis des deutschen Nationalstaates*, München/Berlin: R. Oldenbourg.

Merkel, Wolfgang (1999): *Systemtransformation. Eine Einführung in die Theorie und Empirie der Transformationsforschung*, Opladen: Leske + Budrich.

Mintzel, Alf (1997): *Multikulturelle Gesellschaften in Europa und Nordamerika. Konzepte, Streitfragen, Analysen, Befunde*, Passau: Wissenschaftsverlag Rothe.

Ministerio de Asuntos Exteriores y de Cooperación (2006): *Plan África 2006-2008. Resumen Ejecutivo*, URL: http://www.mae.es/nr/rdonlyres/c4c81869-0e32-470d-8d5f-7a49ad84d5c0/0/planafrica.pdf [14.02.2007].

Ministerio del Interior (2001): *Programa Global de Regulación y Coordinación de Extranjería e Inmigración*, aprobado 30.03.2001, BOE núm. 101, 27.04.2001.

Ministerio de Trabajo y Asuntos Sociales (2005): *Proceso de Normalización de Trabajadores Extranjeros*, 30.12.2005, URL: http://www.mtas.es/balance/proceso_norm.pdf, [19.02.2007].

Ministerio de Trabajo y Asuntos Sociales (2006): *Nota de Prensa*, URL: http://extranjeros.mtas.es/es/general/nota_balance_pateras_20051.pdf, [13.02.2007].

Ministerio de Trabajo y Asuntos Sociales (2007a): *Nota de Prensa* ,URL: http://www.mir.es/dgris/notas_prensa/ministerio_interior/2007/np022103.html, [27.11.2007].

Ministerio de Trabajo y Asuntos Sociales (2007b): *Nota de Prensa: El Gobierno aprueba el Contingente de trabajadores extranjeros de régimen no comunitario en España para 2007*, URL: http://www.tt.mtas.es /periodico, [14.02.2007].

Ministerio de Trabajo y Asuntos Sociales (2007c): *Strategic Plan for Citizenship and Integration 2007-2010 –Executive Summary*, Madrid: MTAS.

Ministerio de Trabajo y Asuntos Sociales, Dirección General Guardia Civíl, Oficina de Relaciones informativas y Sociales: Proyectos para el Control de la Inmigración Irregular, URL: http://www.guardiacivil.org/prensa/actividades/mauritania/especial.pdf, [13.02.2007].

Ministerio de Trabajo y Asuntos Sociales, Gabinete de Comunicación (2005): *Comunidades autónomas y ayuntamientos reciben 120 millones de euros para acogida e integración de los inmigrantes, Nota de Prensa* 18.04.2005, URL: http://www.tt.mtas.es/periodico, [15.04.2006].

MOTTE, Jan and Rainer Ohliger (eds.) (2004): *Geschichte und Gedächtnis in der Einwanderungsgesellschaft. Migration zwischen historischer Rekonstruktion und Erinnerungspolitik*, Essen: Klartext Verlag.

MÜLLER, Marita (1994): *Politische Parteien in Spanien (1977-1982). Interne Konflikte und Wahlverhalten*, Saarbrücken: Verlag für Entwicklungspolitik Breitenbach.

NAGEL, Klaus-Jürgen (2007): El debate sobre la relación entre centro y Autonomías en España, in Walther BERNECKER and Günther MAIHOLD *España: del consenso a la polarización. Cambios en la democracia española*, Madrid/Frankfurt a. M.: Iberoamericana/Vervuert, 265-295.

NOHLEN, Dieter and Andreas HILDENBRAND (2005): *Spanien. Wirtschaft - Gesellschaft - Politik. Ein Studienbuch*, Wiesbaden: Verlag für Sozialwissenschaften.

NORA, Pierre (1998): *Zwischen Geschichte und Gedächtnis*, Berlin: Wagenbach.

NULLMEIER, Frank (2001): Politikwissenschaft auf dem Weg zur Diskursanalyse? in Reiner KELLER et al. *Handbuch Sozialwissenschaftliche Diskursanalyse. Band I: Theorien und Methoden*, Opladen: Leske + Budrich, 285-311.

NUÑEZ SEIXAS, Xosé-Manoel (1993): *Historiographical Approaches to Nationalism in Spain*, Saarbrücken: Verlag breitenbach Publishers.

NUÑEZ SEIXAS, Xosé-Manoel (2001): What is Spanish nationalism today? From legitimacy crisis to unfulfilled renovation (1975-2000), in *Ethnic and Racial Studies*, 42:5, 719-752.

NUÑEZ SEIXAS, Xosé Manuel (2004): Gibt es einen spanischen Nationalismus nach 1975? Zur Rolle des historischen Gedächtnisses im spanischen "patriotischen" Diskurs, in Krzysztof RUCHNIEWICZ and Stefan TROEBST *Diktaturbewältigung und nationale Selbstvergewisserung. Geschichtskulturen in Polen und Spanien im Vergleich*, Wroclaw: Wydawnictwo Uniwersytetu Wroclawskiego, 229-243.

NZZ (2005): *Tauziehen um die Autonomie in Katalonien*, 05.08.2005.

OBERNDÖRFER, Dieter (1993): *Der Wahn des Nationalen. Die Alternative der offenen Republik*, Freiburg/Basel/Wien: Herder.

OBERNDÖRFER, Dieter (1996): Assimilation, Multikulturalismus oder kultureller Pluralismus - zum Gegensatz zwischen kollektiver Nationalkultur und kultureller Freiheit der Republik, in Klaus J. BADE *Migration-Ethnizität-Konflikt. Systemfragen und Fallstudien*, Osnabrück: Universitätsverlag Rasch, 127-147.

OBERNDÖRFER, Dieter (2001): Leitkultur und Berliner Republik. Die Hausordnung der multikulturellen Gesellschaft Deutschlands ist das Grundgesetz, in *Aus Politik und Zeitgeschichte*, 2001:B 1-2, 27-30.

OBERNDÖRFER, Dieter (2003): Zuwanderung und nationale Identität, in Bundesamt für Anerkennung ausländischer Flüchtlinge *50 Jahre. Behörde im Wandel*, Nürnberg: Selbstverlag, 109-120.

OBERNDÖRFER, Dieter (2006): Nation, Multikulturalismus und Migration - auf dem Weg in die postnationale Republik?, in *IMIS-Beiträge*, 7-21.

ORTEGA PÉREZ, Nieves (2003): *Spain: Forging an Immigration Policy*, Migration Information Source, URL: http://www.migrationinformation.org, [10.09.2004].

PAJARES, Miguel (2005): *La Integración Ciudadana. Una perspectiva para la inmigración*, Barcelona: Icaria Editorial.

PALTRIDGE, Brian (2006): *Discourse Analysis. An Introduction*, London/New York: Continuum.

PARK, Robert E. and Ernst W. BURGESS (1969): *Introduction to the Science of Sociology including the Original Index to Basic Sociological Concepts*, Chicago: University of Chicago Press.

PARLAMENT DE CATALUNYA: *Organic Law 6/2006 of the 19th July, on the Reform of the Statute of Autonomy of Catalonia*, URL: http://www.parlament-cat.net/porteso/estatut/estatut_angles_100506.pdf, [19.02.2007].

PASTORE, Ferruccio (2004): *To Regularize or Not to Regularize: Experiences and Views from Europe*, Migration Information Source, URL: http://www.migration information.org, [27.01.2004].

PAYNE, Stanley G. (1991): Nationalism, Regionalism and Micronationalism in Spain, in *Journal of Contemporary History*, 26:3/4, 479-491.

PÉREZ ROYO, Javier (1992): Die Verteilung der Kompetenzen zwischen Staat und Autonomen Gemeinschaften, in Dieter NOHLEN and José Juan GONZÁLEZ ENCINAR *Der Staat der Autonomen Gemeinschaften in Spanien*, Opladen: Leske + Budrich, 103-124.

PUJOL, Jordi and Ramón PI (1996): *Jordi Pujol. Cataluña-España*, Madrid: Espasa Calpe.

PUYOL, Rafael (2003): *La Inmigración en España. ¿Un problema o una necesidad?*, Acto de su toma de posesión como Académico de Número el día 13 de junio de 2001, Lerko Print.

RÄTHZEL, Nora (1997): *Gegenbilder. Nationale Identität durch Konstruktion des Anderen*, Opladen: Leske + Budrich.

REAL DECRETO 2393/2004, de 30 de diciembre, por el que se aprueba el Reglamento a la Ley Orgánica 4/2000, de 11 de enero, sobre derechos y libertades de los extranjeros en España y su integración social, Boletín Oficial de Estado Nr. 6, 07.01.2005, URL: http://extranjeros.mtas.es/es/normativa_jurisprudencia/Nacional/RD2393-04.pdf, [19.02.2007].

REIG TAPIA, Alberto (2007): El debate sobre el pasado y su importancia para el presente, in Walther BERNECKER and Günther MAIHOLD *España: del consenso a la polariza-*

ción. Cambios en la democracia española, Madrid/Frankfurt a. M.: Iberoamericana/ Vervuert, 167-202

RENAN, Ernest (1996): Was ist eine Nation? Rede am 11. März 1882 an der Sorbonne, in Sabine GROENEWOLD *Ernest Renan: Was ist eine Nation? Rede am 11. März 1882 an der Sorbonne. Mit einem Essay von Walter Euchner?* Hamburg: Europäische Verlagsgesellschaft, 7-39.

RIGAU I OLIVER, Irene (2003): La inmigración extranjera en Catalunya: presente y futuro, in Gemma AUBARELL *Perspectivas de la Inmigración en España. Una Aproximación desde el Territorio*, Barcelona: Icaria editorial, 9-34.

ROTENSTREICH, Natan (2003): Volksgeist, in The Electronic Text Center at the University of Virginia Library *The Dictionary of the History of Ideas*, Vol. 4, Charlottesville, Electronic Text Center, URL: http://etext.virginia.edu, pp. 491ff, [22.03.2007].

RUÍZ DE HUIDOBRO, José María (2000): La Ley Orgánica 4/2000, in *Migraciones*, 2000:7, 57-88.

RUOFF, Michael (2007): *Foucault Lexikon*, Paderborn: Wilhelm Fink Verlag.

SÁEZ ARANCE, Antonio (2004): Auf der Suche nach einem neuen "demokratischen Zentralismus"? Nationalkonservativer Geschichtsrevisionismus im Spanien der Jahrtausendwende, in Krzysztof RUCHNIEWICZ and Stefan TROEBST *Diktaturbewältigung und nationale Selbstvergewisserung. Geschichtskulturen in Polen und Spanien im Vergleich*, Wroclaw: Wydawnictwo Uniwersytetu Wroclawskiego, 267-273.

SÁNCHEZ PRIETO, Juan María (2001): Nación Española y Nacionalismos, in Andrés DE BLAS, *et al. La nación española: historia y presente*, Madrid: Fundación para el analisis y los estudios sociales, 153-179.

SCHLEE, Beatrice (2008): *Die Macht der Vergangenheit. Demokratisierung und politischer Wandel in einer spanischen Kleinstadt*, Baden-Baden: Nomos-Verlag.

SCHMIDT, Peer (2005): *Kleine Geschichte Spaniens*, Bonn: Bundeszentrale für politische Bildung.

SCHNAPPER, Dominique (1994): The debate on immigration and the crisis of national identity, in Martin BALDWIN-EDWARDS and Martin A. SCHAIN *The Politics of Immigration in Western Europe*, Essex: Frank Cass, 127-139.

SCHNAPPER, Dominique, Pascale KRIEF and Emmanuel PEIGNARD (2003): French Immigration and Integration Policy. A Complex Combination, in Friedrich HECKMANN and Dominique SCHNAPPER *The Integration of Immigrants in European Societies. National Differences and Trends of Convergence*, Stuttgart: Lucius & Lucius, 15-44.

SERRA, Albert (2005): Spain, in Jan NIESSEN, Yongmi SCHIBEL and Cressida THOMPSON *Current Immigration Debates in Europe: A Publication of the European Migration Dialogue*, Brüssel: Migration Policy Group, 1-28.

SHAFIR, Gershon (1995): *Immigrants and Nationalists. Ethnic Conflict and Accomodation in Catalonia, the Basque Country, Latvia, and Estonia*, Albany: State University of New York Press.

SILVA BARRERA, Emilio (2004): The Importance of Remembrance in the Transition to Democracy in Spain, in Krzysztof RUCHNIEWICZ and Stefan TROEBST *Diktaturbewältigung und nationale Selbstvergewisserung. Geschichtskulturen in Polen und Spanien im Vergleich*, Wroclaw: Wydawnictwo Uniwersytetu Wroclawskiego, 69-74.

SMITH, Anthony D. (1971): *Theories of Nationalism*, London: Duckworth.

SMITH, Anthony D. (1991): *National Identity*, London: Penguin Books.

SNOW, David A. *et al.* (1986): Frame Alignment Processes, Micromobilization, and Movement Participation, in *American Sociological Review*, 51:4, 464-481.

STERNBERGER, Dolf (1990): *Verfassungspatriotismus*, Frankfurt a. M.: Insel Verlag.

STRAUSS, Anselm and Juliet CORBIN (1996): *Grounded Theory: Grundlagen Qualitativer Sozialforschung*, Weinheim: Beltz Psychologie Verlags Union.

SUÁREZ-NAVAZ, Liliana (1997): Political Economy of the mediterranean rebordering: New ethnicities, new citizenships, in *Stanford Humanities Review*, 1997:5.2, 174-200.

SUBIRATS, Joan (2002): *El "éxito" de la (no) política de inmigración, El País*, 15.02.2002.

SÜDDEUTSCHE ZEITUNG (2004): *Das Ende der Arroganz*, 16.03.2004, 3.

SUNDERHAUS, Sebastian (2007): Regularization programs for undocumented migrants, in *Migration Letters*, 4:1, 65-76

SUTHERLAND, Claire (2005): Nation-building through discourse theory, in *Nations and Nationalism*, 11:2, 185-202.

TAZ (2006): *Wahlschlappe für Sozialisten in Katalonien*, 03.11.2006, 10.

TERMES, Josep (1984): *La immigració a Catalunya i altres estudis d'història del nacionalisme català*, Barcelona: Editorial Empúries.

TIBI, Bassam (2001): Leitkultur als Wertekonsens. Bilanz einer mißglückten deutschen Debatte, in *Aus Politik und Zeitgeschichte*, 2001:B 1-2, 23-26.

TORNOS, Andrés, Rosa APARICIO GÓMEZ and Mercedes FERNÁNDEZ GARCÍA (2004): *El Capital Humano de la inmigración*, Madrid: Ministerio de Trabajo y Asuntos Sociales.

TRIANDAFYLLIDOU, Anna (2001): *Immigrants and National Identity in Europe*, London/ New York: Routledge.

UNITED NATIONS POPULATION DIVISION: *Qinquennial estimates and projections, Birth rate, crude, per 1,000 population [code 13580]*, URL: http://unstats.un.org/pop/dvariables/dretrieval.aspx [20.12.2007].

VALANDRO, Franz (2002): *A Nation of Nations. Nationalities' Policies in Spain*, Frankfurt a. M.: Peter Lang.

VAN DIJK, Teun A. (1993): *Elite Discourse and Racism*, London/New Delhi: Sage Publications.

VAN DIJK, Teun A. (1984): *Prejudice in Discourse. An Analysis of Ethnic Prejudice in Cognition and Conversation*, Amsterdam/Philadelphia: John Benjamins Publishing Company.

VAN DIJK, Teun A. (1985): Introduction: Levels and Dimensions of Discourse Analysis, in Teun A. VAN DIJK *Handbook of Discourse Analysis. Vol. 2: Dimensions of Discourse*, London: Academic Press, 1-11.

VAN DIJK, Teun A. (1997a): Discourse as Interaction in Society, in Teun A VAN DIJK *Discourse as Social Interaction. Discourse Studies: A Multidisciplinary Introduction. Volume II*, London/Thousand Oaks/New Delhi: Sage Publications, 1-37.

VAN DIJK, Teun A. (ed.) (1997b): *Discourse as Social Interaction. Discourse Studies: A Multidisciplinary Introduction. Volume II,* London/Thousand Oaks/New Delhi: Sage Publications.

VAN DIJK, Teun A. (ed.) (1997c): *Discourse as Structure and Process. Discourse Studies: A Multidisciplinary Introduction. Volume I,* London/Thousand Oaks/New Delhi: Sage Publications.

VAN DIJK, Teun A. (1997d): The Study of Discourse, in Teun A VAN DIJK *Discourse as Structure and Process. Discourse Studies: A Multidisciplinary Introduction. Volume I,* London/Thousand Oaks/New Delhi: SAGE Publications, 1-34.

VAN DIJK, Teun A. (2001): Principles of Critical Discourse Analysis, in Margaret WETHERELL, Stephanie TAYLOR and Simeon J. YATES *Discourse Theory and Practice. A Reader*, London/Thousand Oaks/New Delhi: Sage Publications, 300-317.

VAN DIJK, Teun A. *et al.* (1997): Discourse, Ethnicity, Culture and Racism, in Teun A VAN DIJK *Discourse as Social Interaction. Discourse Studies: A Multidisciplinary Introduction. Volume II*, London/Thousand Oaks/New Delhi: Sage Publications, 144-180

VARELA, Javier (1999): *La Novela de España. Los Intelectuales y el Problema Español*, Madrid: Taurus.

VELASCO, Juan Carlos (2002): Patriotismo Constitucional y Republicanismo, *Claves de la Razón Práctica*, 125, 33-40.

VILLAGRAS I HERNÀNDEZ, Fèlix (2006): *Frances Xavier Llorens i Barba: cultura i política a la Catalunya del segle XIX*, PHD thesis presented to the Universitat de Barcelona, Facultat de Geografia i Història, Departament d'Història Contemporània the April 26, 2006, URL: http://www.tesisenxarxa.net/TDX-0615106-114946/#documents.

VON HIRSCHHAUSEN, Ulrike and Jörn LEONHARD (2001): Europäische Nationalismen im West-Ost-Vergleich: von der Typologie zur Differenzbestimmung, in Ulrike VON HIRSCHHAUSEN and Jörn LEONHARD *Nationalismen in Europa. West-und Osteuropa im Vergleich*, Göttingen: Wallstein Verlag, 11-45.

WALDMANN, Peter (1990): *Militanter Nationalismus im Baskenland*, Frankfurt a. M.: Vervuert Verlag.

WEBER, Max (1922): *Wirtschaft und Gesellschaft*, Tübingen: Mohr.

WEBER, Max (1948): The Nation, in H. H. GERTH and C. WRIGHT MILLS *From Max Weber: Essays in Sociology*, London: Routledge & Kegan Paul, 171-179.

WEISS, Gilbert and Ruth WODAK (2003): Introduction: Theory, Interdisciplinarity and Critical Discourse Analysis, in Gilbert WEISS and Ruth WODAK *Critical Discourse Analysis. Theory and Interdisciplinarity*, Houndsmills, Basignstoke: Palgrave Macmillan, 1-32.

WESSLER, Hartmut (1999): *Öffentlichkeit als Prozeß. Deutungsstrukturen und Deutungswandel in der deutschen Drogenberichterstattung*, Opladen: Westdeutscher Verlag.

WINTER, Ulrich (2004): Spaniens Intelektuelle: Eine neue Diskussionskultur und die Debatte um Identitäten und "Erinnerungsorte" (1976-2002), in Walther BERNECKER and Klaus DIRSCHERL *Spanien heute. Politik-Wirtschaft-Kultur*, Frankfurt a. M.: Vervuert Verlag, 631-656.

WODAK, Ruth *et al.* (1998): *Zur diskursiven Konstruktion nationaler Identität*, Frankfurt a. M.: Suhrkamp.

ZAPATA-BARRERO, Ricard (2002): *El turno de los inmigrantes. Esferas de Justicia y Políticas de Acomodación*, Madrid: Ministerio de Trabajo y Asuntos Sociales.

ZAPATA-BARRERO, Ricard (2004a): *Inmigración, innovación política y cultura de acomodación en España*, Barcelona: Fundació CIDOB.

ZAPATA-BARRERO, Ricard (2004b): *Multiculturalidad e inmigración*, Madrid: Editorial Sintesis.

ZAPATA-BARRERO, Ricard (2005a): Construyendo una filosofía pública de la inmigración en Catalunya: los términos del debate, in *Revista de derecho migratorio y extranjería*, 2005:10, 9-38.

ZAPATA-BARRERO, Ricard (2005b): Inmigración en la España plural: un debate pendiente, in *El País*, 20.06.2005.

ZAPATA-BARRERO, Ricard (2006a): *Immigració i Govern en Nacions Minoritàries: Flandes, el Quebec i Catalunya en perspectiva?*, Barcelona: Fundació Ramon Trias Fargas.

ZAPATA-BARRERO, Ricard (2006b): The Muslim community and Spanish tradition. Maurophobia as a fact, and impartiality as a desideratum, in Tariq MODOOD, Anna

TRIANDAFYLLIDOU and Ricard ZAPATA-BARRERO *Multiculturalism, Muslims and Citizenship. A European Approach*, London: Routledge, 143-161.

ZAPATA-BARRERO, Ricard (2007): Immigration, Self-Government and Management of Identity. The Catalan Case, in Michel KORINMAN and John LAUGLAND *The long March to the West*, Vallentine: Mitchell, 179-202.

ZAPATA-BARRERO, Ricard (2008): Policies and public opinion towards immigrants: the Spanish case, in *Ethnic and Racial Studies*, 2008, 1-20, URL: http://dx.doi.org/10.1080/01419870802302280, [24.11.2008].

2. ANALYSED DOCUMENTS

Central State

P1: E-I-Gov-Portavoz-AdmPubl-Piqué-Acebes-04-02-2000rtf.rtf: Presidencia del Gobierno (2000): Rueda de Prensa del Consejo de Ministros, 04.02.2000, URL: http://www.lamoncloa.es, [13.01.2006].

P2: E-I-Gov-Portavoz-Just-Piqué-Mariscal-11-02-2000rtf.rtf: Presidencia del Gobierno (2000): Rueda de Prensa del Consejo de Ministros, 11.02.2000, URL: http://www.lamoncloa.es, [13.01.2006].

P3: E-I-Gov-Portavoz-MTAS-Piqué-Pimentel-14-01-2000rtf.rtf: Presidencia del Gobierno (2000): Rueda de Prensa del Consejo de Ministros, 14.01.2000, URL: http://www.lamoncloa.es, [13.01.2006].

P4: E-I-Gov-Portavoz-MTAS-Piqué-Pimentel-18-02-2000rtf.rtf: Presidencia del Gobierno (2000): Rueda de Prensa del Consejo de Ministros, 18.02.2000, URL: http://www.lamoncloa.es, [13.01.2006].

P5: E-I-Gov-Portavozl-Piqué-31-03-2000rtf.rtf: Presidencia del Gobierno (2000): Rueda de Prensa del Consejo de Ministros, 31.03.2000, URL: http://www.lamoncloa.es, [13.01.2006].

P6: E-I-Gov-Pres-19-01-2000rtf.rtf: Presidencia del Gobierno (2000): Conferencia de Prensa del Presidente del Gobierno, Don José María Aznar, y del Primer Ministro de Bélgica, Guy Verhofstadt, 19.01.2000, URL: http://www.lamoncloa.es, [01.03.2005].

P7: E-I-Gov-MinInterior-MayorOreja-04-03-2000.rtf: El País (2000): Entrevista a Jaime Mayor Oreja, 04.03.2000, Madrid.

P8: E-I-Gov-MTAS-Aparicio-23-02-2000.rtf: El País (2000): "La dimisión de Pimentel no es negativa para el PP", Entrevista a Juan Carlos Aparicio (Ministro de Trabajo), 23.02.2000, Madrid.

P9: E-I-Gov-Presidente-Aznar-17-02-2000.rtf: Entrevista al Presidente del Gobierno, Don José María Aznar, en el programa "El Matí" de Catalunya Radio, 17.02.2000, Barcelona, URL: http://www.aznar2000pp.es, [24.01.2006].

P10: E-I-Gov-Presidente-Aznar-24-02-2000.rtf: Entrevista al Presidente del Gobierno, Don José María Aznar, en el programa "Buenos días" de RNE, 24.02.2000, Madrid, URL: http://www.aznar2000pp.es, [24.01.2006].

P11: E-I-Gov-Presidente-Aznar-27-02-2000.rtf: El Mundo (2000): Entrevista con José María Aznar, 27.02.2000, Madrid.

P12: E-I-Gov-Presidente-Aznar-05-03-2000.rtf: Mitin del Presidente del Partido Popular y Presidente del Gobierno Don José María Aznar, 05.03.2000, Las Palmas, URL: http://www.aznar2000pp.es, [24.01.2006].

P13: E-II-Opp-SecrMigrPSOE-Rumi Ibanez-08-12-2000.rtf: Consuelo Rumí Ibañez (2000): Inmigración y Sentido de Estado, in: OTR, 08.12.2000, URL: http://213.9.180.227/NuevasPoliticas-NuevosTiempos/Documentos/Intervenciones-Articulos-Entrevistas/articuloCR-OTR-8-Diciembre2000.htm, [24.01.2006].

P14: E-II-Opp-SecrMigrPSOE-Rumi Ibanez-16-12-2000.rtf: Consuelo Rumí Ibañez (2000): El PP cierra la puerta, in: Cambio 16, 16.12.2000, URL: http://213.9.180.227/NuevasPoliticas-NuevosTiempos/Documentos/Intervenciones-Articulos-Entrevistas/articuloCRCambio16Diciembre2000.htm, [24.01.2006].

P15: E-II-Opp-SecrOrgPSOE-Blanco-04-12-2000.rtf: El Socialista (2000): Entrevista a José Blanco, Secretario de Organización del PSOE, 04.12.2000, URL: http://213.9.180.227/NuevasPoliticas-NuevosTiempos/Documentos/Intervenciones-Articulos-Entrevistas/entrevistaJB_elsocialista041200.htm, [24.01.2006].

P16: E-II-Opp-SecrPolEcPSOE-Sevilla-12-11-2000.rtf: ABC (2000): Entrevista a Jordi Sevilla, Secretario de Política Económica del PSOE, 12.11.2000, Madrid.

P17: E-II-Opp-secrPolSoc-DeLaEncina-19-12-2000.rtf: El País (2000): La inmigración es el reto de España en el siglo XXI, Entrevista a Salvador De la Encina, Secretario de Política Social e Inmigración de la comisión ejecutiva regional del PSOE, Andalucía, 19.12.2000, Madrid.

P18:   Auszüge E-II-DSCongreso-CO_096-07-11-2000.rtf: Cortes Generales, Diario
        de Sesiones del Congreso de los Diputados, Comisiones, Justicia e Interior, Año
        2000, VII Legislatura, Núm. 96, Sesión núm. 9, 07.11.2000.

P19:   E-II-Gov-Portavoz-Cabanillas-28-12-2000rtf.rtf: Entrevista al Ministro Porta-
        voz del Gobierno, Don Pio Cabanillas, en el Programa „Buenos Días", De Radio
        Nacional de España, 28.12.2000, Madrid.

P20:   Auszüge E-II-DSCongreso-PL_044-24-11-2000.rtf: Cortes Generales, Diario
        de Sesiones del Congreso de los Diputados, Pleno y Diputación Permanente,
        Año 2000, VII Legislatura, Núm. 44, Sesión plenaria núm. 42, 24.11.2000.

P21:   Auszüge E-II-DSCongreso-PL_046-29-11-2000.rtf: Cortes Generales Diario de
        Sesiones del Congreso de los Diputados, Pleno y Diputación Permanente, Año
        2000, VII Legislatura, Núm. 46, Sesión plenaria núm. 44, 29.11.2000.

P22:   E-II-DSCongreso-CO_137-28-12-2000komplett.rtf: Cortes Generales Diario
        de Sesiones del Congreso de los Diputados, Comisiones, Justicia e Interior, Año
        2000, VII Legislatura, Núm. 137, Sesión núm. 15, 28.12.2000.

P23:   E-II-Gov-Portavoz-Agr-CiencTec-Cabanillas-Arias-Birulés-22-12-2000.rtf:
        Presidencia del Gobierno (2000): Rueda de Prensa del Consejo de Ministros,
        22.12.2000, URL: http://www.lamoncloa.es, [13.01.2006].

P24:   E-II-Gov-Portavoz-CiencTec-Cabanillas-Birulés-10-11-2000.rtf: Presidencia
        del Gobierno (2000): Rueda de Prensa del Consejo de Ministros, 10.11.2000,
        URL: http://www.lamoncloa.es, [13.01.2006].

P25:   E-III-Gov-MTAS-Caldera-02-01-2005.rtf: El País (2005): El nuevo reglamento
        de extranjería, "Lo razonable es un 10% de inmigrantes", Entrevista a Jesús Cal-
        dera, Ministro de Trabajo y Asuntos Sociales, 02.01.2005, Madrid.

P26:   E-III-Gov-Pres-Zapatero-14-02-2005.rtf: Entrevista al Presidente del Gobierno
        en el Programa "Protagonistas" de Punto Radio, 14.02.2005, Madrid.

P27:   E-III-Gov-Pres-Zapatero-18-02-2005.rtf: Entrevista al Presidente del Gobierno
        en el Programa "Hoy por Hoy", de Cadena Ser, 18.02.2005, Madrid.

P28:   E-III-Gov-Presidente-Zapatero-02-01-2005.rtf: El Periódico (2005): Zapa-
        tero: "El apoyo de Batasuna al plan Ibarretxe lo empeora", Entrevista a José Luis
        Rodríguez Zapatero, Secretario General del PSOE y Presidente del Gobierno,
        02.01.2005, Barcelona.

P29:   E-III-Gov-SecrInm-Rumi Ibanez-07-02-2005.rtf: El País (2005): Los Pro-
        blemas de los Inmigrantes. Entra en vigor el Reglamento de Extranjería.
        "Ésta es la última oportunidad para los empresarios que contratan a 'sin pape-

les", Entrevista a Consuelo Rumí Ibanez, Secretaria de Estado de Inmigración, 07.02.2005, Madrid.

P30:   E-III-Gov-SecrPolMunPSOE-Cuesta-25-01-2005.rtf: La   Razón   (2005): Cuesta: "El plan Ibarretxe implica aplicar la receta de los asesinos", Entrevista a Álvaro Cuesta, Secretario de Política Municipal y Libertades Públicas del PSOE, 24.01.2005, Madrid.

P31:   E-III-Gov-Vicepresidenta-Fernandez de la Vega-08-02-2005.rtf: Telemadrid (2005): Entrevista a Teresa Fernández de la Vega, Vicepresidenta Primera del Gobierno, en el programa "El Circulo de Primera Hora", Telemadrid 08.02.2005, Madrid,   URL: http://www.telemadrid.es/contenidos/html/elcirculo/pagina_ teresavega2.htm, [24.01.2006].

P32:   E-III-Opp-PP-Gallardón-28-02-2005.rtf: TVE1 (2005): Entrevista a Alberto Ruiz Gallardón, Alcalde de Madrid, PP, en el programa "Desayunos de TVE", 24.02.2005, Madrid.

P33:   E-III-Opp-PPC-Piqué-18-01-2005.rtf: Cadena Cope (2005): Entrevista a Josep Piqué (PP), en el programa "La Mañana" de Cadena Cope, 18.01.2005, Madrid.

P34:   E-III-Opp-PPC-Piqué-23-02-2005.rtf: Antena 3 (2005): Entrevista a Josep Piqué (PP), en el programa "El Ruedo Ibérico"de Antena 3, 23.02.2005, Madrid.

P35:   E-III-Opp-SecrGenPP-Acebes-08-02-2005.rtf: Cadena Cope (2005): Entrevista a Àngel Acebes (PP), en el programa "La Mañana" de Cadena Cope, 08.02.2005, Madrid.

P36:   E-III-Opp-SecrGenPP-Acebes-PortInmPSOE-Hernando-09-02-2005.rtf: El País (2005): Europa, el 'efecto llamada' y el control policial. La política migratoria agrava la confrontación entre los dos grandes partidos, Entrevista a Ángel Acebes, Secretario General, PP y Antonio Hernando, Portavoz de Inmigración del PSOE, 09.02.2005, Madrid.

P37:   E-III-Opp-SecrPolSocPP-Pastor-23-03-2005.rtf: Cadena Onda Cero (2005): Entrevista a Ana Pastor (PP), en el programa "Herrera en la Onda" de Cadena Onda Cero, 23.03.2005, Madrid.

P38:   Auszüge E-III-DSCongreso-Co-214-02-03-2005.rtf: Cortes Generales Diario de Sesiones del Congreso de los Diputados, Comisiones, Interior, Año 2005, VIII Legislatura, Núm. 214, Sesión núm. 10, 02.03.2005.

P39: Auszüge E-III-DSCongreso-PL_066-02-02-2005.rtf: Cortes Generales Diario de Sesiones del Congreso de los Diputados, Pleno y Diputación Permanente, Año 2005, VIII Legislatura, Núm. 66, Sesión plenaria núm. 61, 02.02.2005.

P40: Auszüge E-III-DSCongreso-PL_069-09-02-2005.rtf: Cortes Generales Diario de Sesiones del Congreso de los Diputados, Pleno y Diputación Permanente, Año 2005, VIII Legislatura, Núm. 69, Sesión plenaria núm. 64, 09.02.2005.

P41: Auszüge E-III-DSCongreso-PL_071-23-02-2005.rtf: Cortes Generales Diario de Sesiones del Congreso de los Diputados, Pleno y Diputación Permanente, Año 2005, VIII Legislatura, Núm. 71, Sesión plenaria núm. 66, 23.02.2005.

P42: Auszüge E-III-DSCongreso-PL_073-08-03-2005.rtf: Cortes Generales Diario de Sesiones del Congreso de los Diputados, Pleno y Diputación Permanente, Año 2005, VIII Legislatura, Núm. 73, Sesión plenaria núm. 68, 08.03.2005.

P43: Auszüge E-III-DSCongreso-PL_074-09-03-2005.rtf: Cortes Generales Diario de Sesiones del Congreso de los Diputados, Pleno y Diputación Permanente, Año 2005, VIII Legislatura, Núm. 74, Sesión plenaria núm. 69, 09.03.2005.

P44: Auszüge E-III-DSCongreso-PL_077-16-03-2005.rtf: Cortes Generales Diario de Sesiones del Congreso de los Diputados, Pleno y Diputación Permanente, Año 2005, VIII Legislatura, Núm. 77, Sesión plenaria núm. 72, 16.03.2005.

P45: E-III-DSCongreso-Co-203-01-03-2005.rtf: Cortes Generales Diario de Sesiones del Congreso de los Diputados, Comisiones, Trabajo y Asuntos Sociales, Año 2005, VIII Legislatura, Núm. 203, Sesión núm. 18, 01.03.2005.

P46: E-III-Gov-Pres-Zapatero-23-03-2005.rtf: Presidencia del Gobierno (2005): Conferencia de prensa del Presidente del Gobierno después de la reunión del Consejo Europeo, 23.03.2005, Brussels, URL: http://www.lamoncloa.es [13.01.2006].

P47: E-III-Gov-Pres-Zapatero-26-01-2005-b.rtf: Presidencia del Gobierno (2005): Conferencia de prensa del Presidente del Gobierno al finalizar su visita a la República Argentina, 26.1.2005, Buenos Aires, URL: http://www.lamoncloa.es [13.01.2006].

P48: E-III-Gov-Vicpres-Def-Viv-Fernández...-Bono-Trujillo-21-01-2005.rtf: Presidencia del Gobierno (2005): Rueda de Prensa del Consejo de Ministros, 21.01.2005, URL: http://www.lamoncloa.es, [13.01.2006].

P49: E-III-Gov-Vicpres-Ec-Agr-Fernández...-Solbes-Espinosa   04-02-2005.rtf: Presidencia del Gobierno (2005): Rueda de Prensa del Consejo de Ministros, 04.02.2005, URL: http://www.lamoncloa.es, [13.01.2006].

P50:   E-III-Gov-Vicpres-Ec-Fernández...-Solbes-25-02-2005.rtf: Presidencia   del Gobierno (2005): Rueda de Prensa del Consejo de Ministros, 25.02.2005, URL: http://www.lamoncloa.es, [13.01.2006].

P51:   E-III-Gov-Vicpres-MTAS-Fernández...-Caldera-04-03-2005.rtf: Presidencia del Gobierno (2005): Rueda de Prensa del Consejo de Ministros, 04.03.2005, URL: http://www.lamoncloa.es, [13.01.2006].

P52:   E-III-Gov-Vicpres-MTAS-Fernández...-Caldera-28-01-2005.rtf: Presidencia del Gobierno (2005): Rueda de Prensa del Consejo de Ministros, 28.01.2005, URL: http://www.lamoncloa.es, [13.01.2006].

P53:   E-III-Gov-Pres-Zapatero-25-01-2005-b.rtf: Presidencia del Gobierno (2005): Discurso del Presidente del Gobierno después de su reunión con el Presidente de la República Argentina, 25.1.2005, Buenos Aires, URL: http://www.lamoncloa. es [13.01.2006].

P54:   E-III-Gov-Pres-Zapatero-25-01-2005.rtf: Presidencia del Gobierno (2005): Discurso del Presidente del Gobierno en su encuentro con la colectividad española en Argentina, 25.1.2005, Buenos Aires, URL: http://www.lamoncloa.es [13.01.2006].

P55:   E-III-Gov-SecrGenPSOE-Zapatero-12-03-2005.rtf: Oficina de Prensa Federal del PSOE (2005): Intervención del Secretario General en el Comité Federal del PSOE, 12.03.2005, Madrid.

P56:   E-III-Gov-SecrOrgPSOE-Blanco-24-01-2005.rtf: Oficina de Prensa Federal del PSOE (2005): "La hoja de ruta del cambio en España" Conferencia de José Blanco, Secretario de Organización del PSOE, 24.01.2005, Club Siglo XXI, URL: http://www.psoe.es, [23.01.2006].

P57:   E-IV-Gov-SecrRelIntPSOE-Jímenez-10-2005.rtf: Trinidad Jiménez (2005): Una política internacional para el siglo XXI, El Socialista, 10.2005, URL: http://www.elsocialista.es, [23.01.2006].

P58:   E-IV-Gov-Zapatero-26-10-2005.rtf: José Luis Rodríguez Zapatero (2005): "Europa es la respuesta", The Guardian, 26.10.2005, London.

P59:   E-IV-Gov-Presidente-Zapatero-15-10-2005-c.rtf: Cadena Ser (2005): Entrevista al Presidente del Gobierno en el programa "A vivir que son dos días" de la Cadena SER, 15.10.2005, Madrid.

P60:   E-IV-Gov-PresidentePSOE-Chaves-09-10-2005.rtf: El País (2005): La Reforma del Estatuto Catalán. "El PP no puede quedarse al margen del proceso de pacto que se tiene que dar en el Congreso", Entrevista a Manuel Chaves, Presidente del PSOE, 09.10.2005, Madrid.

P61: E-IV-Gov-SecrMovSocPSOE-Zerolo-23-10-2005.rtf: La Gaceta de Canarias (2005): Zerolo: "PP y CC han destruido lo poco que había en servicios públicos", Entrevista a Pedro Zerolo, Secretario de Movimientos Sociales y Relaciones con las ONG, 23.10.2005.

P62: E-IV-Opp-PP-Zaplana-05-10-2005.rtf: Antena 3 (2005): Entrevista a Eduardo Zaplana (PP), en el programa "Rueda Ibérico" de Cadena Antena 3, 05.10.2005, Madrid.

P63: E-IV-Opp-SecrAutPP-Saez de Santamaria-24-10-2005.rtf: Telemadrid (2005): Entrevista a Soraya Sáez de Santa María (PP), en el programa "Circulo a Primera Hora" de Cadena Telemadrid, 24.10.2005, Madrid.

P64: Auszüge E-IV-DSCongreso-CO_358-06-10-2005.rtf: Cortes Generales Diario de Sesiones del Congreso de los Diputados, Comisiones, Trabajo y Asuntos Sociales, Año 2005, VIII Legislatura, Núm. 358, Sesión núm. 26, 06.10.2005.

P65: Auszüge E-IV-DSCongreso-PL_109-14-09-2005.rtf: Cortes Generales Diario de Sesiones del Congreso de los Diputados, Pleno y Diputación Permanente, Año 2005, VIII Legislatura, Núm. 109, Sesión plenaria núm. 101, 14.09.2005.

P66: Auszüge E-IV-DSCongreso-PL_112-21-09-2005.rtf: Cortes Generales Diario de Sesiones del Congreso de los Diputados, Pleno y Diputación Permanente, Año 2005, VIII Legislatura, Núm. 112, Sesión plenaria núm. 104, 21.09.2005.

P67: Auszüge E-IV-DSCongreso-PL_115-28-09-2005.rtf: Cortes Generales Diario de Sesiones del Congreso de los Diputados, Pleno y Diputación Permanente, Año 2005, VIII Legislatura, Núm. 115, Sesión plenaria núm. 107, 28.09.2005.

P68: Auszüge E-IV-DSCongreso-PL_118-05-10-2005.rtf: Cortes Generales Diario de Sesiones del Congreso de los Diputados, Pleno y Diputación Permanente, Año 2005, VIII Legislatura, Núm. 118, Sesión plenaria núm. 110, 05.10.2005.

P69: Auszüge E-IV-DSCongreso-PL_120-18-10-2005.rtf: Cortes Generales Diario de Sesiones del Congreso de los Diputados, Pleno y Diputación Permanente, Año 2005, VIII Legislatura, Núm. 120, Sesión plenaria núm. 112, 18.10.2005.

P70: Auszüge E-IV-DSCongreso-PL_121-19-10-2005.rtf: Cortes Generales Diario de Sesiones del Congreso de los Diputados, Pleno y Diputación Permanente, Año 2005, VIII Legislatura, Núm. 121, Sesión plenaria núm. 113, 19.10.2005.

P71: E-IV-DSCongreso-CO_377-28-09-2005.rtf: Cortes Generales Diario de Sesiones del Congreso de los Diputados, Comisiones, Interior, Año 2005, VIII Legislatura, Núm. 377, Sesión núm. 21, 28.09.2005.

P72: E-IV-DSCongreso-CO_383-10-10-2005.rtf: Cortes Generales Diario de Sesiones del Congreso de los Diputados, Comisiones, Interior, Año 2005, VIII Legislatura, Núm. 383, Sesión núm. 22, 10.10.2005.

P73: E-IV-Gov-Vicpres-Ec-Fernández...-Solbes-23-09-2005.rtf: Presidencia del Gobierno (2005): Rueda de Prensa del Consejo de Ministros, 23.09.2005, URL: http://www.lamoncloa.es, [13.01.2006].

P74: E-IV-Gov-Vicpres-Ec-Fernández...-Solbes-28-10-2005.rtf: Presidencia del Gobierno (2005): Rueda de Prensa del Consejo de Ministros, 28.10.2005, URL: http://www.lamoncloa.es, [13.01.2006].

P75: E-IV-Gov-Vicpres-Fernández...-21-10-2005.rtf: Presidencia del Gobierno (2005): Rueda de Prensa del Consejo de Ministros, 21.10.2005, URL: http://www.lamoncloa.es, [13.01.2006].

P76: E-IV-Gov-Vicpres-Interior-Fernández...-Alonso-30-09-2005.rtf: Presidencia del Gobierno (2005): Rueda de Prensa del Consejo de Ministros, 30.09.2005, URL: http://www.lamoncloa.es, [13.01.2006].

P77: E-IV-Gov-Vicpres-Just-Fernández...-López-A.-07-10-2005.rtf: Presidencia del Gobierno (2005): Rueda de Prensa del Consejo de Ministros, 07.10.2005, URL: http://www.lamoncloa.es, [13.01.2006].

P78: E-IV-Gov-Vicpres-MTAS-Fernández...-Caldera-13-10-2005.rtf: Presidencia del Gobierno (2005): Rueda de Prensa del Consejo de Ministros, 13.10.2005, URL: http://www.lamoncloa.es, [13.01.2006].

P79: E-IV-Gov-Zapatero-15-10-2005-b.rtf: Presidencia del Gobierno (2005): Conferencia de prensa del Presidente del Gobierno, del Presidente de Uruguay y del Ministro de Asuntos Exteriores después de la Cumbre Iberoamericana, 15.10.2005, Salamanca, URL: http://www.lamoncloa.es, [13.01.2006].

P80: E-IV-Gov-Zapatero-17-10-2005.rtf: Presidencia del Gobierno (2005): Conferencia de prensa del Presidente del Gobierno y del Primer Ministro de la República Francesa, 17.10.2006, Barcelona, URL: http://www.lamoncloa.es, [13.01.2006].

P81: E-IV-Gov-Zapatero-27-10-2005.rtf: Presidencia del Gobierno (2005): Conferencia de prensa del Presidente del Gobierno después de la reunión del Consejo Europeo, 27.10.2005, London, URL: http://www.lamoncloa.es, [13.01.2006].

P82: E-IV-Gov-Zapatero-29-09-2005.rtf: Presidencia del Gobierno (2005): Conferencia de prensa del Presidente del Gobierno y del Primer Ministro de Marruecos después de la Reunión de Alto Nivel hispano-marroquí, 29.09.2005, Sevilla, URL: http://www.lamoncloa.es, [13.01.2006].

P83:   E-IV-Gov-PresidentePSOE-Zapatero-03-09-2005.rtf: Oficina de Prensa Federal
        del PSOE (2005): Intervención de José Luis Rodríguez Zapatero en el Comité
        Federal del PSOE, 03.09.2005, URL: http://www.psoe.es, [23.01.2006].

P84:   E-IV-Gov-Zapatero-14-10-2005.rtf: Presidencia del Gobierno (2005): Discurso
        del Presidente del Gobierno en la inauguración de la XV Cumbre Iberoameri-
        cana, 14.10.2005, Salamanca, URL: http://www.lamoncloa.es, [13.01.2006].

P85:   E-IV-Gov-Zapatero-15-09-2005.rtf: Presidencia del Gobierno (2005): Discurso
        del Presidente del Gobierno en el "Council on Foreign Relations" de Nueva
        York, 15.09.2005, New York, URL: http://www.lamoncloa.es, [13.01.2006].

P86:   E-IV-Gov-Zapatero-15-10-2005.rtf: Presidencia del Gobierno (2005): Discurso
        del Presidente del Gobierno en la clausura de la XV Cumbre Iberoamericana,
        15.10.2005, Salamanca, URL: http://www.lamoncloa.es, [13.01.2006].

P87:   E-IV-Gov-Zapatero-21-09-2005.rtf: Presidencia del Gobierno (2005): Discurso
        del Presidente del Gobierno en el Pleno del Congreso sobre la Asamblea General
        de la ONU y la participación española en misiones de mantenimiento de la paz,
        21.09.2005, Madrid, URL: http://www.lamoncloa.es, [13.01.2006].

P88:   E-II-Gov-Blanco-SecrOrgPSOE Oct-Nov-Dic 2000.rtf: El Socialista (2000):
        Entrevista a José Blanco, Secretario de Organización y acción electoral, PSOE,
        Oct-Dic. 2000, 16-19.

P89:   E-II-Gov-Zapatero-Oct-Dic 2000.rtf: José Luís Rodriguez Zapatero (2000):
        Trabajar por el interés colectivo y en defensa de lo público, El Socialista, Oct-
        Dic. 2000, 16-19.

P90:   E-II-Opp-PSOE zum Ley de Extranjeria 24-11-2000.rtf: PSOE (2000): Posición
        del PSOE sobre la Ley d Extranjería, 24.11.2000, URL: http://213.9.180.227/
        NuevasPoliticas-NuevosTiempos/NuestrasPoliticas/Politica   Migratoria/posi-
        cion_ley_extranjeria.htm, [24.01.2006].

P91:   E-II-Opp-PSOE zum Ley Extranjeria 14-12-2000.rtf: PSOE (2000):
        "La Reforma de la Ley de Extranjería en el Senado", 14.12.2000, URL:
        http://213.9.180.227/NuevasPoliticas-NuevosTiempos/NuestrasPoliticas/Poli-
        tica Migratoria/reforma_ley_extranjeria_senado.htm, [24.01.2006].

P92:   E-II-Opp-PSOE zum Plan Greco 27-12-2000.rtf: PSOE (2000): Valoración del
        Programa Global de Extranjería y Migración presentado por el Gobierno y Pro-
        puestas de Modificación del PSOE, 27.12.2000, URL: http://213.9.180.227/
        NuevasPoliticas-NuevosTiempos/NuestrasPoliticas/PoliticaMigratoria/plan_
        greco.htm, [24.01.2006].

P93:   E-III-Opp-Comunicado PP 15-03-2005.rtf: Oficina de Información del PP (2005): Comunicación de los Gobiernos Locales del PP sobre las políticas de inmigración y su incidencia en las corporaciones locales, 15.03.2005.

P94:   E-III-Opp-Comunicado PP sobre PolInmGov 08-02-2005.rtf: Oficina de Información del PP (2005): Comunicado del Partido Popular "Inmigración: Los Diez Errores del Gobierno Socialista", Madrid, 8 de febrero 2005.

P95:   E-I+II-Gov-Auszüge aus Programa Electoral PP 2000.rtf: PP (2000): Elecciones Generales 2000. El Compromiso del Centro, Programa Electoral del Partido Popular, Madrid.

P96:   E-I+II-Opp-Auszüge aus Programa Electoral PSOE 2000.rtf: PSOE (2000): Programa Electoral, PSOE. Elecciones Generales 2000, Madrid.

P97:   E-III+IV-Gov-Auszüge aus Programa Electoral PSOE 2004.rtf: PSOE (2004): Merecemos una España mejor. Programa Electoral Elecciones Generales 2004, Madrid.

P98:   E-III+IV-Opp-Auszüge aus Programa Electoral PP 2004.rtf: PP (2004): Avanzamos juntos. Programa de Gobierno del Partido Popular, Elecciones Generales 2004, Madrid.

P99:   E-PROGRAMA GRECO 30-03-2001.rtf: Ministerio del Interior (2001): Programa Global de Regulación y Coordinación de Extranjería e Inmigración, aprobado 30.03.2001, BOE núm. 101, 27.04.2001.

Catalonia

P1:   CAT- Opp-Article Joan Saura 09-03-2001.rtf: Joan Saura (2001): Inmigración y cuestión nacional, El País, 09.03.2001, Madrid.

P2:   CAT-Gov-Article-Entrevista Artur Mas CiU 27-10-2003.rtf: El País (2003): "Defenderemos un nuevo estatuto dentro de la legalidad", Transcripción del debate con Artur Mas en el aula, 27.10.2003, Madrid.

P3:   CAT-Gov-Article-Entrevista Piqué PP 28-10-2003.rtf: El País (2003): "Es difícil encontrar una administración tan centralista como la catalana", Transcripción del debate mantenido con Josep Piqué en el aula, 28.10.2003, Madrid.

P4:   CAT-Gov-Article Carod-Rovira ERC 20-01-2004.rtf: Josep Lluis Carod Rovira (2004): "Siguem educats, parlem català", Avui, 20.01.2004, Barcelona.

P5:   CAT-Gov-Article Joan Saura IC-V 11-07-2005.rtf: Joan Saura (2005): "Diversitat nacional i cohesió territorial", Segre, 11.07.2005.

P6:   CAT-Gov-Article Joan Saura IC-V 13-05-2005.rtf: Joan Saura (2005): "¿Qué quiere Catalunya?", La Vanguardia, 13.05.2005, Barcelona.

P7:   CAT-Gov-Article Joan Saura IC-V 27-12-2005.rtf: Joan Saura (2005): "Diversidad e igualdad, un falso dilema", El País, 27.12.2005, Madrid.

P8:   CAT-Gov-Article Josep Bargalló ERC 11-09-2004.rtf: Josep Bargalló (2004): "Cohesió social i projecte nacional", El País, 11.09.2004, Madrid.

P9:   CAT-Gov-Article Josep Bargalló ERC 12-07-2005.rtf: Josep Bargalló (2005): "La reforma estatutària no és metafísica: dóna capacitat de gestió en atur, immigració i vivenda", El Periódico, 12.07.2005, Barcelona.

P10:   CAT-Gov-Article Josep Bargalló ERC 30-06-2005.rtf: Josep Bargalló (2005): "La immigració, cosa de tots", El Periódico, 30.06.2005, Barcelona.

P11:   CAT-Gov-Article Lidia Santos PSC 19-07-2004.rtf: Lídia Santos (2004): "Voler és poder: la gestió en l'àmbit de l'estrangeria", Avui, 19.07.2004, Barcelona.

P12:   CAT-Gov-Artículo Adela Ros ERC 03-09-2004.rtf: Adela Ros (2004): "Un falso debate", El País, 03.09.2004, Madrid.

P13:   CAT-Gov-Pres-Maragall PSC 03-06-2005.rtf: Pasqual Maragall (2005): "El tsunami europeo", El Periódico, 03.06.2005, Barcelona.

P14:   CAT-Gov-Pres-Maragall PSC 11-09-2005.rtf: Pasqual Maragall (2005): "Catalunya ha de tornar a mirar lluny", Avui, 11.09.2005, Barcelona.

P15:   CAT-Opp-Article-Entrevista Carod-rovira ERC 27-10-2003.rtf: El País (2003): "Hay que superar la Cataluña dual creada por CiU y PSC", Transcripción del debate mantenido con Josep Lluis Carod Rovira en el aula, 27.10.2003, Madrid.

P16:   CAT-Opp-Article-Entrevista Maragall PSC 24-10-2003.rtf: El País (2003): "Los catalanes no pedimos lo mismo que los vascos", Transcripción del debate mantenido con Pasqual Maragall en el aula, 24.10.2003, Madrid.

P17:   CAT-Opp-Article Maragall PSC 29-06-2001.rtf: Pasqual Maragall (2001): ¿"Impasse"?, El País, 29.06.2001, Madrid.

P18:   CAT-Opp-Article Miret i Serra CIU 04-11-2005.rtf: Àngel Miret i Serra (2005): "Immigració I Polítiques Públiques", El Punt, 04.11.2005.

P19:   CAT-Opp-Article Montilla PSC 2002.rtf: José Montilla (2002): "Políticas de realidades ante la inmigración", El Periódico, 24.05.2002, Barcelona.

P20:   CAT-Opp-Artículo Angel Miret CiU 22-09-2004.rtf: Àngel Miret i Serra (2004): "Identidad y migración", El País, 22.09.2004, Madrid.

P21:   CAT-Gov-Entrevista Duran i Lleida CIU El País 12-11-2003.rtf: El País (2003): Preguntas a Josep Antoni Duran i Lleida, 12.11.2003, Madrid.

P22:   CAT-Gov-Entrevista Adela Ros ERC 19-04-2004.rtf: El Diari dels Estudiants (2004): "L'immigrant ha de tenir expectatives de millora", Entrevista a Adela Ros, 19.04.2004.

P23:   CAT-Gov-Entrevista Artur Mas CIU El País 12-10-2003.rtf: El País (2003): "Cerrar la puerta al nuevo estatuto sería malo para Cataluña y España", Entrevista a Artur Mas, 12.10.2003, Madrid.

P24:   CAT-Gov-Entrevista Campuzano CiU 24-02-2000.rtf: El País (2000): "La reforma de la Constitución no puede ser un tabú", Entrevista a Carles Campuzano, 24.02.2000, Madrid.

P25:   CAT-Gov-Entrevista Mas CIU El Pais 14-11-2003.rtf: El País (2003): "Sería un fraude dar la presidencia a Carod", Entrevista a Artur Mas, 14.11.2003, Madrid.

P26:   CAT-Opp-Entrevista Carod-Rovira ERC El País 11-11-2003.rtf: El País (2003): "Si Cataluña quiere ser soberana lo será, guste o no a Madrid", Entrevista a Josep Lluís Carod-Rovira, 11.11.2003, Madrid.

P27:   CAT-Opp-Entrevista Maragall PSC 09-11-2003.rtf: Enric Company (2003): "El soberanismo es una vía muerta antes de nacer", El País, 09.11.2003, Barcelona.

P28:   CAT-Opp-Entrevista Maragall PSC 10-06-2002.rtf: Avui (2002): Entrevista a Pasqual Maragall, President del PSC, 10.06.2002, Barcelona.

P29:   CAT-Opp-Entrevista Maragall PSC 21-05-2002.rtf: La Vanguardia (2002): Entrevista a Pasqual Maragall, 21.05.2002, Barcelona.

P30:   CAT-Opp-Entrevista Maragall PSC 30-06-2002.rtf: El Periódico (2002): Entrevista a Pasqual Maragall, 30.06.2002, Barcelona.

P31:   CAT-Opp-Entrevista Maragall PSC El Pais 13-11-2003.rtf: El País (2003): "Pactar con CiU sería una estafa", Entrevista a Pasqual Maragall, 13.11.2003, Barcelona.

P32:   CAT-Opp-Entrevista Maragall PSC Tardor 2001.rtf: Joan Tápia (2001): Entrevista a Pasqual Maragall, Nov. 2001.

P33:   CAT-Opp-Entrevista Montilla La Vanguardia 05-03-2001.rtf: La Vanguardia (2001): "La actitud confusa de Pujol ante la inmigración alimenta bajas pasiones", Entrevista a José Montilla, 05.03.2001, Barcelona.

P34:   CAT-Opp-Entrevista Montilla PSC 07-07-2002.rtf: La Vanguardia (2002): "Los inmigrantes ilegales o se regularizan o se expulsan", Entrevista a José Montilla, 07.07.2002, Barcelona.

P35:   CAT-Opp-Entrevista Saura IC-V El País 19-10-2003.rtf: El País (2003): "Las posibilidades de CiU se acabarían si ERC dijera que apuesta por un gobierno de izquierdas", Entrevista a Joan Saura, 19.10.2003, Barcelona.

P36:   Auszüge Bases per a un nou Estatut 04-2003.rtf: CiU (2003): "Bases per a un nou Estatut nacional de Catalunya", Barcelona.

P37:   Auszüge Koalitionsvertrag Tripartit 12-2003.rtf: IC-V, PSC, ERC (2003): Acord per a un govern catalanista i d'esquerras a la Generalitat de Catalunya, 14.12.2003, Barcelona.

P38:   pla Immigració 2001-2004.rtf: Generalitat de Catalunya (2001): "Pla Interdepartamental d'Immigració 2001-2004", aprovat en la sessió del Govern de la Generalitat, 18.07.2001, Barcelona.

P39:   Pla Immigració 2005-2008 I.rtf: Generalitat de Catalunya, Departament de Benestar i Família, Secretaría per a la Immigració (2005): Pla de Ciutadanía i Immigració 2005-2008, Barcelona.

P40:   Pla Immigració 2005-2008 Zusammenfassung.rtf: Generalitat de Catalunya, Departament de Benestar i Família, Secretaría per a la Immigració (2005): Pla de Ciutadanía i Immigració 2005-2008. Recull d'idees claus, Barcelona.

P41:   CAT-Gov-Conference Duran i Lleida CIU 15-11-2001.rtf: Josep A. Duran i Lleida (2001): "Decisius per a Catalunya", Conferència al Col.legi de Periodistes de Catalunya, 15.11.2001, Barcelona.

P42:   CAT-Gov-Conference Duran i Lleida CIU 25-10-2001.rtf: Josep A. Duran i Lleida (2001): "Vers la Normalització Religiosa a Catalunya", Conferència, 25.10.2001, Barcelona.

P43:   CAT-Gov-Pres- Pujol 12-02-2001.rtf: Generalitat de Catalunya (2001): Discurso del president Pujol: "La relació nord-sud en la Mediterrània del segle XXI: una visió des de Catalunya", 12.02.2001, URL: http://www.gencat.net.

P44:   CAT-Gov-Pres-Maragall PSC 15-06-2005.rtf: Generalitat de Catalunya (2005): Discurso del president Maragall: "Un finançament per al progrés econòmic i social de Catalunya", 15.06.2005, URL: http://www.gencat.net.

P45:   CAT-Gov-Pres-Maragall PSC 01-07-2005.rtf: Generalitat de Catalunya (2005): Discurso del president Maragall: "Signatura del primer conveni de la Llei de Barris", 01.07.2005, URL: http://www.gencat.net.

P46:   CAT-Gov-Pres-Maragall PSC 02-09-2004.rtf: Generalitat de Catalunya (2004): Discurso del president Maragall: "Inauguració del Congrés Mundial "Moviments Humans i Immigració", en el marc del Fòrum 2004", 02.09.2004, URL: http://www.gencat.net.

P47:   CAT-Gov-Pres-Maragall PSC 06-04-2005.rtf: Generalitat de Catalunya (2005): Discurso del president Maragall: "Conferència 'Catalunya 2005: Un programa de reformas'", 06.04.2005, URL: http://www.gencat.net.

P48:   CAT-Gov-Pres-Maragall PSC 06-05-2005.rtf: Generalitat de Catalunya (2005): Discurso del president Maragall: "Discurs institucional sobre la nova etapa del Govern de la Generalitat de Catalunya", 06.05.2005, URL: http://www.gencat.net.

P49:   CAT-Gov-Pres-Maragall PSC 10-06-2005.rtf: Generalitat de Catalunya (2005): Discurso del president Maragall: "Inauguració de la Trobada Empresarial de Rialp", 10.06.2005, URL: http://www.gencat.net.

P50:   CAT-Gov-Pres-Maragall PSC 13-01-2005.rtf: Generalitat de Catalunya (2005): Discurso del president Maragall: "Catalunya 2005: un any de respostes", 13.01.2005, URL: http://www.gencat.net.

P51:   CAT-Gov-Pres-Maragall PSC 18-10-2005.rtf: Generalitat de Catalunya (2005): Discurso del president Maragall: "Debat de Política General", 18.10.2005, URL: http://www.gencat.net.

P52:   CAT-Gov-Pres-Maragall PSC 20-06-2005.rtf: Generalitat de Catalunya (2005): Discurso del president Maragall: "Discurs del president de la Generalitat en la inauguració de 12è Congrés de la UGT a Catalunya", 20.06.2005, URL: http://www.gencat.net.

P53:   CAT-Gov-Pres-Maragall PSC 22-03-2004.rtf: Generalitat de Catalunya (2004): Discurso del president Maragall: "Catalunya oberta: una estratègia econòmica", 22.03.2004, URL: http://www.gencat.net.

P54:   CAT-Gov-Pres-Maragall PSC 27-05-2004.rtf: Generalitat de Catalunya (2004): Discurso del president Maragall: "Una propuesta catalana para la España plural", 27.05.2004, URL: http://www.gencat.net.

P55:   CAT-Gov-Pres-Pujol 01-02-2001.rtf: Generalitat de Catalunya (2001): Discurso del president Pujol: "Globalización e identidad", 01.02.2001, URL: http://www.gencat.net.

P56:   CAT-Gov-Pres-Pujol 04-07-2000.rtf: Generalitat de Catalunya (2000): Discurso del president Pujol: "Ante el gran reto de la inmigración", 04.07.2000, URL: http://www.gencat.net.

P57: CAT-Gov-Pres-Pujol 08-10-2002.rtf: Generalitat de Catalunya (2002): Discurso del president Pujol: "Inauguració de la mostra 'Cataluña tierra de acogida'", 08.10.2002, URL: http://www.gencat.net.

P58: CAT-Gov-Pres-Pujol 10-05-2001.rtf: Generalitat de Catalunya (2001): Discurso del president Pujol: "Acte d'inauguració de l'exposició CATALUÑA, TIERRA DE ACOGIDA ", 10.05.2002, URL: http://www.gencat.net.

P59: CAT-Gov-Pres-Pujol 10-09-2001.rtf: Generalitat de Catalunya (2001): Discurso del president Pujol: "Missatge del president amb motiu de l'11 de setembre de 2001", 10.09.2001, URL: http://www.gencat.net.

P60: CAT-Gov-Pres-Pujol 11-03-2002.rtf: Generalitat de Catalunya (2002): Discurso del president Pujol: "Catalunya en el món", 11.03.2002, URL: http://www.gencat.net.

P61: CAT-Gov-Pres-Pujol 17-09-2003.rtf: Generalitat de Catalunya (2003): Discurso del president Pujol: "Desde la Constitución hasta hoy", 17.09.2003, URL: http://www.gencat.net.

P62: CAT-Gov-Pres-Pujol 18-09-2001.rtf: Generalitat de Catalunya (2001): Discurso del president Pujol: "El porvenir de Europa no depende solo de la política", 18.09.2001, URL: http://www.gencat.net.

P63: CAT-Gov-Pres-Pujol 21-06-2001.rtf: Generalitat de Catalunya (2001): Discurso del president Pujol: "Llengua, cultura i economia dels països petits a la Unió Europea", 21.06.2001, URL: http://www.gencat.net.

P64: CAT-Gov-Pres-Pujol 22-06-2001.rtf: Generalitat de Catalunya (2001): Discurso del president Pujol: "Cloenda de la segona edició de les Jornades de debat 'CATALUNYA DEMÀ'", 22.06.2001, URL: http://www.gencat.net.

P65: CAT-Gov-Pres-Pujol 23-05-2001.rtf: Generalitat de Catalunya (2001): Discurso del president Pujol: "Globalització i identitat", 23.05.2001, URL: http://www. gencat.net.

P66: CAT-Gov-Pres-Pujol 26-09-2000.rtf: Generalitat de Catalunya (2000): Discurso del president Pujol: "XIII Encontre Internacional Homes i Religons: Oceà de Pau, religions i cultura en diàleg", 26.09.2000, URL: http://www.gencat.net.

P67: CAT-Gov-Pres-Pujol 27-07-2001.rtf: Generalitat de Catalunya (2001): Discurso del president Pujol: "Cataluña, tierra de acogida", 27.07.2001, URL: http:// www.gencat.net.

P68: CAT-Gov-Speech Artur Mas CIU 21-10-2002.rtf: Artur Mas (2002): Conferéncia: Catalunya sense límits: els nous horitzons del nostre projecte de país, 21.10.2002.

P69:   CAT-Gov-Speech Pujol CIU 23-10-2003.rtf: Jordi Pujol (2003): Conferència: "1975-2003", 23.10.2003, Palau de Congressos de Catalunya Barcelona.

P70:   CAT-Opp-Conference Carod-Rovira ERC 04-06-2002.rtf: Josep Lluís Carod-Rovira (2002): "Immigració: Drets Socials, Deures civils", Conferència.

P71:   CAT-Opp-Speech Carod-Rovira ERC 22-04-2003.rtf: Josep Lluís Carod-Rovira (2003): "L'hora de Catalunya. Nous Horitzons per al Segle XXI, Conferència en el *Col·legi de Periodistes de Catalunya. Barcelona.*

P72:   CAT-Opp-Speech Maragall PSC 06-09-2001.rtf: Pasqual Maragall (2001): "Més ambició per Catalunya", Conferència, 06.09.2001.

P73:   CAT-Opp-Speech Maragall PSC 25-07-2001.rtf: Pasqual Maragall (2001): "Immigració i ciutadania", Discurs d'obertura de la Jornada de Debat organitzada pel PSC de Barcelona, Barcelona.

P74:   CAT-Opp-Speech Pujol CIU 10-11-2004.rtf: Jordi Pujol (2004): "Gent i País", Conferència del Molt honorable senyor Jordi Pujol, Institut d'Estudis Catalans, Barcelona, 10.11.2004.

P75:   CAT-Opp-Speech Pujol CIU 14-02-2005.rtf: Jordi Pujol (2005): "Reflexions que ara toca fer", Conferència a càrrec del Molt honorable senyor Jordi Pujol, ESADE, Barcelona, 14.02.2005.

P76:   Auszüge CiU Wahlprogramm Katalonien 2003.rtf: CiU (2003): "Tu ets primer", Programa electoral CiU, Eleccions al Parlament de Catalunya 2003, Barcelona.

P77:   Auszüge PP Wahlprogramm Katalonien 2003.rtf: PP (2003): Programa electoral PP, Eleccions al Parlament de Catalunya 2003, Barcelona.

P78:   Auszüge PSC Wahlprogramm Katalonien 1999.rtf: PSC (1999): "Nuevas Oportunidades para Cataluña", Programa electoral PSC, Eleccions al Parlament de Catalunya 1999, Barcelona.

P79:   Auszüge PSC Wahlprogramm Katalonien 2003.rtf: PSC (2003): Programa Elecciones al Parlament de Catalunya 2003, Barcelona.

P80:   ERC Wahlprogramm-Migration Katalonien 2003.rtf: ERC (2003): Resum del programa de govern d'ERC. Eleccions al Parlament de Catalunya 2003, Barcelona.

P81:   IC-V Wahlprogramm Katalonien -Propuestas Inm-2003.rtf: IC-V (2003): Propuestas Inmigración, Eleccions al Parlament de Catalunya 2003, Barcelona.

P82:   Auszüge-DSCP-P-010 15-03-2000.rtf: Diari de Sessions del Parlament de Catalunya, Número 10, VI Legislatura, Ple del Parlament, Sessions plenàries núm. 7 i 8, 15.03.2000.

P83: Auszüge-DSCP-P-033 15-11-2000.rtf: Diari de Sessions del Parlament de Catalunya, Número 33, VI Legislatura, Ple del Parlament, Sessions plenàries núm. 24, 15.11.2000.

P84: Auszüge-DSCP-P-043 07-02-2001.rtf: Diari de Sessions del Parlament de Catalunya, Número 43, VI Legislatura, Ple del Parlament, Sessions plenàries núm. 27, 07.02.2001.

P85: Auszüge-DSCP-P-045 21-02-2001.rtf: Diari de Sessions del Parlament de Catalunya, Número 45, VI Legislatura, Ple del Parlament, Sessions plenàries núm. 28, 21.02.2001.

P86: Auszüge-DSCP-P-046 07-03-2001.rtf: Diari de Sessions del Parlament de Catalunya, Número 46, VI Legislatura, Ple del Parlament, Sessions plenàries núm. 29 i 30, 07.03.2001.

P87: Auszüge-DSCP-P-050 19-04-2001.rtf: Diari de Sessions del Parlament de Catalunya, Número 50, VI Legislatura, Ple del Parlament, Sessions plenàries núm. 32, 19.04.2001.

P88: Auszüge-DSCP-P-052 16-05-2001.rtf: Diari de Sessions del Parlament de Catalunya, Número 52, VI Legislatura, Ple del Parlament, Sessions plenàries núm. 33 i 34, 16.05.2001.

P89: Auszüge-DSCP-P-058 27-06-2001.rtf: Diari de Sessions del Parlament de Catalunya, Número 58, VI Legislatura, Ple del Parlament, Sessions plenàries núm. 38 i 39, 27.06.2001.

P90: Auszüge-DSCP-P-068 07-11-2001.rtf: Diari de Sessions del Parlament de Catalunya, Número 68, VI Legislatura, Ple del Parlament, Sessions plenàries núm. 43 i 44, 07.11.2001.

P91: Auszüge-DSCP-P-082 03-04-2002.rtf: Diari de Sessions del Parlament de Catalunya, Número 82, VI Legislatura, Ple del Parlament, Sessions plenàries núm. 54 i 55, 03.04.2002.

P92: Auszüge-DSCP-P-084 17-04-2002.rtf: Diari de Sessions del Parlament de Catalunya, Número 84, VI Legislatura, Ple del Parlament, Sessions plenàries núm. 56, 17.04.2002.

P93: Auszüge-DSCP-P-087 16-05-2002.rtf: Diari de Sessions del Parlament de Catalunya, Número 87, VI Legislatura, Ple del Parlament, Sessions plenàries núm. 57, 16.05.2002.

P94: Auszüge-DSCP-P-088-089 29 u. 30-05-2002.rtf: Diari de Sessions del Parlament de Catalunya, Número 88, VI Legislatura, Ple del Parlament, Sessions plenàries núm. 58 i 59, 30.05.2002.

P95:   Auszüge-DSCP-P-091 13-06-2002.rtf: Diari de Sessions del Parlament de Catalunya, Número 91, VI Legislatura, Ple del Parlament, Sessions plenàries núm. 60 i 61, 13.06.2002.

P96:   Auszüge-DSCP-P-114 13-02-2003.rtf: Diari de Sessions del Parlament de Catalunya, Número 114, VI Legislatura, Ple del Parlament, Sessions plenàries núm. 73, 74 i 75, 13.02.2003.

P97:   Auszüge-DSCP-P-119 26-03-2003.rtf: Diari de Sessions del Parlament de Catalunya, Número 119, VI Legislatura, Ple del Parlament, Sessions plenàries núm. 81, 26.03.2003.

P98:   Auszüge-DSCP-P-124 04-06-2003.rtf: Diari de Sessions del Parlament de Catalunya, Número 124, VI Legislatura, Ple del Parlament, Sessions plenàries núm. 85 i 86, 04.06.2003.

P99:   Auszüge DSCP-P 008 14-03-2004.rtf: Diari de Sessions del Parlament de Catalunya, Número 8, VII Legislatura, Ple del Parlament, Sessions plenàries núm. 14, 15 i 16, 14.03.2004.

P100:   Auszüge DSCP-P 011 21-04-2004.rtf: Diari de Sessions del Parlament de Catalunya, Número 11, VII Legislatura, Ple del Parlament, Sessions plenàries núm. 20 i 21, 21.04.2004.

P101:   Auszüge DSCP-P 012 05-05-2004.rtf: Diari de Sessions del Parlament de Catalunya, Número 12, VII Legislatura, Ple del Parlament, Sessions plenàries núm. 22, 05.05.2004.

P102:   Auszüge DSCP-P 014 26-05-2004.rtf: Diari de Sessions del Parlament de Catalunya, Número 14, VII Legislatura, Ple del Parlament, Sessions plenàries núm. 24, 26.05.2004.

P103:   Auszüge DSCP-P 016 u. 017 16 u. 17-06-2004.rtf: Diari de Sessions del Parlament de Catalunya, Número 16, VII Legislatura, Ple del Parlament, Sessions plenàries núm. 25, 17.06.2004.

P104:   Auszüge DSCP-P 047 12-05-2005.rtf: Diari de Sessions del Parlament de Catalunya, Número 47, VII Legislatura, Ple del Parlament, Sessions plenàries núm. 58 i 59, 12.05.2005.

P105:   Auszüge DSCP-P 049 02-06-2005.rtf: Diari de Sessions del Parlament de Catalunya, Número 49, VII Legislatura, Ple del Parlament, Sessions plenàries núm. 61, 02.06.2005.

P106:   Auszüge2-DSCP-P-046 07-03-2001.rtf: Diari de Sessions del Parlament de Catalunya, Número 46, VI Legislatura, Ple del Parlament, Sessions plenàries núm. 29 i 30, 07.03.2001.

P107: DSPC-C 123 02-02-2001.rtf: Diari de Sessions del Parlament de Catalunya, Número 123, VI Legislatura, Comissió d'Estudi sobre la Política d'Immigració a Catalunya, Sessió núm. 12, 02.02.2001.

P108: DSPC-C 186 26-04-2005.rtf: Diari de Sessions del Parlament de Catalunya, Número 186, VII Legislatura, Comissió Permanent de Legislatura sobre Immigració, Sessió núm. 4, 26.04.2005.

P109: DSPC-C 206 19-05-2005.rtf: Diari de Sessions del Parlament de Catalunya, Número 206, VII Legislatura, Comissió Permanent de Legislatura sobre Immigració, Sessió núm. 5, 19.05.2005.

P110: DSPC-C 222 20-06-2005.rtf: Diari de Sessions del Parlament de Catalunya, Número 222, VII Legislatura, Comissió Permanent de Legislatura sobre Immigració, Sessió núm. 6, 20.06.2005.

P111: DSPC-C 223 14-04-2000.rtf: Diari de Sessions del Parlament de Catalunya, Número 223, VI Legislatura, Comissió d'Estudi sobre la Política d'Immigració a Catalunya, Sessió núm. 2, 7, 8, 9, 10 i 11, 14.04.2000.

P112: DSPC-C 224 16-02-2001.rtf: Diari de Sessions del Parlament de Catalunya, Número 224, VI Legislatura, Comissió d'Estudi sobre la Política d'Immigració a Catalunya, Sessió núm. 13, 14, 15, 16 i 17, 16.02.2001.

P113: DSPC-C 28 28-04-2000.rtf: Diari de Sessions del Parlament de Catalunya, Número 28, VI Legislatura, Comissió d'Estudi sobre la Política d'Immigració a Catalunya, Sessió núm. 3, 28.04.2000.

P114: DSPC-C 38 13-04-2004.rtf: Diari de Sessions del Parlament de Catalunya, Número 38, VII Legislatura, Comissió sobre Immigració, Sessió núm. 2, 13.04.2004.

P115: DSPC-C 44 26-05-2000.rtf: Diari de Sessions del Parlament de Catalunya, Número 44, VI Legislatura, Comissió d'Estudi sobre la Política d'Immigració a Catalunya, Sessió núm. 4, 26.05.2000.

P116: DSPC-C 54 09-06-2000.rtf: Diari de Sessions del Parlament de Catalunya, Número 54, VI Legislatura, Comissió d'Estudi sobre la Política d'Immigració a Catalunya, Sessió núm. 5, 09.06.2000.

P117: DSPC-C 71 23-06-2000.rtf: Diari de Sessions del Parlament de Catalunya, Número 71, VI Legislatura, Comissió d'Estudi sobre la Política d'Immigració a Catalunya, Sessió núm. 6, 23.06.2000.

P118: DSPC-C 84 27-09-2004.rtf: Diari de Sessions del Parlament de Catalunya, Número 84, VII Legislatura, Comissió Permanent de Legislatura sobre Immigració, Sessió núm. 3, 27.09.2004.

P119:   Auszüge BOPC-197-18-06-2001 Document Comissió d'Estudi.rtf: Bulletí Oficial del Parlament de Catalunya: Document de la Comissió d'Estudi sobre la Política d'Immigració a Catalunya (260-00001/06), 18.06.2001.

P120:   Auszüge BOPC-368-10-12-2002 Carta d'acolliment.rtf: Bulletí Oficial del Parlament de Catalunya Nr. 368: Proposició de llei sobre la Carta d'acolliment per a les persones nouvingudes a Catalunya, 10.12.2002.